T0332813

Beginning Design for 3D Printing

Joe Micallef

Apress®

Beginning Design for 3D Printing

ISBN-13 (pbk): 978-1-4842-0947-9

ISBN-13 (electronic): 978-1-4842-0946-2

Managing Director: Welmoed Spahr
Lead Editor: Michelle Lowman
Technical Reviewer: Alex Chen
Editorial Board: Steve Anglin, Louise Corrigan, Jonathan Gennick, Robert Hutchinson, Michelle Lowman, James Markham, Susan McDermott, Matthew Moodie, Jeffrey Pepper, Douglas Pundick, Ben Renow-Clarke, Gwenan Spearing, Steve Weiss
Coordinating Editors: Kevin Walter and Mark Powers
Copy Editor: Kim Wimpsett
Compositor: SPi Global
Indexer: SPi Global
Artist: SPi Global

Distributed to the book trade worldwide by Springer Science+Business Media New York, 233 Spring Street, 6th Floor, New York, NY 10013. Phone 1-800-SPRINGER, fax (201) 348-4505, e-mail orders-ny@springer-sbm.com, or visit www.springeronline.com. Apress Media, LLC is a California LLC and the sole member (owner) is Springer Science + Business Media Finance Inc (SSBM Finance Inc). SSBM Finance Inc is a Delaware corporation.

For information on translations, please e-mail rights@apress.com, or visit www.apress.com.

Apress and friends of ED books may be purchased in bulk for academic, corporate, or promotional use. eBook versions and licenses are also available for most titles. For more information, reference our Special Bulk Sales–eBook Licensing web page at www.apress.com/bulk-sales.

Any source code or other supplementary material referenced by the author in this text is available to readers at www.apress.com/9781484209479. For detailed information about how to locate your book's source code, go to www.apress.com/source-code/. Readers can also access source code at SpringerLink in the Supplementary Material section for each chapter.

Contents at a Glance

Contents

About the Author

Joe Micallef spent 10 years working as a graphic designer before pursuing a Masters degree in animation at the University of Southern California. At USC Joe became the university's Adobe Scholar and also was awarded an Annenberg Fellowship that required him to collaborate with USC's Virtebi School of Engineering. Through this collaboration Joe began to conceptualize workflows that combined animation and 3D printing. After attaining his Masters, Joe provided his media expertise to various manufacturing organizations for training, marketing, and advocacy purposes. He has deep experience creating models for 3D printing, animation and video games simultaneously, and teaches modeling and animation at Pasadena City College.

About the Technical Reviewer

Alexander Chen is the Class of 2018 at Duke University, North Carolina. He is pursuing a bio-medical engineering degree with plans to work on prosthetics in the future. He is heavily involved with volunteering at a non-profit called Palos Verdes on the Net (PVNet) where he managed the educational programs and gained his experience with 3D printers. In high school, he has spent time to teach youth hands-on science learning skills in his non-profit organization – Science Study Buddies. Due to the inspiration from his science research teacher, he founded the Science Study Buddies program to enhance and enrich youth science learning skills and critical thinking processes through fun, hands-on science activities. He has also done 5 years of intensive research in photovoltaics, that has led to various accolades on the national and international level.

CHAPTER 1

■■■

What's Possible with 3D Printing?

Game-changing, groundbreaking, enabling, and *disruptive* are just a few of the many words used to describe the growing manufacturing technology known as 3D printing. As an established means of making things (3D printing is more than 30 years old and was conceived by Chuck Hull in 1983), 3D printing is an additive fabrication process that can turn digital computer-generated geometry into physical objects using a variety of materials through a layer-by-layer building process. Because of many recent developments, this amazing process of making things has become a mainstream means of production and is now being utilized by companies large and small, startups, schools, hobbyists, designers, and artists in a wide range of industries.

What makes 3D printing unique among other manufacturing technologies is that it is easily accessible, opening the doorway for anyone, with the desire, to turn their ideas into physical products, parts, tools, and works of art. Part of this accessibility can be found in a range of online services that allow those interested to peruse and output 3D-printable content. As a valuable resource, the Web is a grand showcase of 3D-printable objects, sculptures, and parts waiting to be discovered. With nothing more than an Internet connection, access to 3D-printable content is only few clicks away, making it easy to download and purchase 3D-printable products.

Yet, while anyone can access 3D-printable content online, eventually aspiring 3D designers will want to create 3D-printable objects of their own. Thankfully, with the wide range of free modeling software tools available, there are many opportunities for designers from all walks of life to begin the modeling process. While, some may be more comfortable with jumping right in and exploring on their own, others might be overwhelmed by the many tools and techniques available. Therefore, for those who want a deeper insight on where and how to get started, this book, *Beginning Design for 3D Printing*, has been written to cover a wide range of design and modeling techniques for 3D printing.

Through the course of this book you will be introduced to step-by-step design techniques to build up modeling skills for 3D printing. Since this book follows the belief that 3D printing should be accessible to everyone, the workflows presented will take advantage of a broad range of 3D software tools that are freely available online. Some of the software tools introduced have intuitive interfaces and are easy to learn. A few 3D tools will be a bit more complicated, but since this book is using a pathway approach to educate, new users should have no problems if they begin their journey with the basic 3D modeling methods presented in the early chapters and then proceed along the path to learn more intermediate and advanced techniques presented in the later chapters. More seasoned modelers may find this book to be a handy reference as well since it will touch upon a variety of methods for generating 3D structures along with providing different ways to validate files to ensure success in the 3D printing process.

Before I begin discussing the modeling process for 3D printing, this initial chapter will provide a glimpse into the growing list of objects, structural forms, and products being created with the 3D printing process. If you are completely new to 3D printing, this chapter will provide you with an overview of what is possible and inform you of the growing trends shaping 3D printing's continuing evolution. Knowing what is and isn't possible will help you get a firmer understanding of what 3D printing is capable of and ideally will provide you with the confidence that your own ideas and designs are 3D printable. The many 3D-printed objects and trends featured in this first chapter will let your own imagination take flight as you begin the journey into the world of design for 3D printing.

1

Enter a New Era of Design with 3D Printing

The motivation to be creative—the spark of ingenuity that motivates us to design, craft, construct, and manufacture—is a basic human desire. Like Leonardo da Vinci, many of us have, in the back of our minds, a blueprint for an amazing idea, a working machine, or a beautiful piece of art. (In fact, many modern-day designers have 3D printed some of da Vinci's original illustrations, as shown in Figure 1-1.) Our desire to build and create is no different from the motivation that inspired great artists and engineers to bring the marvels of civilization into existence. Every day, a new concept is born in countless imaginations—ideas for products and things that would make the world a better place. Yet, we often cast such plans aside with the perception that they would be too complex, costly, and time-consuming to build. Self-doubt often sets in, and our most practical plans get thrown into the bin of abandoned dreams.

Figure 1-1. *An original illustration of a polyhedral structure by Leonard da Vinci and a 3D-printed version created in Blender and printed using Deezmaker's Bukito 3D printer*

But now 3D printing has made the inconceivable possible: the transformation of our digitally dreamt-up ideas into multidimensional reality. Through this growing 3D-printing phenomena, many barriers of production can be overcome, enabling the artist, designer, and manufacturer in all of us to bring our ideas into fruition. With this remarkable digital technology, a new world of fabrication awaits where anybody can turn computer-generated models into real-world objects. In schools, libraries, community spaces, local businesses, and online, many da Vinci dreams are now becoming 3D-printed reality.

As someone reading this book, you've probably developed an interest in 3D printing and are eager to take advantage of this incredible technology. But a 3D-printed product or work of art is only as good as the design put into it, and poorly conceived designs cost time and money. To harness 3D printing's true potential, a proficiency in design is extremely important. The excitement of 3D printing quickly fades when the final output fails to live up to its initial promise. Having the design skills to model objects for 3D printing is no trivial matter, and unfortunately, with the many software tools available, there is no single design solution to create a 3D-printable product. New, eager designers are faced with an overwhelming number of techniques to learn, which include spline-based modeling, polygonal box modeling, digital organic sculpting, parametric workflows, high-precision solid modeling, and even a bit of computer programming. Thankfully, many free 3D modeling programs are available that will allow a new designer to gradually learn the 3D modeling process. Open source applications and easy-to-learn software tools such as FreeCad, OpenScad, Tinkercad,

123D apps, Microsoft Builder, Blender, and Sculptris (Figure 1-2) allow eager designers to become familiar with the necessary basics (such as navigating 3D space and combining geometric shapes) to build simple objects that will enable them to start printing their own customized 3D objects.

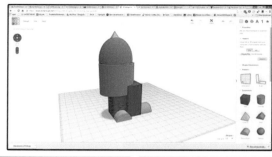

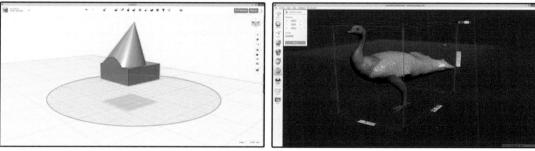

Figure 1-2. *Free applications from Autodesk (Tinkercad on top, 123D Design at the lower left, and Meshmixer at the lower right) can help newcomers learn 3D modeling skills right away*

The Importance of Universal Access

The best way to begin learning the design process is to explore the design tools that are freely available. Owning a 3D printer is not requirement for becoming a designer of 3D-printed objects since universal access is one characteristic that separates 3D printing from other manufacturing technologies. Through the Web, 3D designers can build geometry using web-based apps and then 3D print final products using a web-based service bureau. This universal access to 3D printing is enabled through online services such as Thingiverse, Shapeways, Sculpteo, 3D Hubs, Pinshape, and My Mini Factory. And to see 3D printers in operation, libraries, trade shows, copy shops, maker spaces (Figure 1-3), universities, and other brick-and-mortar spaces also offer firsthand, 3D printing access to the general public. All of these services take advantage of one commonality: they use cloud computing and the Internet to allow 3D print designers to communicate, design, and manufacture (one could say that with 3D printing the factory is in the clouds). Whether it's through downloading 3D-printing software, learning the 3D-printing process through online tutorials, or using online services to correct 3D files, the Internet plays an essential role in the 3D printing process.

If desired, 3D-printing production can be entirely on the cloud, and designers can work remotely to access a wide range of 3D printers. With the proliferation of the Internet, 3D printing holds an advantage over the manufacturing innovations of the past. The Gutenberg Press, the water wheel, blast furnaces, welding torches, kilns, CNC machines, laser cutters, and many more "industrial-age" innovations allowed corporations and privileged artists to pursue their manufacturing and artistic endeavors, but historically these tools were often unavailable to the general public. In the "digital age," access to 3D printing is a resource that is merely an Internet connection away. Therefore, not owning software or 3D printing hardware shouldn't stop you from asking, "Can I build it myself?" With the digital tools that are now freely available online, the answer is yes.

Figure 1-3. *Students at PVNet (an after school training center/makerspace located in Palos Verdes, California) learn 3D modeling skills. Hanging above them are drones they have developed using 3D printed parts*

If access to hardware and software is readily available, the next two most essential ingredients for 3D-printing success are a good imagination and the desire to create objects of your own. Without the designer's inspiration, the engineer's ingenuity, and the artistic desire to explore new shapes and forms, the 3D printer is merely a machine gathering dust or, at most, a glorified copier of inanimate objects.

Whether you're entirely new or you have access to a 3D printer but never had the opportunity to design 3D models of your own, your imagination and creative ambition will be an extremely valuable assets as you enter this amazing age of digital fabrication. The term *digital fabricator* may seem odd at first, but it's a very apt description of someone who uses digital tools to create physical objects. Illustrators and graphic designers wanting to explore design in multiple dimensions, engineers wanting to prototype new ideas, at-home hobbyists with inventive ideas for 3D objects, and entrepreneurs wanting to develop new products are all becoming digital fabricators as they learn how to design for 3D printing.

With 3D printing you turn polygons, curves, and pixels (the fundamental building blocks of computer-generated models) into real-world things. Your digital ideas, born from the imagination, become fabricated, physical objects you can hold in the palm of your hand—and, as the saying goes, if you can imagine it, you can build it. Essentially, when you design for 3D printing, you are turning "bits" into "matter." This process of turning "bits to matter" is a novel approach for manufacturing (some people call this process *reality computing*), and as you enter this world of digital fabrication, consider yourself to be a design pioneer, where your ideas and vision can be transformed into tangible art, tools, parts, and products.

As your experience with 3D printing grows, you will conjure up new things to build, construct, and fabricate while continually being inspired with the possibilities that 3D printing has to offer. Many designers have already awakened to the manufacturing possibilities of 3D printing, and the growing number of real-world "things" being reproduced with 3D printing shows the potential of this amazing technology.

New Creative Possibilities Emerge with 3D Printing

As this 3D-printing revolution unfolds, the lexicon of 3D-printable objects will continue to grow as inventors, designers, and entrepreneurs bring new ideas to life. To inspire your imagination, Figures 1-4 through 1-20 provide several examples of recent 3D-printed objects that showcase the diverse range of what is possible with 3D printing.

3D Printing Everyday Things

Designing everyday things, especially items for the home, is a growing application for 3D printing. Picture frames, vases, lamps, window displays, speaker enclosures, furniture, flowerpots, soap dishes, and wall hooks are just a few of the more commonplace items being produced. Figure 1-4 shows a home environment display created by 3D Print Life (`www.3dprintlife.com`) for the 2015 Consumer Electronic show. The room is stocked with a range of 3D-printed home goods showcasing 3D printing's diverse capabilities.

Figure 1-4. A room demonstrating 3D-printed objects for the home by 3D Printlife (`www.3dprintlife.com`) that appeared at the Consumer Electronics Show (CES) in 2015. Photo courtesy of Jeff Stevens

Reinventing Common Objects

As room interiors become populated with 3D-printed décor, inventive makers will find ingenious ways to reimagine everyday household items with 3D printing. Designers can give common, household items new shape and structure by taking advantage of 3D printing's ability to produce complex and nontraditional forms. For example, Rich Olson used his design expertise to create a spherical, nontraditional 3D-printed stereo speaker enclosure. Taking advantage of 3D printing's design flexibility, Olson was able to deviate from the traditional rectangular box design that is typically associated with speaker enclosures, bringing a new form factor to speaker design, as shown in Figure 1-5. The easy availability of 3D printing and open source tools has driven Olson to develop new, unique concepts and bring designs such as the spherical enclosure into existence. As an independent inventor, Olson is free to experiment with 3D printing for a number of his creations, which are featured on his web site, `http://nothinglabs.com/`. The design of the spherical enclosure was done with OpenSCAD, which is a free, downloadable parametric solid modeling tool. (Tutorials on how to use OpenSCAD are featured throughout this book.)

Figure 1-5. *Rich Olson of Nothing Labs (`http://nothinglabs.blogspot.com/`) created this hanging "Death Star" speaker enclosure using OpenSCAD. Photo courtesy of Rich Olson*

3D Printing in Schools

From the living room to the school room, the educational value of 3D printing cannot be ignored as academic institutions throughout the world are integrating 3D printing workflows into school curriculums. As part of the learning process, 3D printing can have a profound effect on education, where abstract concepts can be translated and built into physical objects in the classroom. For example, in physics labs, students can re-create turbine engines using 3D printing. For biology, 3D printing can be used to create plastic cutaways of the human body and internal organs. In history classes, teachers can produce 3D-printed historical replicas to supplement written material and increase student engagement. Even math problems can be made more comprehensible with physical models that explain geometry. In one sense, the shop class can be reborn as schools integrate additive manufacturing methods into traditional learning processes.

While many places of higher learning are just starting to catch on to the benefits of 3D printing, some schools have gotten a head start, giving students an advantage in the new additive workflows that will become standard for a range of industries.

One prime example is David Sheffler's Jet Engine Manufacturing course (that has been taught at the University of Virginia since 2011) where Sheffler's students build a working, one-quarter-scale replica of a Rolls-Royce AE3007 turbofan jet engine (Figure 1-6).

Figure 1-6. *A working, one-quarter-scale replica of a Rolls-Royce AE3007 turbofan jet engine created by Professor David Sheffler's students in his Jet Engine Manufacturing course that has been taught at the University of Virginia since 2011*

Some 3D-printed classroom projects lead to actual end-user projects where students become inventors. For example, at Design Technology Fab Lab located at Pasadena City College, students use 3D printing to create specialized maps for the visually impaired.

Under the guidance of 3D printing expert Joan Horvath, the Design Technology Pathway students at Pasadena City College use their design knowledge for 3D printing to manufacture tactile map (Figure 1-7) for visually handicapped students at the Frances Blend School located in Los Angeles.

Figure 1-7. *Here, Pasadena City College students present 3D-printed books for the visually impaired, which was project developed in PCC's Design Technology program*

Pushing the Boundaries of Sculpture, Structure, and Form

Artists such as Kevin Mack, Gil Bruvel, Bathsheba Grossman, Joshua Harker, and many more are pushing the boundaries of sculpture using 3D printing. Artists are using 3D printing to explore highly complex shapes with visually mesmerizing structures that defy gravity and challenge common artistic conventions.

Mack uses his expertise as an academy-award winning visual-effect artist to design and then 3D print mesmerizing sculptures that would be impossible to manufacture by any other means. Mack uses a variety of software tools and computational algorithms to create flowing and intricate structures that push the boundaries of 3D printing (Figure 1-8).

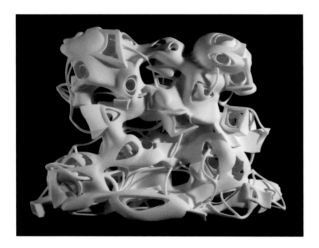

Figure 1-8. *Standing Mind Over Matter by Kevin Mack (`www.kevinmackart.com`). Photo courtesy of Kevin Mack*

3D Printing to Complement Traditional Sculpture

Sculpture artists such as Tim King and Bridgette Mongeon are using 3D printing to supplement preexisting workflows. In some circumstances, artists are using 3D printing to explore a larger sculpture on a smaller scale, or 3D printing is used in combination with other sculptural mediums.

Sometimes a sculpture is created through traditional means using a lost-wax cost process, where the initial artistic work is sculpted out of clay and used to create a mold, which is filled with wax. The process takes several months, while the wax mold is treated with sand layers to create a ceramic shell and then the initial wax is burned away. The new mold is then used for a bronze casting for the sculpted work. Other times the sculpture is created digitally using tools such as Pixologic's ZBrush and then output using a CNC machine to carve out the various forms.

With all the effort put into the lost-wax casting process, 3D printing enables artists to make unlimited reproductions of their original works. This capability to mass produce the original allows artists to market their work to a much wider audience by leveraging the 3D data scanned from the original.

Bridgette Mongeon has perfected the art of leveraging data from her sculpted originals. Mongeon's monumental Tiger sculpture is located on the campus of the Grambling State University Campus. The original tiger sculpture began as a digital file that was then carved from polyurethane foam using a CNC machine. Final details were added by hand with a layer of clay, and then the complete sculpture was finalized through a bronze casting process. Since the tiger began as a digital file, it was a straightforward task to output the digital version for 3D printing. The 3D-printed version can then be repurposed as a smaller sculpture and potentially jewelry. Figure 1-9 illustrates the four main steps in the process.

Figure 1-9. *The bronze Tiger by Bridgette Mongeon goes through four complete stages of production. From left to right, the tiger began as a digital file, was then CNC'ed and sculpted in clay, was cast in bronze, and was then output as a 3D-printed statue*

Tim King works in a similar fashion and uses the lost-wax process to create his bronze cast originals. King then takes advantage of 3D scanning to create 3D-printed versions using a variety of 3D printers. His bronze statue, Daddy's Balance, began as a class sculpture before going through the lost-wax-casting process. After the bronze version was completed, King used 3D scanning to digitize the bronze version for 3D printing. From the digital file, several versions were printed in a variety of materials, which included a metal version, a plastic version, and a resin version (Figure 1-10).

Figure 1-10. *King uses the lost-wax casting process to create his bronze statue titled Daddy's Balance. After the bronze version was complete, 3D scanning was used to create several 3D-printed replicas. From left to right is the original clay sculpture, a 3D-printed version in metal, and a 3D-printed version in plastic*

Engineering Impossible Objects

Mathematicians and engineers are using 3D printing to create complex clockwork objects and mathematically derived geometric forms. One of the more fascinating aspects of 3D printing is that fully assembled machines can be 3D printed in one pass, with embedded, operational gears and interconnected parts.

With the rise of 3D printing, gear-based 3D-printed objects have grown in popularity among engineers. Figure 1-11 shows a gear sphere designed by Paul Nylander. Gear spheres are highly complex mechanical globes where each gear cog must be in perfect alignment in order for all gears to rotate properly. Many of these "gear spheres," when 3D-printed and fully assembled, would be impossible to accomplish with any other type of manufacturing technology.

Figure 1-11. *Nylander's Gear Sphere. More of Nylander's work can be found at* www.bugman123.com. *Photo courtesy of Paul Nylander*

Another gear-sphere creation is the Mechaneu created by Toru Hasegawa at Proxy Design Studios (http://proxyarch.com). Similar to Nylander's gear sphere, the Mechaneu is printed fully assembled. One part of Hasegawa's design process involves the development of sophisticated algorithms to create intricate texturing on the gears (Figure 1-12).

Figure 1-12. *Hasegawa's intricate gear sphere is 3D printed fully operational in SLS plastic nylon. Complex algorithms were used to design the intricate gears. Photo courtesy of Toru Hasegawa*

3D Printing for Architecture

Architectures were some of the very first adoptees of 3D printing as a means to fabricate miniature scale models of large-scale construction projections. Closely following the evolving 3D printing technology, architects and interior designers have found a wide variety of uses for 3D printing such as 3D blueprints, 3D printed wall panels, 3D printed furniture and large scale structures that have been 3D printed in their entirety.

Several well-known institutions are developing the use of 3D printing as a construction method for large-scale structures and homes. Leading the way in this research is Contour Crafting at the University of Southern California. The Contour Crafting layering construction technology developed by Dr. Behrokh Khoshnevis uses a mammoth, large-scale 3D printer that is capable of printing a house in one pass. Currently the Contour Crafting 3D printer uses concrete as its main material but potentially in the future it may print other structural components such a plumbing and electrical systems.

Outside of educational institutions, architectural firms big and small are focusing a great deal of research on using 3D Printing as a means of construction. Companies such as Emerging Objects and Future City Labs are utilizing 3D printing in transform how buildings are developed.

Emerging Objects run by Ron Raels and Virginia San Fratello in Oakland California, focuses on using 3D printing to build large-scale structures with sustainable materials such as salt, sand, wood, and cement. The large-scale, natural looking forms developed through Emerging Object's proprietary 3D printing techniques often consist of interlocking and undulating patterns that help conserve heat and absorb sound (Figure 1-13).

Figure 1-13. *Pictured is Emerging Object's Involute Wall on display at the 3D Printer World Expo in Burbank California. The large-scale, 600lb structure is printed entirely with sand. The wavy, curved surfaces of the Involute Wall absorbs sound waves, and regulates temperature in extreme climates*

In neighboring San Francisco, Future City Labs is an experimental studio and architectural think tank overseen by Jason Kelly Johnson and Nataly Gattegno that explores the intersection of additive technologies and responsive building spaces. Future Cities Lab's design aesthetic involves organic-looking architecture and installations that respond to human feedback. One example is the proposed Paralux bench (Figure 1-14) – an outdoor bench that would be fitted with LEDs and sensors enabling it to react to the person sitting on it. The Paralux prototype concept was 3D printed in a range of materials varying in opacity and hardness, using multi-material Stratasys Objet500 Connex3 3D printer (Figure 1-15).

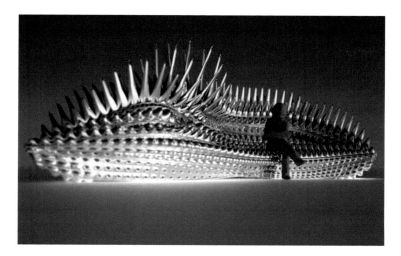

Figure 1-14. *The initial 3D rendering of the Future Cities Lab's Paralux bench spiky, undulating structure would be conceivable with 3D printing*

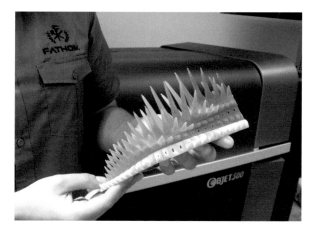

Figure 1-15. *The 3D printed prototype of Future Cities Lab's Paralux bench was printed by Fathom (studiofathom.com) on an Stratays Objet 500 Connex3 for an exhibit at the 2104 3D Printer World Expo in Seattle*

3D-Printed Jewelry and Luxury Items

Designers are turning to 3D printing to create jewelry and luxury items. Exotic materials and precious metals are often used to bring value to a final 3D-printed product. Designers such as Nervous System (consisting of Jessica Roshenkrantz and Jesse Louis-Rosenberg), Tomas Wittelsbach, Igor Knezevic, and Jenny Wu are creating one-of-a-kind works and wearable art that take advantage of the complex forms that are possible only with 3D printing.

Many of the jewelry artists producing 3D-printed jewelry are multiskilled designers who have years of experience creating 3D models in other fields. One of the nice things about designing for 3D printing is that the design knowledge can transfer across disciplines. For example, Igor Knezevic uses his skills as concept artist and background as an architect to create his intricately designed brand of high-end lamps (Figure 1-16).

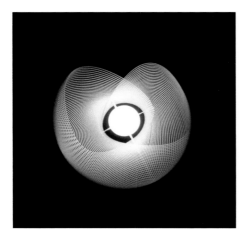

Figure 1-16. *A hypnotic bird's view eye of Igor Knezevic's 3D-printed lamp from his design collection at Alienology (`www.alienology.com/`). Photo courtesy of Igor Knezevic*

Jenny Wu also uses her background in design and architecture to creating compelling forms. The orbiting, encircling curves found in her Papilio Ring is reminiscent of a butterfly's flutter—demonstrating how even the most complex geometries can be created through the 3D printing process (Figure 1-17).

Figure 1-17. *Wu's Papilio ring demonstrates the intricate structures that 3D printing is capable of. More of Wu's can be found at `www.jennywulace.com`. Photo courtesy of Hans Koesters*

3D-Printed Fashion and Wearables

The fashion industry has also become adopters of the 3D printing phenomena, ensuring no fashion item is left untouched by the 3D printing process. Shoes, eyewear, neckties, full-length dresses, hats and undergarments have all been manufactured using a 3D printing process. 3D printing enables fashion designers to push the design of clothing traditional tailoring methods. By investigating the possibilities of 3D scanning combined with 3D modeling software, fashion designers transform couture into a form of wearable architecture where geometrically complex garments are printed in one pass. Designers leading the way in this 3D printing fashion movement include Francis Bitonti, Michael Schimdt, Iris van Herpen, Catherine Wales and Anouk Wipprecht.

Often embedded into a the 3D printed wearable designs are circuitry that allows the 3D printed clothing to react to environmental conditions. A notable example is the Intel Edison Spider Dress designed by Anouk Wipprecht (Figure 1-18) that emulates the predatory instincts of spider through it's sophisticated, 3D–printed, arachnid-like design. The dress is fitted with motion detectors allowing the articulated, spider appendages to react to those who approach it.

Figure 1-18. *The Intel Edison based Robotic Spider Dress designed by Anouk Wipprecht shows the sophisticated geometric couture made possible due to 3D printing. Photo courtesy of Jason Perry*

The Independent Manufacture of 3D-Printed Toys

Toy designers such as Mark Tragesar are using 3D printing to prototype captivating toy designs (Figure 1-19). As an independent toy designer, Tragesar is free to experiment with his own ideas and market his concepts to the toy manufacturing industry. The only limit to what Tragesar can create is his own imagination, which he pushes to the highest degree.

Figure 1-19. *An example of one of Mark Tragesar's 3D-printed toys. More examples of Mark Tragesar's work can be found at* http://insanitoy.com/. *Photo courtesy of Mark Tragesar*

3D-Printed Drones and Robotics

As more drones take to the sky, inventors and students are finding the 3D printer to be the perfect tool to create hard-to-find parts and drone accessories. These same inventors are also creating robots and computer-embedded wearable objects. Some of them are using new 3D printer technology, such as the Voxel8 3D printing (www.voxel8.co/) to print fully 3D print operational drones, complete with 3D-printed embedded circuitry.

Having the 3D printing technology on hand allows students to develop robotics as part of a course or for a personal project. For example, the after-school program at Palos Verdes on the NET Technology Center in Palos Verdes, California, students are taught how to design 3D-printed drones from concept to completion. Figure 1-20 shows a drone created via 3D printing by the PVNet students specifically for the Palos Verdes Fire Department.

Figure 1-20. *A drone created with 3D-printed parts by the students at PVNet (edu.pvnet.com) in Palos Verdes, California. The claw at the bottom of the drone was 3D-printed using carbon fiber filament*

The Migration to 3D Printing

Drones and robots are just a small sampling of what students and at-home inventors are exploring with 3D printing. Some of the more recent and inventive 3D-printed creations include a 3D-printed lawn mower, 3D cosplay accessories, 3D printed bridges, a 3D printed vacuum cleaner, a complete 3D-printed guitar, and a full-scale 3D-printed motorcycle—and as the adoption of 3D printing progresses, you will begin to see many more objects that were once created by traditional manufacturing methods migrate to a 3D printing process (you can find a timeline of 3D-printed designs in Appendix A). As more products become manufactured via 3D printing, skilled designers and engineers will be needed to convert preexisting models from traditional manufacturing into new, 3D-printable formats. The design engineers involved in this conversion can consider themselves to be pioneers of digital manufacturing as they translate traditionally manufactured products into 3D-printable products for the first time.

Quite a few of these pioneering designers have already begun this great migration into the world of 3D printing, and there are many more newcomers entering this "wild west" stage of experimentation and discovery. Right now, 3D printing is on the threshold of becoming mainstream, which is great timing for startups and inventive individuals who want to be the first to capitalize on 3D printing's manufacturing capabilities. Just as the World Wide Web grew from a digitally text-based communications tool to the ubiquitous, multimedia, social broadcasting platform that it is today, we are witnessing the beginning stages of 3D printing becoming an important manufacturing platform with many engaged designers excited about the prospects ahead.

The push to use 3D printing as a direct manufacturing process is a relatively recent phenomena. Many may be surprised to learn that 3D printing has been around for more than 30 years. The patent for the first 3D printer was developed by Chuck Hull in 1984. Back then, the first 3D printers were known as *rapid prototyping machines* and used a process known as *stereolithography*. The stereolithographic process is a popular form of 3D printing that continues to be used today and utilizes ultraviolet light to solidify a liquid resin (other stereolithographic processes use lasers). Initially, inaccuracies and weaknesses in the first materials being used (the first stereolithographic machines used photopolymer plastics that were brittle and prone to distortions) made the early 3D printers unsuitable for direct manufacturing.

While early-on 3D printings couldn't be used for direct manufacturing, it was useful for prototyping concepts in the early stages of the manufacturing process. The practitioners benefitting the most from these initial rapid prototyping/stereolithography machines were architects, industrial designers, researchers, universities, and manufacturers who used the stereolithographic prototypes for testing, research, and analysis. It was only just recently that advancements in 3D printing's capabilities (probably in the last five to ten years) have enabled industries, professionals, hobbyists, entrepreneurs, and home consumers to become aware of 3D printing's potential for direct manufacturing of final parts, custom products, and personalized works of art. The improvements leading the way for wider adoption and direct manufacturing include new material technologies along with advancements in 3D modeling software. University research, open source initiatives, crowdsourcing, and the maker movement have also pushed many of these advancements forward in recent years. Innovations coming from both highly regarded institutions and at-home tinkerers have led to the development and proliferation of 3D printers that are faster, portable, affordable, and more efficient.

Evolving Material Technologies

One factor behind 3D printing's popularity is the diverse range of materials that have been developed or adapted for the 3D printing process. As previously mentioned, when 3D printing was initially developed, one of the first materials being used was a liquid photopolymer. While fine for prototyping purposes, because of its weak structural integrity, the photopolymer-based material had a limited application, making it impractical for final products. Today's plurality of material offerings include thermoplastic filaments, liquid resins, and a variety of solid powders, providing enough variety to make 3D-printed objects far more useful for a wider range of applications.

FDM/FFF (3D Printing with Filament)

Currently, among desktop users of 3D printing, the most common material type used for 3D printing is thermoplastic filament. The 3D printing process that uses filament is referred to as either fused deposition modeling (FDM) or fused filament fabrication (FFF) 3D printing. Thermoplastic filament comes in coiled spools and in two distinct varieties: polyactic acid (PLA) and acrylonitrile butadiene styrene (ABS). Understanding the unique properties of PLA and ABS filament is part of the design process—both have unique chemical properties that make each suitable for certain applications. PLA filament is derived from organic chemical compounds, has a lower melting temperature, and is used for more detailed objects. ABS is derived from synthetic chemicals, has a higher metal temperature, and has greater material strength, making it more suitable for parts where strength is a necessity. Both PLA and ABS come in a broad array of colors.

To expand upon their material properties, there are several varieties of filament that have been combined with other materials (known as composite filaments), enabling owners of FDM printers to print in faux wood, stone, and various metals. For example, the Stratsys-owned company Makerbot produces composite PLA (http://store.makerbot.com/filament/composite), which comes in maple wood, limestone, bronze, and iron varieties. Some filaments, such as the Ninja Flex (www.ninjaflex3d.com/) enable the additive manufacturing of flexible products. There is also a carbon fiber filament that can be used for durable parts. The company Proto-Pasta (www.proto-pasta.com/) sells a number of "exotic" filaments, which includes conductive filament (for 3D-printed electronics) and magnetic filament.

Binderjet (Powderbed) 3D Printing

Other printers, beside FDM/FFF models, can print in a broader variety of materials that include stone-like gypsum. ZCorp printers (now owned by 3D Systems) use a process called *binderjetting* that uses a liquid polymer to bond together power material to create stone-like objects. The liquid used is the main agent that binds the powdered material together.

The binderjet process can work with a variety of materials in powder form. The original material used in the process was either starch or gypsum. Many new materials have been developed for the power-bed process, such as sand, acrylics, ceramics, calcium carbonate, and sugar.

By integrating the infusion of dyes into the process, the binderjet process can also print in full color and is often the choice printer artists and for "3D-printed" selfies.)

SLS

Selective laser sintering is similar to the binderjet process but uses a laser to melt plastic powders and plastic powder composites. Instead of binding material together with a liquid, a laser is used to melt material in a process called *sintering*.

Typical materials used in the SLS process are metal, ceramic, glass, and plastic powders.

SLM/DLMS

Selective laser melting (SLM) and direct laser metal sintering (DLMS) use lasers to melt or sinter metal powders to create metal products.

Many metallic materials are being developed to broaden 3D printing's application for direct metal manufacturing (especially in the aerospace industry). Any metal that can be reduced to a powder form is printable. Such 3D printers are beyond the price range of most individuals but can still be accessed through service bureaus such as Shapeways (`www.shapeways.com`). Ultimately, the kinds of metal material that can be output and the strength and durability of those outputted materials are dependent on the type of 3D printer being used.

Multimaterial 3D Printing

Multimaterial machines, such as the Stratasys Connex and Objet machines, can print multiple materials in one pass. The Stratasys process to multimaterial is made possible with a process known as *polyjetting*. Similar to inkjet printing, the polyjet process jets a curable resin but builds up objects layer by layer.

Demonstrating the results of the polyjet, multimaterial process are 3D-printed shoes developed by Pensar, a product development company located in Seattle, Washington. The 3D-printed Pensar shoe was printed on a Stratasys Objet500 Connex3 with a combination of rigid and flexible materials, allowing the shoe to bend yet stay rigid at the heel to properly protect the feet (Figure 1-21).

Figure 1-21. *3D-printed DNA shoes, designed by Alex Diener of Pensar (`http://pensardevelopment.com/`). Photo courtesy of Pensar*

Currently, the Pensar shoe is just a prototype since the polyjet material is not durable for extended athletic use. Ideally, as material research advances, more durable materials will become available, making the Pensar shoe suitable for extended use.

Sustainable Organic Materials

Material research is also enabling the use of natural and sustainable materials such as salt and wood pulp. Included in the development of organic material research that is being put to the test is the development of food-based printers that can produce custom candy, chocolate, and a variety of other culinary creations. Scientists are also using biological-based 3D printers that can output human cells.

This list is not all-conclusive because universities and researchers are developing 3D printers with a broader range of material offerings. This ongoing research, compounded by the many material offerings that already exist, will expand industrial applications for 3D printing, giving 3D print designers more opportunities to create a broader array of 3D-printed products.

At Emerging Objects, Ron Rael and his team have printed structures using a range of sustainable materials such as wood pulp, salt, and paper. Exemplifying the process of using salt, the Saltygloo structure, developed by Ron Rael and his team, is constructed from 3D-printed salt that has been harvested from salt crystallization ponds in Redwood City, California. The final structure is built from 336 translucent, crystalline salt panels and reinforced with aluminum rods (see Figure 1-22).

Figure 1-22. *Ron Rael and his team at Emerging Objects (`www.emergingobjects.com/`) use 3D-printed salt to construct large-scale structures*

Advancements in Software Design

Complementing new material innovations is the ongoing development of software packages specifically geared toward digital design and model production for 3D printing. Just as there are more materials to output to, there are more digital design tools available to create the models that can be output. CAD and animation software packages for 3D modeling have been around for quite a while. Most of these packages were designed for a specific industry intention, such as computer-generated animation, architecture, or manufacturing. For example, tools such as Autodesk's Maya and Maxon's Cinema4D have been developed for animation. But while both of these software packages have robust modeling capabilities, the intention was never specifically for 3D printing, and these packages have many other functions that may or may not be applicable for 3D printing.

Therefore, now that 3D printing is taking off, many software developers are creating dedicated modeling tools more focused on the workflows specific to 3D printing. Some of the workflows being focused on in this new generation of 3D modeling tools include the following: retoplogy algorithms, support generation, the ability to properly orienting models on the print bed, and procedures for validating models for 3D print output. Companies specifically dedicated to 3D-printing design workflows include iMaterialise, Matterhackers, Microsoft Netfab, Shapeways, Sculpteo, Adobe, and Autodesk. These companies are interested in the 3D-printing industry and have therefore developed tools to help ensure that the 3D-printing process runs smoothly. The majority of this book will focus on these various software tools to give an in-depth understanding of preexisting tools along with the new tools that are being developed.

The one workflow that is especially important is the process of validating models for 3D printing to ensure that any model created in 3D software is printable and error free. This will be explained in greater detail in later chapters, but for digital models to print properly, they must be "watertight," meaning that there can be no holes or gaps on the surface of digital model. Digital models must also be free of "nonmanifold geometry," such as extruded edges that have no surface thickness.

Another important process is support generation. Supports are necessary to ensure that the model stays stable during the 3D-printing process. Software tools such as MeshMixer (Figure 1-23) and Cura are capable of generating supports for 3D-printable models.

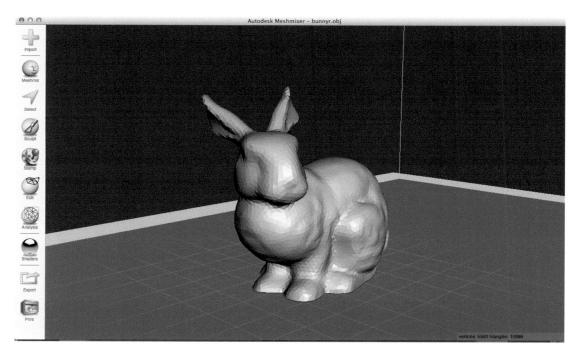

Figure 1-23. *MeshMixer has been a software tool specifically developed by Autodesk for 3D printing. The software was initially conceived by software developer Ryan Schmidt and allows users to connect, repair, and combine 3D models from other 123D apps via the cloud*

Interestingly, another advancement in the evolution software for 3D printing is the integration of 3D-modeling functionality into preexisting design software packages. One example is Photoshop, which has begun to integrate 3D-modeling capabilities in its latest version of its creative cloud application. Photoshop users can now create and manipulate 3D geometry from directly within Photoshop and send their designs directly from Photoshop for 3D printing.

Open Source Initiatives

Many open source initiatives, where software code and hardware designs are freely available to the general public, are helping 3D-printing technology proliferate, allowing newcomers to share their 3D-printed ideas with the world. The open source movement is a natural offshoot of the Internet-based economy, where giving things away for free is a great way to gain publicity and accelerate the adaptation of a product or idea. Helping spread open source 3D printing is one of the founding precepts of the RepRap (`http://reprap.org/`) movement. The RepRap movement helped establish desktop 3D printing by freely giving away plans on how to build a 3D printer. The Rep Rap movement plans to build an open source 3D printer; for more information, see `http://reprap.org/wiki/Eventorbot`.

The RepRap movement is one of the main catalysts behind the first Makerbot (which is probably the most popular desktop 3D printer on the market). RepRap stands for "replicating rapid prototype" and was developed by Dr. Adrian Boyer in 2005. Boyer's intention was to create a machine that could build other 3D printers. The designs for the first RepRap were shared among his colleagues and then distributed under a free software license. Since 2007, the plans have been shared and modified, enabling more people to become owners of low-cost 3D printers. The Makerbot (now owned by Statasys) is based on the RepRap plans.

A number of source initiatives have helped in the development of software for both the creation and validation of 3D-printable models. One popular open source modeling software package is Blender, which can be downloaded at `www.blender.org`. Blender will be featured in more detail in later chapters.

A software tool used specifically to ensure that 3D models are printable is Cura. Figure 1-24 shows the source code for CuraEngine on GitHub. GitHub (`www.github.com`) is great online resource to explore the development of new software tools for 3D printing.

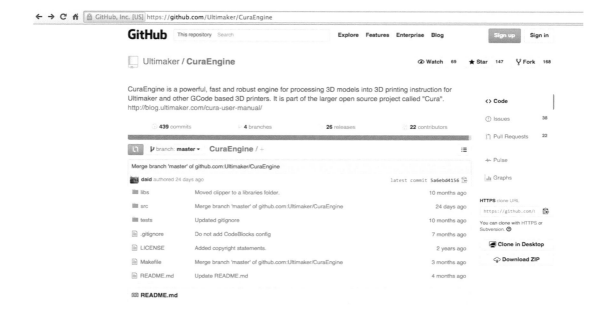

Figure 1-24. *CuraEngine is part of Cura, a 3D printing visualization/validation tool that has been made openly available to the 3D-printing community. Learn more at* `https://github.com/Ultimaker/CuraEngine` *and* `https://ultimaker.com/en/products/software`

Larger corporations such as Autodesk are also contributing to the open source movement. For instance, Autodesk has announced the world's first 3D-printing operating system known as Spark (`http://spark.autodesk.com/`).

Crowdfunding Driving the Development of New Machines

Crowdfunding sites such as Kickstarter and IndieGoGo are helping launch new 3D-printing business ventures along with the development of new 3D printer machines and technologies. Through crowdfunding, entrepreneurs gain a portion of their funding from a supportive public appreciative of the new technology.

Since 2011, there has been more than 60 crowdfunded printers; several are now available for sale and have become successful. Some of more successfully funded campaigns include the 3D Micro (`https://printm3d.com/themicro/`), which received $3,401,361, and the Form1, which received $2,945,885 (`http://formlabs.com/en/products/form-1-plus/`).

The decision to use Kickstarter to fund a new 3D printer can be a challenging proposition for many startups. Many new 3D printer manufacturers underestimate the amount of money it takes to bring a new 3D printer into the marketplace. Oftentimes more than crowdfunding alone is needed for manufacturers to gain success in the marketplace. To raise the necessary capital, successful 3D printer brands often use funding from venture capitalists and angel investors, in addition to the crowdfunding campaign, to grow their business.

While crowdfunding can be a gamble for some 3D printer startups, oftentimes it's only a means to enter the bring continued research and development for technology. With a vested interest grown through social networks and an online fan base, the recent proliferation of 3D printing can be partially attributed to recent crowdfunding campaigns. Without crowdfunding, many 3D printer brands would not find their way onto the desktops of consumers and businesses.

These many crowdsourcing campaign initiatives have created a highly competitive marketplace for 3D printers in general, and to gain market dominance, some crowdfunded 3D printer manufacturers have dropped the prices of their machines quite dramatically. At one point it was impossible to find a 3D printer for less than $20,000. Now 3D printers exist within a broad range of affordability. Some 3D printers are now available for about $300.

Successful crowd campaigns have also helped draw in angel investors, innovators, and entrepreneurs to establish startup companies focused on 3D printing. The promise of 3D printing, combined with crowdfunding, is tempting many would-be entrepreneurs to take the plunge and turn a dream into a potential business. One example is Own Phones (`http://ownphones.com/`)—an idea developed by Itamar Jobani who is using 3D printing to create custom Wi-Fi headphones (Figure 1-25). Through Kickstarter, Jobani raised more than $700,000. Without Kickstarter and the use 3D printing as the main means of manufacturing his designs, Own Phones may not be possible.

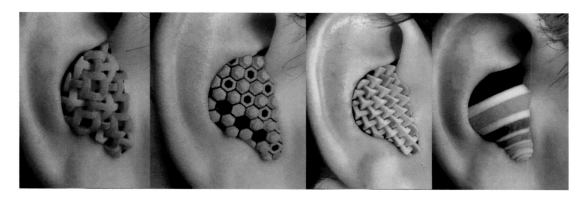

Figure 1-25. *Jobani's customizable Own Phones wireless headphones were made possible thanks to a successful Kickstarter campaign. Photo courtesy of Own Phones*

The New Maker Culture

Finally, there is a growing culture for making things and, in a way, a reemergence of a "shop class" culture—something that has faded away from many schools in recent years because of funding deficits. This new desire to build and construct can be seen through several growing initiatives: the maker movement, pathway education programs, STEM education, and many startups developing new wearables and products for the Internet of Things.

The maker movement can be seen in a number of growing Maker Fairs that take place throughout the world. These maker events draw thousands of individuals who are proficient in a range of manufacturing techniques. This enthusiastic group of hobbyist engineers progressively promotes 3D printing as the means to invent new products and explore advanced technology.

In addition to the Maker movement, there are many educational programs being implemented to encourage students to learn advanced technology skills that promote 3D printing. These educational initiatives include pathway programs and science, technology, engineering, and math (STEM) programs that help students stay focused in their field of study. Many of the pathway programs being implemented in community colleges focus on design, engineering, and manufacturing. These programs integrate 3D printing into curriculums to fuel engagement and create a results-driven education experience.

Together, the maker movement, education pathways, and STEM programs are introducing students to 3D-printing technology to provide design and production skills for the additive manufacturing careers that lie ahead. From these educational endeavors, a maker-based culture of learning is inspiring larger, more established companies, factories, and institutions to explore new 3D printing design methodologies and incorporate 3D printing into their preexisting workflows.

New Ventures Grow with 3DP Democratization

The developments featured in the previous sections are contributing growth factors influencing 3D printing's current popularity. Caught in this wave of innovation are businesses new and old, from large corporations to lone individuals, who are becoming more attracted to the possibilities enabled by 3D printing and multidimensional manufacturing. This collective of 3D-printing innovators comes from all walks of life and are helping pave the way to democratize manufacturing. In turn, as this democratization process grows, we are beginning to see more and more individuals independently turning their imagined ideas into physical objects. In this democratized manufacturing movement, the date is tangible, and the imagination is palpable. This ability to dream up new ideas and manufacture them through 3D printing is accessible to everyone, and this is what makes 3D printing such an interesting prospect for the beginning designer.

> *"When you produce something yourself instead of purchasing it, that changes your relationship to it. You are empowered by it."*
>
> —Amtel corporation (author unknown)

Since 3D printing is making everyday individuals the new drivers of innovation, many people with no background in manufacturing are waking up to the possibility that they can contribute a new idea, product, or invention to the marketplace and society. Engaged in an ongoing, online conversation about of what is possible, these participants of the 3D-printing process are showcasing a broad range of 3D-printable ideas and products for a wide range of industries. Through this engaging online discussion, innovation is accelerating, spreading the knowledge of 3D printing quickly. It is here, through the Web, that the democratization process is quickly spurring the desire for more individuals to access 3D-printing technology. Online marketplaces, forums, and social networks are inspiring the creation of new designs and products, giving birth to new business ventures that many have never thought of. This online proliferation of 3D-printable ideas is also impacting an incredibly diverse range of industries. Fashion, culinary arts, aerospace engineering, architecture, automotive design, visual effects, medical device manufacturers, and many more industries are all exploring the use of 3D printing as part of their manufacturing processes.

From this online evolution, 3D printing is becoming an equalizing force in the world of industrial manufacturing, enabling lone individuals to compete with larger companies. The evolution of 3D printing, in a way, is analogous to desktop publishing. Before desktop publishing existed, the publishing process was available only to privileged individuals, authors, journalists, and academics, and getting an idea to print was a lengthy process. It was necessary to work with a typesetter and a printing press operator to a get a professional-looking page of text with illustrations and photographs printed. There were other options available, but the process was cumbersome. It wasn't until the introduction of PageMaker software from Aldus and the LaserWriter printer from Apple Computer that publishing was made available to the masses. As desktop publishing grew, the technology enabling it become more affordable, making it far easier for lone individuals to get their ideas printed. Incredibly, 3D printing predates desktop publishing by one year—the concept of desktop publishing wasn't conceived until 1985, one year after Chuck Hall invented stereolithography.

Just as desktop publishing opened the doors and allowed new ideas to reach a larger audience, 3D printing is allowing new inventions, art, and products to flourish and grow. Already, a number of novel applications and intriguing startups are being established, with many companies springing up to take advantage of the technology, disrupting traditional manufacturing methods with new 3D printing processes. These new enterprises include Organovo, which is using 3D technology to print human tissue (www.organovo.com); Sugarlabs, which is creating 3D printing edible objects (http://the-sugar-lab.com/); Local Motors, a company specializing in 3D printing cars (https://localmotors.com); Metamason, which is creating medical devices; and Made In Space, which is developing 3D-printing technologies for off-world manufacturing.

As 3D printing startups continue to grow, new designers will be needed to produce 3D models for a broad range of applications. The diverse commodities now being manufactured with 3D printing range from cars to candy and from aerospace parts to artificial organs and are establishing a new growing market for 3D print designers. Even electronic objects, such as flashlights, smartphones, hearing aids, drones, and loud speakers may soon be entirely printed with a 3D-printing process. As products that were created with subtractive, industrial technologies migrate to new 3D printing workflows design, considerations will be brought to the fore, and many questions need to be answered. What are digital design techniques that can be used to create objects that are lighter, stronger, and better constructed? Can objects be customized for a specific end user? Can we cut material costs by designing objects more efficiently? As we enter what appears to be a "nothing off-limits era" of digital fabrication, many 3D printing design challenges await. From simple to complex and from functional to abstract, 3D printing is giving designers the opportunity to investigate a wide range of design possibilities.

Design Collapses

The desire to pursue new design concepts with 3D printing has led to a cross-pollination of ideas across seemingly unrelated industries. There is now a growing list of professionals using similar design workflows to build, fabricate, and design three-dimensional objects. This list includes engineers, medical researchers, architects, fashion designers, jewelry artists, chefs, sculptors, mechanics, carpenters, roboticists, industrial designers, VFX artists, and animators. Fields both technical and artistic are finding commonalities in the process of design. As new 3D printing ventures are being explored, there is a growing synergy between a diverse range of professions. The phrase "design is collapsing" refers to this growing synergy, where separate design disciplines are collapsing into a singular design methodology. Designers are now borrowing techniques from unrelated professions and using universal design principles to explore new fields outside their initial interest. With these universal principles, 3D printing professionals are finding it easy to transition into new careers. Architects are becoming fashion designers. Engineers are becoming artists. Occupations that were once separate and distant have grown closer together using common core design principles that are being reinforced through the 3D printing process. As commonalties unfold among these many fields, a new interdisciplinary class of digital designer is starting to emerge.

When we talk about having an " interdisciplinary skill set," we are referring to someone who has an understanding of universal design principles and how they can apply these skills across a broad range of disciplines. Universal design skills would include basic design theory concepts such as contrast, rhythm, scale, texture, positive/negative space, radiation, dominance, and the interrelationship of forms. Just about every profession involved in the fields of construction, design, and fabrication shares these basic principles. Interdisciplinary design skills provide a universal toolkit, allowing digital fabricators to tackle a wide range of production challenges and help ensure the economic viability of 3D print designer.

With interdisciplinary design, the joy of discovery occurs when we juxtapose the shapes and forms from uniquely distinct industries. For example, an architect may find inspiration in forms associated with biology. A culinary artist is using engineering principles to explore the shape of food. Fashion designers may find influences in aerospace design. With 3D you may have already seen the influence of seemingly opposing ideas in strangely shaped electronic devices, jewelry, and 3D-printed foods. These various mashups of established ideas is allowing us to imagine new, cleverly manufactured products ranging from aerospace parts to wearable robotics. As you will progressively explore the world of 3D-printed design, you too will find ways combine a diverse range of influences into new works of art.

Much of the exploration and experimentation that permits this interdisciplinary approach is deeply rooted in the digital 3D modeling software that gives design practitioners the freedom to mix and match ideas in new and interesting ways. While the industrial application may be different, the design principles remain the same, and these principles are bonded together through digital technologies. While learning these tools may be challenging at first, having the creative flexibility to adapt to new software tools while adhering to universal design principles is a great asset for employment.

Additive vs. Subtractive

As you begin to explore design for 3D printing, it's important to understand the differences between subtractive and additive manufacturing. Subtractive manufacturing is associated with traditional manufacturing and often involves cutting up materials and assembling the resulting pieces into its final form. Sometimes this act of reassembly involves welding, gluing, or nailing the pieces back together. A simple example of subtractive manufacturing would be the construction of birdhouse, which would require sawing pieces of wood and then nailing and fitting the resulting planks to make the final birdhouse. Other subtracting processes for manufacturing involve the manipulation of material by scraping, cutting, or chiseling—such as the CNC process of carving away from a block of material or the sculpting of a human bust by chiseling away the form from the alabaster.

Before the advent of 3D printing, subtractive manufacturing was really the only option for manufacturing. Most complex and intricately curved shapes were impossible to make by any other means. One of the downfalls of subtractive manufacturing is that it involves using several machines in order to make complex shapes possible, and this can be time-consuming and expensive. A subtractive pipeline can include a number of these processes: CNC, drop hammering, laser cutting, water-jet cutting, and welding.

One step in the subtractive manufacturing, which is actually more of an additive process, involves the use of liquid materials, whether they are plastic or molten metals, to make new forms. Adhering globs and bits of material together, transforming malleable material or using a mold with hardening liquid material is another step in the traditional, additive manufacturing process. Molds are often essential as a first step. Whether through molten metal or soft clay, the manufacturing method of building up material through a pouring or sculpting process is the closest preexisting traditional approach that is similar to the 3D process. But there are three main differences. First, with 3D printing, molds and dies are not necessary. Second, except with some 3D metal additive processes, there is no need to "bake" the material to create a hard, final object. Third, there is no need for post manipulation of the printed object to ensure that the final output matches the original design specifications. With some traditional operations in a subtractive manufacturing pipeline, objects can deform during the industrial manufacturing process. For example, some metal objects that have been physically formed using large industrial drop hammers suffer from a condition known as "springback," and they must be adjusted to go back into their proper specified shape. In the digital world of 3D printing, the shape of the 3D-printed object is a true duplicate of the initial 3D file that was designed in the modeling software. The 3D-printed file will appear the same every time, matching the original digital design.

Understanding the limitations of subtractive manufacturing, you can easily see how 3D printing offers a new approach to building three-dimensional objects. 3D printing is a straight route from digital file to final part. Some have dubbed the 3D-printing process as a "mind-to-part" workflow, meaning that there are no intermediate steps or assembly processes necessary to construct the final 3D-printed object. All that is needed is the designer, a software program, and the 3D printer. Already there is talk that complex supply chains used in traditional, subtractive manufacturing (where parts are built as multi-piece assemblies through dies, metal pours, CNC, and welding) will be supplanted by the more simplified 3D printing, or additive manufacturing.

Growing Objects

The additive process of 3D printing is sometimes referred to as *growing an object*. To some, that may seem peculiar since the word *grow* has organic connotations unfitting for a mechanical machine that builds something. But, if you have ever had the opportunity to watch a 3D printer in action, growing an object is an apt way to describe the process because materials are deposited layer by layer.

This layer-by-layer process depends upon the type of 3D printer being used. Some machines emit plastic material (known as *filament*) through a hot end, which is connected to an extruder; others use lasers to fuse material together in a bed of powder. Regardless of the additive process being used, the act of creating a 3D part is also universally known as "growing a part."

The 3D-printing process of growing a part is analogous to the formation of coral, or the calcification of a shell where thin substrates form one layer upon the other to create the final calcified object. Upon examination of coral or seashells, the organic complexity of this additive process is readily apparent. This organic complexity can be found throughout nature. Spiraling forms, vegetation branching off in random directions, vines revolving around one another, web-like structures, and other cellular patterns are quite common.

Exploring other natural processes, where layering is evident, such as the growth of fungi, plants, and sediments, can help designers better understand the complexity achievable with 3D printing. In fact, many 3D print designers often use organic forms to influence the shapes of the objects they are developing. Examples include the Spirula speakers by Akame, the jewelry and architectural elements created by Nervous System, and Neri Oxman's futuristic fashion.

While the organic way of growing objects sometimes may produce results that feel alien yet strangely compelling, this process of additively creating is something that we should already feel comfortable with. As humans we are naturally attuned to the process of stacking and layering. If you have stacked blocks together and built something out of Legos, you are already familiar with the additive process of construction.

Knowing that we all have, intuitively at one point or the other, used mud, clay, or building blocks in an additive way can help us feel more confident with tackling some of the more complex software tools used for 3D printing. Most CAD and modeling software packages operate in a similar fashion, where shapes are gradually combined to create the final product to be printed. There even exists an app that lets us convert a real-world Lego model into a digital file suitable for 3D printing.

The Paradigm Shift in Design and Manufacturing: Is This the Beginning of a Manufacturing Renaissance?

The notion that parts and products can be "grown" excites the imagination, making 3D printing appear like something out of science fiction. Besides being a subject of curiosity, the growing popularity of 3D printing, and the respective media attention it receives, makes many believe we are entering a manufacturing renaissance where anything is possible.

This renaissance term is often overused for marketing purposes—companies and organizations wishing to engage an audience describe themselves as entering a "renaissance" when they release a new product or undergo a branding change. But the word *renaissance* has positive connotations conveying change, artistic quality, the proliferation of knowledge, and the democratization of learning skills (it isn't surprising that many companies have an affinity with the terms), and these concepts can be inspiring to new designers entering the field of 3DP. Realistically, it may take some time for 3D printing to gain the renaissance status, and only time will tell if the term is truly applicable. Currently, what makes 3D printing fit for the description is its ability to enable anyone to become the sole master of the 3D printing production process, from the initial conception of an idea to its final 3D-printed output.

This urge to be a master of the design process may have begun in the Renaissance where books and libraries grew thanks to Gutenberg's press machine. From that point forward, human and machines have worked together to make life easier and the world more understandable through the dissemination of knowledge and creativity. If I were to give the creative process of 3D printing a historical frame of reference, where humans first used machines for mass production, it may have begun with Gutenberg—or even perhaps from an earlier inventor who came before him.

Like the Gutenberg press, desktop computing, and the Web, 3D printing is a transformative technology that allows for the proliferation of ideas across a wide audience. In 3D printing's case, these ideas take the form of physical objects or virtual 3D models. Just as the Gutenberg press was instrumental in spreading knowledge in the Renaissance by enabling the mass production of books, 3D printing is instrumental for spreading the knowledge of manufacturing in the digital age by enabling anyone to produce the objects they desire.

Indeed, the designers who are now taking advantage of 3D printing have the same desires as Gutenberg, Thomas Edison, Henry Ford, da Vinci, Chuck Hall, and the other great inventors who have come before them. The ability to freely utilize freely distributed knowledge, whether it's through books or digital transmission, compels us to dream, design, and invent. This same urge to create and invent is how 3D printing technology was born from the mind of Hull, who toiled with photopolymers to create the first 3D-printed object. Therefore, the origin of 3D printing is more than the evolution of machine; it is the product of humanity's desire to invent and create.

TERMINOLOGY USED IN THIS BOOK

Before getting too deep into the design for 3D printing, I will discuss a number of terms that may be confusing to new designers starting off.

The use of term *traditional* and *conventional* will be used throughout this book to define design, construction, and manufacturing methods that do not use 3D printing technology as a means of fabrication. This is not to disparage conventional techniques in any way since many conventional methods of manufacturing can complement the 3D-printing process.

The distinction is necessary in order to compare and contrast 3D printing with other manufacturing techniques. Examples of traditional or conventional manufacturing methods that have been in dominance in factories and manufacturing facilities include CNC, water jets, presses, lathes, welding, and other tools that bend, carve, combine, and deform to transform materials into new shapes. The terms *traditional* and *conventional* also fall into the category of legacy technologies, in other words, manufacturing methods that are starting to decline. An example of conventional legacy method would be metal-cutting machines that have been replaced by water jets and lasers.

3D printing can also be used as an over-arching term describing a broad range of processes, all of which build objects using a layer-by-layer process.

Also, the terms *3D printing* and *additive manufacturing* can be used interchangeably. Some sources may distinguish between the terms and describe *3D printing* as a subset of additive manufacturing. Indeed, much debate on this subject could arise to help classify the two terms. But since 3D printing is being adopted by many entrepreneurs to create real-world usable products (and not just prototypes), it can be trivial to distinguish between the two.

One may argue that the term *additive manufacture* is reserved for larger companies and enterprises, but 3D printing opens up the manufacturing process to everyone—giving students, at-home hobbyists, artists, and designers the opportunity to bring 3D-printed concepts to the marketplace. Two prime examples of additive manufacturing from startups and lone individuals include 3DPrintlife and Michael Aylesworth, which have 3D-printed products for sale online store at Amazon.com `www.amazon.com/gp/node/index.html?ie=UTF8&me=A1V9JQ2VE1JCFX&merchant=A1V9JQ2VE1JCFX&qid=1417780678`).

Finally, you may see the abbreviation 3DP many times. This is just a simple way to say 3D printing.

Summary

This chapter provided some valuable insight into what is currently being created with 3D printing and where 3D printing is headed in order to bring clarity, direction, and, most importantly, inspiration to the design process for 3D printing.

Now that we have explored a full range of 3D-printed products and works of art, newcomers and veterans alike should now have the creative confidence that it is possible to turn their ideas into 3D-printed reality. The information herein will help up-and-coming 3D print designers navigate the many software tools and workflows used during the 3D-printing design process. Smile and congratulate yourself because you are now taking the first steps enabling you to conquer the design methodologies, software tools, and production techniques that will help you master this amazing technology.

■ ■ ■

CHAPTER 2

Exploring Design Techniques for 3D Printing

As you learned in Chapter 1, the applications for 3D printing (additive manufacturing) are extremely diverse. With a very broad range of industrial applications being impacted by 3D printing (which include the fine art, aerospace, automotive, toy design, construction, fashion, medical devices, entertainment, and culinary arts industries) and with many more applications that have yet to be discovered, it would appear that almost any object being manufactured using traditional (subtractive) methods can now just as easily be manufactured with 3D printing. This is enlightening news to the many artists, designers, and engineers on the quest to 3D print their first objects. Since it appears nothing is off-limits, many makers are now eager to learn the design techniques being used for the 3D-printing process so they too can be part of this manufacturing revolution.

This chapter will break down the design process for 3D printing, with an analysis of the workflows and various techniques being used for 3D modeling. The chapter will also discuss the modeling process, the components of 3D models, and the freely available software tools that will allow anyone to create their own 3D models. The beginning of this chapter will survey a variety of techniques being used in the 3D-printing community. At the end of the chapter you'll find a rundown of the 3D modeling applications that are used in the modeling exercises in the remaining chapters of this book. The purpose of this chapter is to explore a wide variety tools and techniques to illustrate that there are many ways to create designs for 3D printing. Again, it is important to note that the majority of tools mentioned (with a few exceptions) are free and available to anyone with Internet access.

You Become the Factory

Designing objects for 3D printing can be a fun, creatively fulfilling, and even financially lucrative opportunity for those wanting to enter this expanding field of digital, additive manufacturing. As a 3D-print designer, you can have total control over the means of production. From the first design sketch to the final 3D-printed part, you can work with confident independence on an idea of your own creation. You can be in complete control of every aspect of the production process, from the initial design to the final sale. You become the factory, which can provide a great sense of personal satisfaction knowing that any dreamt-up design can be turned into a part, product, or work of art without any outside assistance.

The independent spirit associated with 3D printing is one of the main reasons behind its growing popularity. 3D printing democratizes the act of making things, putting the process of manufacturing into the hands of the individual. With minimal startup costs (you probably need to own or have access to a computer or laptop to get started) and little up-front experience, there are few barriers denying entry. The allure of being in control of the means of production and the desire to have a hand in the creative process are attracting many people to this emerging means of "making things." With the growing ecosystem of digital design software and wide range of affordable 3D printer hardware, 3D printing is now affordable and accessible to everyone. Since anyone can now take advantage of the technology, it is a great time for small groups and individuals to learn and discover design processes for 3D printing and even start manufacturing companies of their own.

Reviewing Your Design Options

Even though 3D printing has been around for 30 years, for the general public, it has only just recently become a mainstream means of making things, and there is much to learn (and teach) about the design skills necessary to build 3D-printable objects. The great thing about entering the field now is that you are not alone in your desire to learn. The majority of designers, artists, and engineers in the world have little or virtually no 3D-print design experience, and you will be in good company as you tackle the design challenges associated with 3D printing for the first time. Even at universities throughout the world, 3D-printing curriculum has yet to be thoroughly developed, and the knowledge of how to design for 3D printing is just starting to take shape.

Therefore, in this growing landscape of fresh ideas, it's an exciting time to learn and grow with the technology. As you progressively gain more modeling skills and design techniques for 3D-printable objects, you will begin to uncover more ways to explore 3D printing's true potential—and even contribute to the learning process. Many of the techniques you will find here may inspire other novel approaches for turning your ideas into printable products and ideally lead the way to even more exciting design possibilities. But, before we get started, it is always good to take the time to creatively reflect upon the many different design approaches already being utilized by the 3D-print community. This will give you a better understanding of the 3D-print design process.

Generating Ideas for 3D Printing: Where to Begin

When approaching 3D modeling for the first time, many may wonder where to begin. Most people will consider CAD to be the only means to create 3D models, but recent advances in 3D software and web-based design tools make it easier than ever to design content for 3D printing. Outside of traditional CAD modeling, there are many new options to create 3D content, including web-based applications that can turn flat sketches into 3D designs, techniques that turn photographs into 3D models, and organic sculpting tools that let designers create 3D models using "digital clay." The following sections run through the various techniques that both newcomers and experienced engineers will appreciate.

The Importance of Sketching to Developing Ideas

One of the easiest ways to begin thinking about the design process for 3D printing is to begin with a simple sketch or doodle of the object you want to create. These simple doodles are sometimes called *thumbnails*, *wireframes*, *whiteboard sketches*, or *napkin sketches* because they are often derived and dreamt up during quick moments of inspiration, in lunch meetings, during presentations, or in short conversations where the only effective way of visualizing an idea is through a quick sketch. These sketches are usually nothing more than rough scribbles that are simple and concise and can act as rudimentary blueprints for greater ideas (Figure 2-1). Sketching can be an iterative process, where the spark of inspiration is drawn on a scrap piece of paper and then refined as a series of thumbnails back at the office.

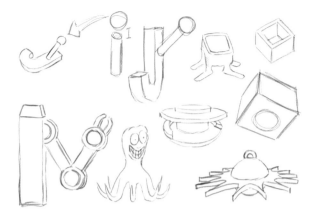

Figure 2-1. *The brainstorm process for 3D modeling should begin with a series of sketches*

■ **Note**   The term *thumbnail* is commonly used to describe small, descriptive sketches usually drawn by art directors and industrial and graphic designers to help illustrate variations in a concept or design. Such sketches are usually tiny and quickly drawn in a series to visualize and brainstorm a broad range of ideas.

Even in the digital age, where many ideas are born on the screen, quick sketches by hand help designers realize the look and feel of the final product they are designing for 3D printing. Sketchbooks are essential for these moments of inspiration, and as time goes on, you will find yourself building a library of sketches representing the many things you want to produce with a 3D printer.

Turn a 2D Drawing into a 3D Object to Create Jewelry, Decorative Objects, and Tiny Intricate Parts

Sketches are more than a means to help brainstorm new ideas; there now exists a variety of software-driven techniques that will turn a scanned 2D drawing, sketch, or image into a 3D object. If you are apprehensive about 3D modeling or need a quick solution to create a 3D model, using a software conversion process to turn a 2D image into a 3D object offers a viable solution. Professionals who take advantage of this process include jewelers who need to create small, intricate objects and artists who take need to take an image from a client (such as a logo) and quickly convert it to a 3D project. Note that this process works best with grayscale images and is not appropriate for photographs (in other words, you couldn't use this process to turn a photo of a person into a 3D object). Various methods for converting 2D sketches into 3D drawing are explained in the next section.

Web Sites That Will Turn 2D Drawings into 3D Objects

There are several digital tools and online applications that will let you turn these quick napkin sketches into 3D-printable geometry objects, More precisely, you can turn a 2D image into an `.stl` file, which the common file format for a 3D printable object.

■ **Note**   The .stl file format was developed by Charles Hull to allow CAD software to output suitable files for 3D printing. Most standard CAD and computer modeling programs will export an .stl file. The .stl format is often used as an abbreviation of stereolithography and also stands for Standard Tessellation Language.

Basically, these software tools will turn simple black-on-white drawings into real 3D objects that you can later modify and edit in various other 3D applications. The typical workflow is that you begin with a simple two-dimensional black (or shades of gray) sketch on white. You can then scan or take a photo of that image (which is easy to do if you own a smartphone), e-mail it your computer (most likely a .jpeg file), and open that image in Photoshop for further editing. From there you can upload/import the image to a number of 2D-to-3D conversion applications. Many of these applications are free web-based apps and therefore easily accessible if you have access to the Internet. All of these apps will convert your 2D image into a 3D object and extrude the two-dimensional sketch into a three-dimensional object (Figure 2-2). The range of grayscale tones in the images you import into the apps will often determine the elevation of the 3D object that you output. From there, most of these 2D-to-3D conversion applications will let you export or download an .stl file that you can modify in another 3D design program. If you are satisfied with the final outputted 3D objects, you can send it directly to your 3D printer or a 3D-printing service bureau for final output.

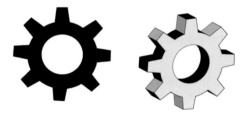

Figure 2-2. *A 2D gear and the extruded 3D version*

■ **Note**   An image that uses gradiations of gray to create an elevated 3D object is called a *height map*.

There are a number of web-based software tools that are readily available (for free) for this conversion process. These web-based tools can be found on the following websites: www.selva3d.com, www.3defy.com, and www.shapeways.com. Also, there are several free 3D modeling applications that are capable of turning two-dimensional images into 3D geometry as well, such as OpenSCAD (available for download at www.openscad.org)and Blender (available for download at www.blender.org/). Both OpenSCAD and Blender are discussed in greater detail later in this chapter. The process of using www.selva3d.com and www.shapeways.com is discussed in the following sections.

Selva3D

A simple approach is two converting a 2D image to 3D geometry offered by the web site www.selva3d.com (Figure 2-3). Simply go to www.selva3d.com, choose any JPEG image on your hard drive, upload it via the "Choose file" button, and then click the Transform button. The web site may take up to 10 minutes to process the file, but once the process is complete, a "Download .stl" button will appear allowing you to download the 3D .stl version of the file to your hard drive.

Figure 2-3. *The interface to upload a 2D image to* `www.selva3d.com`

Selva3D is a web-based application that turns a 2D grayscale into a height map. The image is extruded into 3D geometry. The resulting geometry has a faceted exterior, appearing as a series of connected triangles as seen in Figure 2-3. These triangles are more properly referred to as *faces* or, in computer graphic terms, *polygons*. The process of generating the faces that make up the geometric composition of the newly 3D object is known as *tessellation* (Figure 2-4).

Figure 2-4. *An example of the facted 3D geometry created in Selva3D*

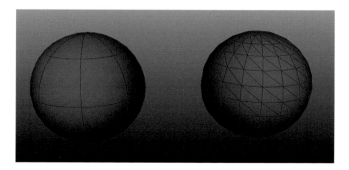

Figure 2-5. *Left: A 3D representation of a sphere constructed from curves before tessalation. Right: The representation of the sphere after tessalation. The tessalated sphere is now composed of planar, triangular faces to represent the curvature of the sphere*

■ **Note** A tessellated surface is a faceted, geometric, 3D surface composed of repeated planar faces. Each individual face will be three- or four-sided, but typically three-side faces (in other words, triangular faces) are the most common. Together, these planar faces form the geometric structure of a 3D object. The process of tessellation turns any type of geometry into a series of faceted faces. To be 3D printed, all 3D models must be tessellated.

Shapeways

Similar to Selva3D, on the Shapeways web site there is an app called 2D to 3D (www.shapeways.com/creator/2dto3d) where the same premise applies (Figure 2-6). Upload a black-and-white or grayscale image to the Shapeway's 2D to 3D app, and the app will extrude that image into a 3D object. The Shapeway's 2D to 3D web app has added functionality that enables users to determine the width and thickness of their final 3D creations. Users can then upload the file directly to Shapeways to be 3D printed or can download the results as an .x3db file. Unfortunately, not too many applications will allow the import of the .x3db file for further manipulation. One of the few applications that will open the .x3db file is Netfabb, which will then allow users to export the file as an .stl.

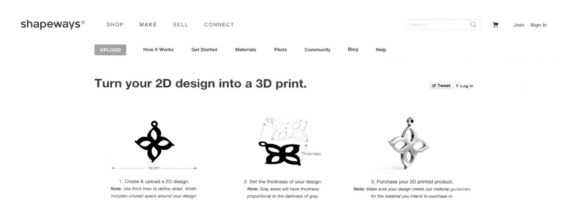

Figure 2-6. *The 2D to 3D app found on* www.shapeways.com/creator/2dto3d *also converts 2D images into 3D geometry*

■ **Note** The X3DB file format is associated with X3D, a royalty-free open standards file format and runtime architecture to represent and communicate 3D scenes and objects using XML, developed by the Web3D Consortium.

Other Options to Turn 2D Images into Geometry

Here are some other options to turn 2D images into geometry.

Pixologic's ZBrush

Most of the other programs work in similar fashion but may have a steeper learning curve than Selva3d. For example, Pixologic's ZBrush has an innovative feature called Shadow Box (Figure 2-7) which will turn 2D, grayscale, silhouetted images (in computer graphic terms these grayscale images are often called *alpha masks*) into 3D geometry. The ZBrush Shadow Box feature is a cube that will project three images placed on their X, Y, and Z faces to generate the 3D geometry.

Figure 2-7. *Pixologic's ZBrush Shadow Box feature can generate geometry from 2D images*

Adobe Photoshop and Illustrator CC

If you own Adobe Photoshop CC, you can explore grayscale height maps in more detail by using the New Mesh from Layer feature in Photoshop's 3D menu (Figure 2-8). There are many other features to explore in Photoshop CC as well that will extrude 2D graphic elements 3D geometry. Photoshop CC will allow designers to send 3D files directly to online service bureaus for 3D printing. If you can afford Adobe Creative Cloud, Photoshop CC is a great tool to have in your 3D-printing design arsenal.

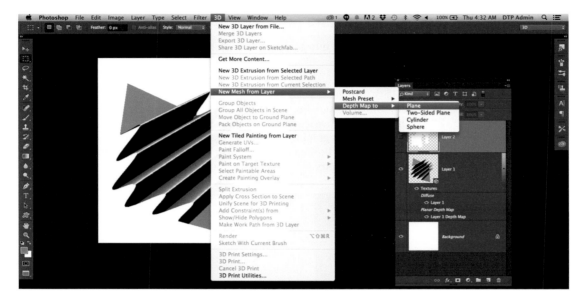

Figure 2-8. *Photoshop CC's New Mesh from Layer function can convert grayscale images to 3D objects*

Both height maps and alpha masks, in ZBrush and Photoshop, can allow designers to create inset and carved patterns on the surface of their objects (Figure 2-9). This can be a great way to add a bit of flair and texture to normally flat surfaces. This technique will be discussed in later chapters.

Figure 2-9. *A graphic design created in Adobe Illustrator has been used to create an inset design on the picture frame in ZBrush*

Another option is use a 2D vector program such Illustrator CC to explore a broad range of silhouettes (Figure 2-10) to brainstorm interesting graphic patterns that can be converted to alpha masks and height maps. By exploring gradients, vector symbols, typography, and various masking techniques in these 2D design applications, you can build up an alpha library of part silhouettes that can be referred to for quick part generation.

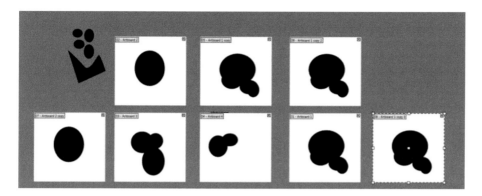

Figure 2-10. *A number of 2D images designed in Adobe Illustrator will be used to create 3D geometry in another program*

The benefit to using a flat silhouette to generate 3D geometry is that it can save a lot of time. For example, you can extract 3D information from a 2D blueprint to quickly make parts for engineering purposes or use architectural blueprints to quickly make 3D architectural models.

Regardless of which program you choose to use, 3D parts created using a 2D-to-3D parts conversion program can be a launching point for more sophisticated designs when imported into other programs such as 123D Design, Meshmixer, and Tinkercad.

Take Advantage of Online Model Databases to Create and Modify Objects

Once you have completed your first round of sketches for that amazing 3D-printable creation, you will be eager to begin designing right away. But before you open up your first design program, don't reinvent the wheel. I mean this literally, because a particular wheel (or any part that is essential to your design) may already exist. If a wheel is an important part of your design, you may want to explore some of the many 3D model databases online to investigate whether a 3D wheel model already exists to suit your needs. Possibly, you can download a wheel that has already been designed and, if its copyright policy permits, utilize that wheel in your project. This can save you valuable time. Remember, if you decide to download objects for your design, you must follow standard copyright procedures. You should also ask the original creator for permission.

Brainstorming New Ideas

Online databases can also be a great source of inspiration. One of the most basic questions a first-time designer may ask is "What should I make?" There are web sites that sell 3D-printable content (sometimes they give models away for free), such as Thingiverse and Pinshape, that can give designers a general idea of what types of projects are being pursued for 3D printing. When brainstorming new ideas, these sites can become important assets in your research.

Thingiverse

For 3D model databases, Thingiverse has a large following in the 3D-printing community. As a smorgasbord of 3D printable objects, Thingiverse is a collection of downloadable files that have been created by skilled modelers and CAD artists who want to share their ideas with the 3D-printing community.

Anything found in Thingiverse's expanding 3D database can be downloaded as an `.stl` and imported into a majority of the 3D modeling software tools featured in this book. The full spectrum of 3D-printable items in Thingiverse's catalog ranges from practical to whimsical to downright ridiculous.

■ **Note** Users who download files on Thingiverse must follow the Creative Commons license agreement (Figure 2-11). As stated in the Creative Commons license agreement, files can be downloaded and modified as long as the original designer is given proper attribution. The Creative Commons license also forbids the commercial sale of the downloaded files.

Figure 2-11. *Always look for the Creative Commons logo and follow the Creative Commons copyright licensing agreement when downloading 3D objects from other sources*

Pinshape

Pinshape (Figure 2-12) is another great site to explore for inspiration. Pinshape is meant to be an economic enabler for 3D printing where designers can showcase and sell their digital products to the growing demographic of 3D printer owners who are searching for content.

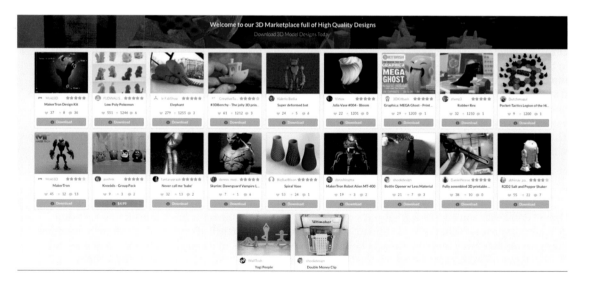

Figure 2-12. *A example of the many downloadable file available at* `www.pinshape.com`

As its name implies, Pinshape is a digital pin board for multidimensional shapes. Similar to Pinterest, Pinshape allows those who sign up to organize their favorite "shapes" into boards. Pinshapers can follow one another, leave comments, and like preferred designs. Printable 3D content can be purchased (some items are free) and downloaded as an STL file.

Pinshape also provides 3D printing for those without access to a 3D printer. There are more than 35 materials to choose from including hard white plastic, resin, sterling silver, ceramics, and wax.

Other 3D Model Database Options

Besides Thingiverse and Pinshape, there are many other 3D model repositories to explore, such as MyMiniFactory, TurboSquid, and Pond5. All these sites operate in their own unique way. Note that not all sites will let you download files for free.

A final place for inspiration is Pinterest (`www.pinterest.com`). While you cannot download `.stl` files from Pinterest, what you will find is a crowdsourced, constantly expanding visual record of a wide variety of 3D-printed designs that can be a great resource when brainstorming new ideas. A number of Pinterest users now place 3D-printed objects into specific categories (cars, toys, jewelry, fashion, mathematical objects, and so on). Because of its popularity, Pinterest is highly recommended as a place to research the latest innovations in 3D-printed design and to learn about what is trending in the world of 3D printing.

Reverse Engineering Is Essential

The explorations of sites such Pinshape and Thingiverse allow designers to see what projects have already been pursued and therefore let designers know about what ideas have yet to be discovered. Take the time to reverse engineer 3D models that interest you. The analysis of many of the projects found on these sites can provide a valuable insight into how computer-generated models are constructed.

■ **Note** Reverse engineering is the process of taking apart an assembled object and figuring out how it works.

Curiosity will be a driving force behind in your journey as a 3D-print designer, and in your research in how things are made, you will uncover the fascinating inner workings and assembly processes of many objects, especially mechanical objects with moving parts, that will help in your own design efforts. Opening up and examining `.stl` files in your preferred model package will allow you to reverse engineer models. This is an essential means to learn how things are built. Simply rotating and observing an object in 3D space may also give you insight into how other objects are designed. This detailed examination may help you find flaws that you may want to avoid in your designs.

Also take the time to research patents on Google and explore "exploded views" of objects. An exploded view (Figure 2-13) will help you understand the components that make up a particular design, but your goal is not to copy these designs but to make them more efficient by taking advantage of the structural complexity that is allowed in the additive design process. As you observe exploded views, you will find more efficient ways to combine multiple parts into a singular object. Many of the screw and bolts that are present in objects predating digital fabrication will be unnecessary in your 3D-printable designs.

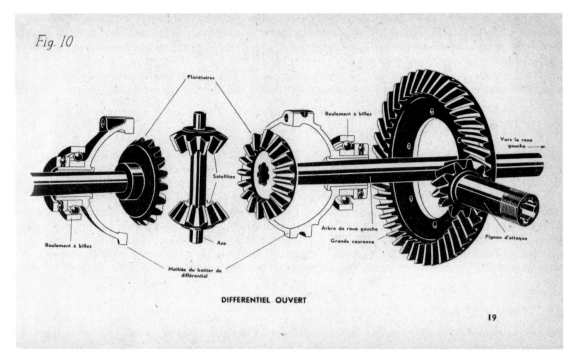

Figure 2-13. *An example of an exploded view. The original image is from Agence Eureka's Flickr account (`https://www.flickr.com/photos/taffeta/8739692374/in/photostream/`).*

Many times you will be asked to build simple objects such as wall switch mount covers, wall hooks, and other common household accessories. Reserve engineering and exploring the design methods of other artists will aid you in the development of your own designs and even help you understand how more complicated objects such as clockwork gears and intricate, articulated toys are built.

Mashup Manufacturing and Kit Bashing

When brainstorming new 3D-printable ideas, a fun exercise is to "mash up" your meshes and modify an original 3D model. Having access to downloaded .stl files using an online database, designers can combine .stl files in interesting ways to create new variations or to add design elements to preexisting objects.

In many 3D programs, the procedure to combine many meshes into a singular tessellated mesh is called a *Boolean operation*. For those new to the modeling process, a Boolean operation is an easy way to combine, intersect, and subtract multiple meshes to build more intricate composite objects. For example, if any models you download are composed of quads or tris, you can combine and append them to other tessellated meshes to create interesting design possibilities. As mentioned earlier, it may not be necessary to build every component of your model from scratch; find some "starter parts" via a download service. A starter part can be a downloaded file that you can extrapolate, modify, and mash up with parts using Boolean operations in the 3D design program of your choice. For example, you can download wheels from Pinshape, mechanical arms from Thingiverse, and an ATM machine from TurboSquid to make an interesting robot.

Before any Boolean operation is performed, meshes must be watertight. A watertight mesh is important not only for Boolean operations but for 3D printing in general. Meshes that are planar (flat) with gaps and holes on their surface are not considered watertight. These meshes will cause errors when Boolean operations are applied and will not print properly.

Nonmanifold geometry is the common term to describe bad meshes that are not watertight. A watertight mesh is any mesh that is manifold, completely enclosed, and without any gaps in the surface topology. Sometimes you may come across a mesh that isn't watertight, or you may accidentally create meshes that are not watertight during the modeling process. To ensure all meshes are watertight, applications such as Netfabb and Meshmixer have functions that can repair watertight meshes. The process of creating watertight meshes will be discussed in later chapters.

■ **Note**   Watertight meshes are essential for 3D printing. For a 3D model to print properly, it must be completely enclosed, with no gaps, holes, or breaks in the surface. Imagine if your 3D model was filled with water; if there are gaps in the model, it will "leak," which can cause the 3D-printing operation to fail. Solid model packages such as Solidworks will create watertight meshes automatically, but most other modeling packages won't.

This process of combining random parts, whether through Booleans or another process, to make something completely new is called *kit bashing*. Kit bashing (or *greebling*) is a process that existed before the digital age, where motion-picture prop artists salvage small plastic parts from store-bought modeling kits to provide industrial authenticity to their imaginative designs.

With the many modeling options already discussed, ranging from using 2D-to-3D conversations tools to downloading `.stl` files from online databases, it is conceivable that someone with little modeling experience could use kit bashing to begin the 3D-modeling process. Free downloadable software such as Meshmixer is a great kit-bashing tool that can aid in this process. Kit-bashed ideas include everything from personalized jewelry to customizable toys. Thingiverse even provides a category for base objects that can be customized for kit bashing, inviting designers to modify the original Thingiverse files as they want.

The Components of a Mesh

For kit bashing to take place, the 3D models being bashed together must have consistent features. Most importantly, these files must be *meshes*. Any `.stl` file you download will be a mesh by default. And, through the investigation of 3D models online, it will be readily apparent that almost all of the files downloadable for 3D printing will be in `.stl` format (you will occasionally find files in other formats such as `.obj` and `.vrml`).

■ **Note**   A mesh is a 3D polygonal object composed of vertices, edges, and faces. Vertices are connected by edges, and edges define faces to help determine the shape and form of a computer-generated model.

To understand what a mesh is, import two or three `.stl` files into Meshmixer and compare them. Hit the W key in Meshmixer to view the files in wireframe mode. Try this with several models, and you begin to see similarities in the structure you are viewing. As you explore the `.stl` files in wireframe mode, you will see that the files are composed of a repeating pattern of triangles (Figure 2-14). The term for this type of faceted, surface triangulation on a 3D computer-generated model is *tessellation*. A mesh is essentially a computer-generated model composed of tessellated faces (faces are also referred to as *polygons*). At the intersection of each face is a point. Points connect to other points with edges, and the edges determine the shapes of the many faces making up the mesh.

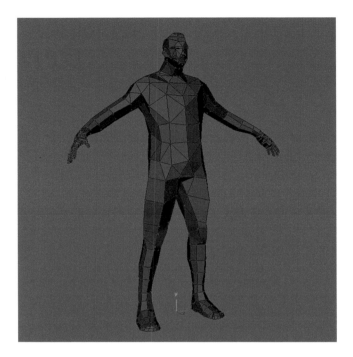

Figure 2-14. *An example of a mesh model of a human character*

■ **Note**   Meshes consist of three essential components: polygons (also called *faces*), edges, and vertices (sometimes called *points*). Two points define an edge, and three or more edges define a polygonal face. All the elements of a mesh can be moved and manipulated to define the shape of the mesh.

The faceted tessellated patterns of triangles on a 3D model are called *tris*. Other file types, such as the .obj file format, may be tessellated with four-sided polygons or quadrangles (often called *quads*). Sometimes you will find .obj files composed of both quads and tris.

As you begin to collect 3D models, you will find unique ways to mix and mash up these faceted meshes. Many CG modeling software applications can import .stl and .obj files. If a modeling software package supports the .stl and .obj formats, most likely that software (such as Autodesk Meshmixer) will have the capability to combine multiple meshes to form a single mesh.

Modeling packages, such as ZBrush and Meshmixer, are especially well suited for kit bashing since they have a variety of efficient functions for combining computer-generated geometry. Autodesk Meshmixer (which is also freely available at www.meshmixer.com/download.html) is an ideal modeling tool to begin exploring various ways to combine 3D geometry. Meshmixer will let you open a folder of .stl parts and integrate those parts onto a larger mesh. Pixologic's ZBrush has a tool that operate in a similar fashion called Insert Multi-Mesh Brushes(Figure 2-15). This brush is an ingenious concept that is enabling artists to quickly combine models. Each single brush can contain more than 30 unique geometric elements that can be quickly applied and combined while sculpting in ZBrush. The many .stl files in your collection can be imported into ZBrush and be used as an insert multimesh brush (Meshmixer and ZBrush will be discussed in more detail in later chapters).

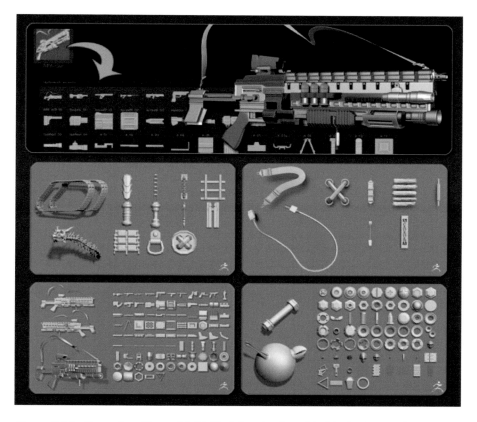

Figure 2-15. Examples of Insert Multi-Mesh brushes found in Pixologic ZBrush

Meshes, Curves, and Solids

Potentially you may find files in different formats such as `.iges`, `.step`, and `.parasolid`. A number of these file formats come from CAD and solid modeling software programs and are commonly used by engineers. If you come across one of these files and if you happen to have a software package that is capable of opening them (such as Rhino, Solidworks Maya, Invento, or Fusion 360), you will see that, structurally, they are different from `.stl` meshes in their geometric composition. Most likely, models with a file extension of `.iges`, `.step`, and `.parasolid` will be composed of curves. Objects composed of curves are a bit less complicated than meshes. The lines that define a curved-based object are economical. When comparing a curved-based object and a meshed object side-by-side, there tends to far less visual information in the curved-based model.

Curve-Based Models

Many engineers prefer curve-based objects. Curves are defined mathematically and are resolution independent, meaning the curves will retain the surface flow regardless of the computer's screen resolution (that is, curves always appear smooth no matter how closely you zoom in on them). A necessity for industrial manufacturing where the strictest tolerances must be followed, curves can define a model with a high level of precision. Curves come in several varieties such as splines, Beziers, or NURBS (which stands for nonuniform rational Bezier splines). When several curves define the shape of a 3D object, that object is known as a *surface*. Like meshes, curves have components. The fundamental building blocks of a curve are called *edit points* and *control vertices*. Edit points lie directly on the curve's surface, and control vertices are offset from the curve.

■ **Note**   The edit points and control vertices of a curve help define its topology.

Some CAD programs are superior for curve-based modeling, while others are known more for their solid modeling capabilities. Solid modeling programs are distinct from other modeling tools since the focus is on enclosed shapes. The geometrics enclosed in a solid modeling program are watertight by default. Solid modeling tools such as Solidworks have users define solids to build parts, and those parts are combined to create assemblies. In a purely curved-based modeling program, users must create solids from individual curves. Even though curve-based applications have sophisticated controls to aid in the positioning of curves points to create surfaces, these surfaces may not be watertight.

In the past, solid modeling tools and curves-based models were quite distinct, but now the functionality of these engineered tools have overlapped. For example, Rhino was once exclusively a NURBS modeler but has added solid-modeling like functions (called *polysurfaces*). And Solidworks will now let users manipulate curves directly.

Precision-Based vs. Organic-Based Workflows

Rather than get lost in the terms and methodologies defining solid modeling and curve-based tools, beginning modelers can place software modeling tools into three categories (Figure 2-16): precision-based tools for engineering (which use solids and/or curves), organic-based modelers (which use high-resolution meshes), and transitional modeling tools, which combine both meshes and curves. Transitional-based tools are also helpful as conversion tools since they can provide a route to convert high-resolution meshes to curves and vice versa.

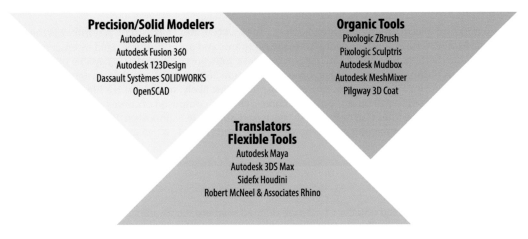

Figure 2-16. *The taxonomy of 3D design software*

Unfortunately, 3D printers cannot utilize curves for 3D printing. Therefore, if a model is to be 3D printed, all curves-based models will become tessellated when saved as `.stl` files for final output. Hence, regardless of an object's original composition (curved-based or mesh-based), every 3D model eventually becomes a 3D mesh in the end.

If you are new to 3D modeling, using curves for the first time can be challenging. To create a cube with curves, each face of the cube must consist of four curves. To define one face, the end points of each curve defining the face(i.e. the corner points where the curves meet), must meet precisely; otherwise, the cube cannot built. Now imagine a more complex object, such as a toy car. The toy car can consist of many solid shapes, and each solid shape must be defined by its own set of curves. Modeling such a toy car can be a tedious process since aligning the curves to create the final geometric shapes can take focus and deliberation. On the other hand, mesh-based polygon models composed of tris or quads will be far easier for beginner modelers to adjust if they haven't had any exposure to a 3D-modeling program. The process of modifying mesh-based models involves selecting faces on the model (the individual polygons on a mesh are called a *face*) and pushing and pulling them to manifest the final form. This process of pushing and pulling faces is often called *extruding* in the various mesh-based modeling packages. While this process of pushing and pulling meshes is a straightforward and rapid means to create a complex geometric shape, it lacks the mathematical precision of curved-based modeling programs.

The decision to use precision-based modeling tools or organic-based modeling tools will ultimately depend on the project being undertaken along with the designer's personal preference. Those who are devoted to curved-based, precision tools usually come from engineering backgrounds where precision is a necessity. Artistically inclined professionals (such as animation artists and toy designers) tend to prefer polygonal modeling software as their means to create complex-shaped geometric forms.

Many will argue the merits of precision-based vs. organic-based tools, but with 3D printing, both methods of modeling, whether curve or polygonal, are equally valid. Having knowledge of both methods is beneficial since such knowledge will allow designers to tackle a broader spectrum of 3D-printing challenges, from engineering to artistic. For 3D-printing design purposes, both methods are recommended and are featured in the later chapters of this book.

High-Resolution Meshes

Since meshes can be built up into elaborate forms rather quickly, mesh modeling allows for free-flowing artistic expression that can be otherwise challenging with curve-based tools. Because of the free-flowing nature of mesh-based modeling, such as painting and sculpting in the real world, designers can get instant gratification when sculpting with meshes. Meshes can be pushed and pulled, extruded, and smoothed in real time, giving immediate feedback to the designers as the model is developed. Meshes allow for free-flow creativity, whereas when using curves, designers must carefully think through their models. With curves there is little room for experimentation.

Meshes are resolution dependent, meaning the number of mesh or polygon faces in the computer-generated model will determine its resolution quality. A low-resolution mesh will be very faceted (some artists prefer this for style for aesthetic purposes). In fact, a popular trend in computer-generated geometry is the highly faceted look found in early video games. High-resolution objects have very tiny polygons. Each polygon in a high resolution can be the size of pixel, and this allows for high-resolution models to be very detailed. Because of this granular resolution, high-resolution modeling programs are analogous to working with digital clay (Figure 2-17), where artists can push, pull, and carve into models to manipulate ultrafine polygonal surfaces. As a trade-off for this high level of detail, high-resolution polygonal objects tend to be memory intensive. Some of the more detailed models creating high-resolution sculpting techniques can easily reach 1GB in size.

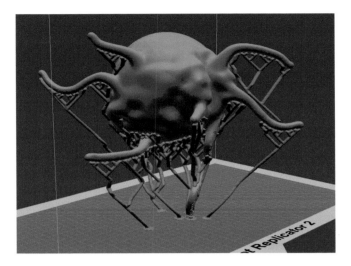

Figure 2-17. A high-resolution (organic) model in Autodesk Meshmixer

While amazingly detailed, these memory-heavy works of art are sometimes met with disapproval by 3D-printing service bureaus since such large-sized files can be difficult to manage. Online services bureaus (such as Shapeways) and brick-and-mortar service bureaus may refuse to 3D print models that are more than 1GB in size. This shouldn't deter you from creating highly detailed meshes since (as explained in later chapters of this book) there are many methods to optimize the size of a mesh while keeping the quality of that mesh intact.

Explore Artistic and Organic Sculpting Techniques

Because of their ultrafine resolutions, models created using organic sculpting methods can be pulled, stretched, and modified very quickly. Some of the more well-known programs that utilize organic modeling techniques include Pixologic ZBrush, Pixologic Sculptris, Autodesk Mudbox, Autodesk Meshmixer, and Pilgway's 3D-Coat.

These tools allow for the real-time manipulation of "digital clay", enabling the development of wide variety of complex geometric forms

If you have ever seen a highly detailed 3D-printed sculpture, most likely it was created from these high-resolution sculpting tools. Many of the tools in these high-resolution modeling programs emulate tools that a real-life sculptor would use. The tools in high-resolution sculpting programs that allow designers to chisel, carve, pull, stretch, grace, smooth, flatten, and twist the forms into the desired shape often begin with a simple sphere of clay, which can make new designers feel more acclimated to the sculpting process.

Since high-resolution sculpting tools found in programs such as Meshmixer, Mudbox, Sculptris, and ZBrush are analogs to tools in the real world, artists who want to create digital models for the first time may find these programs easier to adapt to. The familiarity of these tools enable new modelers to begin the modeling process immediately without the need to learn the cumbersome, and sometimes confusing, methodologies found in more expensive and elaborate CAD modeling programs. In other words, sculpting programs allow for an easier point of entry for the beginning 3D-print artist.

Rather than using curves to precisely determine the form and structure of the digital model, in a high-resolution, digital sculpting program, the forms are gradually built up slowly, and the results are similar to what a sculptor would create in the real world. Because of the amorphous forms and biological-inspired creations derived from these high-resolution tools, modeling software such as ZBrush and Mudbox are often referred to as *organic* modeling tools. With these organic, high-resolution tools, countless sculptures, figurines, and statues of highly realistic animals, creatures, and anthropomorphic forms are being manufactured with 3D printing. In the entertainment industry, the use of high-resolution sculptures can be highly lucrative. Highly detailed creatures and characters from popular films and video games can be modeled efficiently and in high detail. These digital models can then be leveraged for both films and video games. Such models can be 3D printed as well to create multidimensional marketing collateral and toys.

As mentioned, whether you work in precision-based modeling software or in an organic, high-resolution program using meshes, every model you work on, regardless of how it began, will be converted to faceted meshes when it is saved as an .stl file. Essentially, if your model is to be 3D printed, an .stl mesh is the end result of every 3D modeling experience. No matter what modeling tool or process you begin with, everything you create will be converted to a mesh before being sent to the 3D printer.

Using 3D Scanning to Modify Preexisting Objects

Meshes can also be the result of 3D scanning (Figure 2-18), which is a useful means of creating 3D geometry for any project you undertake.

Figure 2-18. *Example of the original object, the mesh resulted from the 3D scan, and the 3D Systems Sense scanner used to scan the object*

Many times a digital sculpture begins as a 3D scan that is then modified in some way. In the past, the data accumulated from 3D scanning posed challenges to 3D modelers. The data from a scan usually takes the form of a dense point cloud. Most cloud points cannot be manipulated effectively without some type of software conversion, and in the past, the process to convert a point cloud to 3D geometry was tedious. Today, software is available to make the point cloud to mesh conversion process far more efficient. Also, many new 3D scanners automatically convert points to meshes, making the scanned data available for immediate manipulation in 3D-modeling software. The cost of owning a 3D scanner has also greatly diminished over the years, allowing more businesses to use 3D scanning as part of their everyday operations. Some 3D scanners can attach directly to an iPad to take accurate scans in minutes, which can then be uploaded and distributed via the cloud.

With this increase in implementation, 3D scanning is being utilized by startups and new businesses in a variety of ways. One interesting trend is the use of 3D scanning, along with 3D printing, to create three-dimensional snapshots/miniature statues as re-creations of family members, pets, and loved ones. Some companies are using licensing agreements with sport franchises and entertainment brands to combine a fan's 3D-scanned face with a preexisting 3D model of a well-known athlete and film/video game character. The final result is 3D printed as a statue or toy to create one-of-kind mementos.

Photogrammetry

Besides 3D scanning, there are other methods that are being used to acquire 3D data to create 3D models. Photogrammetry is a method of converting multiple 2D photographs of a landmark or architectural structure to create 3D models. Photogrammetry involves taking photographs of objects at various angles, finding matching points of reference, and then calculating the distances between various geometric features on the objects represented. These distances can then be used to determine dimensions that can then be translated into 3D geometry.

Photogrammetry is now being used for a variety of purposes. The company XREZ (`www.xrez.com`) uses photogrammetry to create virtual environments for media projects and virtual reality. That photogrammetry data can then be 3D printed, turning large-scale monuments into desktop-sized and physically accurate miniature re-creations (Figure 2-19).

Figure 2-19. *The photogrammetry data of an Eastern Island Moia head prepared and converted into a 3D model by Eric Hanson and Greg Downing from the company Xrez*

Lidar Scanning

Another technology similar to 3D scanning is lidar scanning. Lidar stands for "light detection and ranging" and uses airborne systems, such as drones, to measure landscapes with pulse light to gain 3D information about the earth's surface. This data takes the form of a point cloud, which is a dense collection of vertices that can be triangulated into a mesh and then 3D printed.

One recent project where the lidar scanning method has been put to use is the 3D-printed replication of the landmass of Rancho Palos Verdes in Southern California (Figure 2-20). The 3D print is a true-to-life, miniature replica of the Palos Verdes landslide thanks to lidar technology. The practical purpose of the Rancho Palos Verdes 3D-printed model is to help identify earthquake faults on the Rancho Palos Verdes landmass.

Figure 2-20. *A 3D-printed model of Rancho Palos Verdes created with lidar data created by Ted Vegari and his students at PVNet in Rancho Palos Verdes, California*

Part Databases

Other beneficial applications of 3D scanning are to help develop parts libraries, which can be a useful resource for kit bashing. If you happen to have 3D scanning at your disposal, begin scanning the world around you. Any interesting object you come across be 3D scanned, becoming "base geometry" that can serve as a launch point for 3D modeling project. Nothing is off-limits, and with 3D scanning you can begin to assemble a "digital junk drawer" of 3D-printable parts.

This "digital junk drawer" of reusable 3D-scanned parts will help speed up the design process for 3D printing. Some of the objects you scan will inspire new designs. Weirdly shaped objects, discarded machine parts, and exotically shaped knickknacks can be scanned and reconfigured in countless ways in your 3D-modeling application of choice. Don't overlook the value of common, mundane, everyday objects to provide inspiration for your designs. Use your "digital junk drawer" as a parts database to help fuel future ideas.

For productivity purposes, a preestablished database of parts will allow you to focus more on custom designs. Modeling small parts, such as latches, wall plates, mounts, hooks, and gears, can be time-consuming and unnecessary if they can be imported from a prebuilt parts database.

Iterative Prototyping

3D scanning is also a useful part of the prototyping process, where an initial concept is used to test a product design before final manufacture. In this regard, 3D scanning is a useful application because it can help ensure that prototypes conform to proper measurements. Data from 3D scanning is especially useful when prototypes need to be custom-fit and aligned with other objects. In some circumstances, a 3D-printed prototype is used in manufacturing as a measuring tool (called a *fixture* or *standard*) to ensure parts conform with precise tolerances.

The use of 3D scanning can also help accelerate the modeling process when multiple versions or slight variations are necessary. The initial scanned prototype can then be modified in modeling software. The multiple versions can be 3D printed with slight variations, and the client can pick the preferred version during a final approval process. Iterative prototyping can also be a useful means to improve upon parts in order to make them better.

This process of creating variations in a design can also bring added value to the client/designer relationship and gives a client an opportunity to feel more involved in the design process. When given the opportunity, clients will appreciate that they had a choice in the manufacturing process.

Procedural Modeling Techniques for Mass Customization

One way to explore iterative variations is through procedural techniques. Procedural modeling is a process to help evolve a design. Common examples of procedural models include fractals and L-systems. The application of procedural modeling is just being realized as a means for designers and engineers to test a product and make countless variations (Figure 2-21). Most procedural modeling tools rely on sophisticated computer algorithms that use variables and adjustable parameters to add variation to the design.

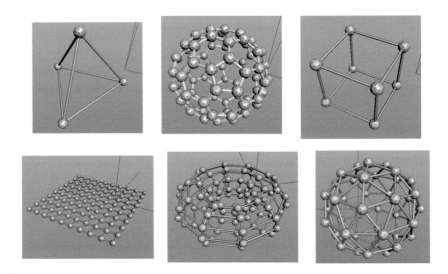

Figure 2-21. *Many design variations are possible with one digital asset, created in Sidefx's Houdini software*

For example, imagine a 3D model of a shoe design with the possibility of built-in parameters. A client or customer could adjust parameters built into the model to create endless variations. Engineers can use iterative prototyping in a similar way. An example would be a part that is meant to hold a heavy load. Variations can be built into the model that would create automatic reinforcements in the model that would automatically increase in proportion to the weight of the load. It wouldn't be necessary to build multiple versions for different loads since algorithms built into the model would react to the input of other variables (such as the weight load the model is meant to carry) and automatically adjust itself as necessary.

When used to create final, end-use products, procedural modeling becomes a great means for mass customization. Designers, new and old, need to be aware of the capabilities of customization since it will enable the creation of 3D models in a more efficient and effective manner. Some software tools are ideal for mass customization, such as Sidefx's Houdini and Grasshopper for Rhino. These software tools can be challenging to use for the beginning modeler since they allow designers to create complex node networks that resemble object programming.

■ **Note** Manufacturing during the Industrial Age evolved from the advancements developed from mass production. In the digital age that we now live in now, mass customization will be a growing trend thanks to the powerful capabilities of 3D printing.

These complex node structures enable designers to create user interfaces called *digital assets*. These digital assets are essentially apps that can be given to a client or another designer to create unlimited variations in models. Any one of these countless variations can then be output as a final product for 3D-printing purposes. Highly complex models can then be modified and adjusted in the app without the need for someone with modeling experience.

The capabilities embedded in these applications can allow for the creations of highly complex models. One parameter could add more wheels to a custom car, another parameter could adjust the scale of the wheels, and another parameter could change the tread on the wheels. End users could then download the custom design into a program such as Meshmixer and push the design even further.

Turning Typography into a Three-Dimensional Object

One of the goals of mass customization is personalization, where printed objects have a greater value because they have been designed to appeal to a person's individual needs and desires. The addition of words and lettering to a design is a great way to enable personalization.

One software tool that makes the addition of type to a 3D model an easy process is Microsoft Builder. It has a number of useful typography functions. This capability is available in other software applications, but few applications extrude and wrap type as efficiently as Microsoft Builder.

Regardless of the application used, the type manipulation functions found in various software modeling packages can provide a great incentive for graphic designers to enter the world of 3D printing. For 3D-printing purposes, designers should take the time to explore the readability of multidimensional types. Some fonts will read well; others won't. Bolder, san-serif fonts are the safest bets for readability purpose. As you take the time to investigate a range of font families, the structures of various letterforms in extruded three-dimensional space may inspire uniquely new ideas.

Typography can added to end-use products in a number of ways. The products themselves can be composed completely from type. Such objects can be functional and personal. Imagine jewelry boxes, pencil cases, pet accessories, and picture frames composed completely out of type, such as a desktop pencil case that spells out the name of the user it belongs to. Other examples are picture toys, such as trucks and robots, constructed out of typography and personalized with the name of child. Nothing is off-limits. A range of interior design objects, such as clocks, lamps, and vases, can be constructed completely from multidimensional words and letterforms.

Explore the Growing World of Material Options

Don't forget that the final output of the 3D-printed object can be customized with the many varieties of materials available. This is something to consider once you are ready to 3D print your designs. At first you will probably want to play it safe with PLA and ABS, but eventually you will discover that here is a growing range of filaments now available for desktop 3D printers that mimic other types of materials such as wood, stone, iron, and bronze. Experimenting with material types can lead to novel approaches for the final 3D-printed product.

Wood filaments give the illusion that a product was handcrafted. Glow-in-the-dark filaments can add an expected element to toys and jewelry. Metallic filaments can give organic objects weight, durability, and an industrial feel.

If you can afford to, you should also take the time to explore other methods of 3D printing beyond fused deposition modeling. Use a service such as Shapeways or Sculpteo to explore flexible materials. If you have the opportunity, experiment with resin-based printers such as Autodesk's Ember, Formlabs' Form1+, or SprintRay's MoonRay 3D printer to discover the higher-resolution capabilities of stereolithography (SLA), resin-based 3D printers.

Ideally, in time, you will become well versed in the variety of materials offered. As your proficiency with 3D printing grows, you will become acquainted with a broader range of material options that enable you to push 3D printing's customization capabilities even further.

Remember: Shape Complexity Is Free

A popular phrase associated with 3D printing is "Shape complexity is free." Essentially this means intricate, complex shapes are no more difficult to print than simple shapes. If the volume of material to output is the same, a simple sphere will take no longer to print than a multigear object.

In traditional manufacturing (that is, manufacturing using subtractive methods), the fabrication of complex objects (sometimes referred to as *complex assemblies*) takes time and deliberation. Using traditional manufacturing methods, the final part or product may need to be assembled in phases using multiple machines and fabrication methods (metal pour, CNC, drop hammer, hydroforming, water jet, laser cutting, welding, and so on). The facilitation of the multistage process of subtractive manufacturing requires the transportation of parts to remote workstations/locations, multiple workers with distinct skill sets, and an approval process for each component being manufactured. This multistepped approach can be time-consuming and expensive. Because of the costs associated with production and the varied manufacturing methods, complex parts need to be carefully planned and engineered before production takes place. In some circumstances, certain structural forms, such as parts with internal voids and implicit geometries, can be impossible to build or simply too cost prohibitive. With 3D printing, many of the production challenges associated with traditional manufacturing can be avoided. Since the 3D-printing process grows objects layer by layer, fully assembled objects can be printed in a single pass. The ability to output "single-pass parts" and fully developed final-use products in a single pass makes the numerous machines and workflows associated with traditional/subtractive manufacturing unnecessary.

■ **Note**   Implicit surfaces (also referred to as *iso-surfaces*) represent a subset of computer-generated geometry that is often highly organic in form and sometimes consists of complex intersections and repetitive shapes. Implicit surfaces are difficult to produce with traditional modeling methods of meshes and curves. In the world of computer graphics, implicit surfaces are created using procedures that blend objects together. Blobby molecules, metaballs, and soft objects are the computer-generative tools typically associated with the creation of implicit surfaces. Voxels (in other words, volume pixel) are data points on a three-dimensional grid and can be used to create implicit surfaces as well.

Therefore, with 3D printing, the label that used to read "Some assembly required" may be a thing of the past. Remember buying a toy as kid, knowing that it had to be "assembled" before you could use it? Unless the design specifically requires it (such a 3D-printed puzzle where the parts are meant to be put together), assemblies are no longer necessary. With the additive processes of 3D printing, fully assembled objects with interconnected pieces, operating gears, embedded circuitry, and articulated joints are totally possible. Designers now can worry less about structural complexities of an object and focus more on the actual design. Before 3D printing, many objects, especially organic forms, would be impossible to build. Traditionally, complex multipart objects would have to be engineered (often using supply chains) for assembly. Engineers would have to spend a great deal of time determining how to ensure that parts connected smoothly together to ensure proper workability. Welded, screwed, snapped-on, and bolted assemblies were commonplace. But now we can begin to visualize objects as whole units. Many objects created through an assembly process can now be redesigned with a focus on maximum efficiency and ergonomic reliability. The multiple pieces of complex assemblies can be merged together in a final design, redesigned to ensure proper strength to weight ratios, and 3D printed as a whole, singular object.

Hod Lipson elaborates in further detail on the nature of shape complexity in his book *Fabricated: The New World of 3D Printing*, where he describes ten principles of 3D principles. His first principle touches on the freedom to design complex structures with 3D printing (that is, free complexity). His other principles branch off from free complexity to discuss the corollaries of free variety and "no assembly required."

> *"Principle one: Manufacturing complexity is free. In traditional manufacturing, the more complicated an object's shape, the more it costs to make. On a 3D printer, complexity costs the same as simplicity. Fabricating an ornate and complicated shape does not require more time, skill or cost than printing a simple block. Free complexity will disrupt traditional pricing models and change how we calculate the cost of manufacturing things."*

—Hod Lipson, from his book Fabricated: The New World of 3D Printing

Exploration his book is highly recommended and can serve as great inspiration for aspiring 3D print designers or additive manufacturing engineers.

The freedom to develop complex shapes is opening new creative doorways and opportunities for artists, designers, and engineers to turn their imaginative ideas into reality. The ability to grow intricate and ornate designs will allow for the exploration of new forms and structures ranging from practical to weird and allow engineers to solve industrial design problems that have hindered production in the past. As more advanced, multimaterial 3D printers enter the marketplace, complexity will be pushed even further with the development of multimaterial objects that can be printed in one pass. The Stratasys Connex and Objet machines are already capable of enabling the single-pass creation of objects with materials ranging from hard and rubber-like to softer, flexible, translucent plastics in a single pass.

All of these innovations are liberating for designers who may have curtailed working on a project because of the potential complexities in the design. Now is the time to bring those ideas to the drawing board and confidently realize that their manufacture is entirely possible.

Your Ultimate Resource for Endless Ideas

One final thought to keep in mind is that the ultimate resource for an endless cascade of 3D-printable ideas is your own imagination, and since in the world of 3D printing "Shape complexity is free," you have the creative freedom to design any object you desire. Ideally you will look beyond the ideas in this chapter to pursue and invent new applications of your own. Remember, we are just beginning to embark on the 3D-printing revolution, and there are countless design concepts and creative ideas waiting to realized.

Since shape complexity is free, don't lock yourself into one school of thought. Be fluid in your mind-set and mix philosophies from both art and engineering. Now is the time to approach manufacturing from a completely new direction. Take this opportunity to develop and invent fully assembled products. Contemplate intricate geometries and visually appealing surfaces while investigating new complex forms. Bring together the methodologies of engineering, fine art, and design and develop aesthetically pleasing artifacts that have a practical purpose.

As you explore these new 3D-printing techniques, many eureka moments await, creating the potential for freelance income and new business opportunities. The growth of 3D printing will establish new opportunities for designers to gain clients, opening the doors to grassroots manufacturing. Indeed, a manufacturing revolution may be possible, but ultimately the success of 3D printing will depend upon designers who develop innovative workflows and ideas that take advantage of the technology. Therefore, the next question you may be asking is, what skills are necessary to get started?

Getting Started with Free 3D Modeling Software

When it comes to learning 3D modeling applications, the gateway to getting started can be found in the many free modeling tools available online. These tools include the free creator apps found on Shapeways, the Autodesk series of 123D apps, Autodesk Tindercad, Autodesk Meshmixer, OpenSCAD, FreeCAD, Microsoft Builder, Pixologic Sculptris, and Blender (Figure 2-22). While many free applications are available, the apps featured here are the more common ones being used by the 3D-printing community.

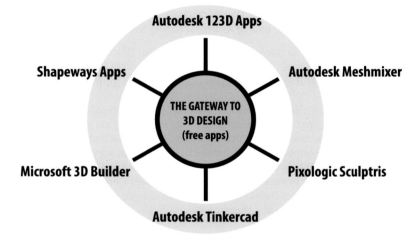

Figure 2-22. *The gateway to learning 3D design can begin with tinkering with the many free design apps that are available*

With many free 3D-modeling packages available online, new users have many opportunities to dabble and find the software tools they feel most comfortable with—a background in neither engineering background nor any previous CAD experience required. There have been discussions circulating online arguing that the design software and CAD used for 3D modeling can be too complicated for the average person. But learning 3D design software tools tends to be a cumulative experience. Beginning with simple web-based apps will allow new users to get acclimated with basic 3D-modeling procedures, giving them the confidence to tackle more intensive 3D design software tools.

My recommendation is to begin with the most accessible, easiest-to-comprehend tools such as Tinkercad and follow a learning pathway to progressively become more proficient in the 3D-modeling process. The design pathway is outlined in Figure 2-23, followed by more in-depth descriptions of each application. The remaining chapters of this book are based on this learning pathway, with each successive chapter focusing on more advanced workflows in the pathway chain.

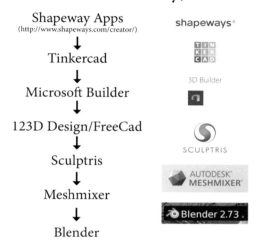

Figure 2-23. *New 3D modelers should follow a learning pathway in order to progressively learn 3D design with the least amount of frustration*

If you have never used a 3D-modeling software package, starting with the simplest tools will eliminate any frustrations you may have in developing your modeling skills. All of these programs available are free and easy to learn if you begin with the simpler applications.

A Summary of the 3D Software Used in This Book

The following sections provide a brief synopses of the software packages used in the remaining chapters.

Autodesk Tinkercad

Tinkercad is probably one of the easier programs to learn in the ecosystem of freely available CAD tools. Tinkercad's main virtue is its accessibility. As a free, web-based app, Tinkercad is available to anyone with online access. This web-based accessibility (unfortunately) is Tinkercad's weakness as well, since large and complex models may cause the Tinkercad interface to slow down to a crawl.

Tinkercad (Figure 2-24) is basically a Boolean solid modeler. The main building blocks in Tinkercad are watertight solids such cubes, spheres, cones, and pyramids. There many unique objects included as well such as paraboloids, half spheres, and hexagon prisms. Users can drag shapes onto a grid and combine or subtract shapes using a group function found in the menu bar. There really isn't a way to adjust the components of the geometric solids—you can only scale, rotate, and move them in 3D space.

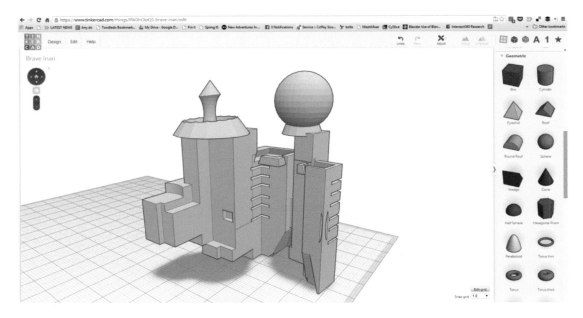

Figure 2-24. *The Tinkercad interface*

Designs in Tinkercad can be exported as `.stl` files and further modified in other programs. Tinkercad is really best for simple geometric objects such as picture frames, boxes, and birdhouses. For beginners, Tinkercad is a great place to begin. The basic framework of an object can be designed in Tinkercad and then exported to another modeling program for more advanced editing.

OpenSCAD

OpenSCAD (Figure 2-25) is quite different from other 3D applications mentioned in this book. OpenSCAD is a free modeling program that allows users to create solid models using code. The interface is a text-based editor, and users will use commands to create objects. For example, the command cube ([2,3,4]) will create a cube that is 2 units wide, 3 units long, and 4 units tall. There are many commands in OpenSCAD to generate a wide range of 3D-printable objects.

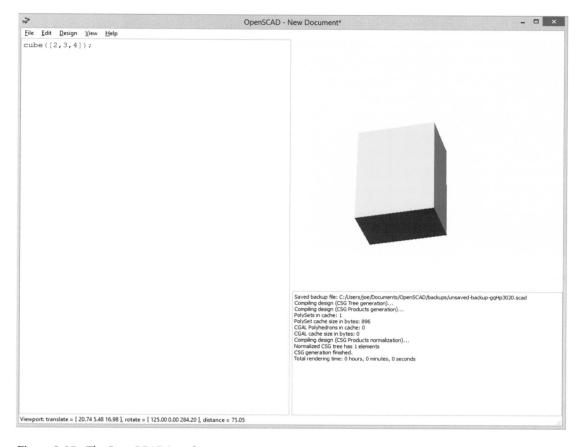

Figure 2-25. *The OpenSCAD interface*

OpenSCAD is great for simple objects required exact precision. Complex objects in OpenSCAD require a great deal of up-front planning, and there is little room for experimentation.

Like the other applications listed here, OpenSCAD can export models as `.stl` files for further modification in other applications.

Microsoft 3D Builder

The main intent of 3D Builder (Figure 2-26) is to make 3D design workflows as easy as possible. 3D Builder contains a library of 3D-printable objects that can be modified quickly for immediate printing. New users can emboss any model with text or images, merge 3D objects together, repair downloaded 3D models, and arrange models flat on the print bed. One goal of 3D Builder is to avoid having nontechnical users needlessly resort to CAD for more common tasks, such as adding text to a prebuilt model or using Boolean operations to create a mold.

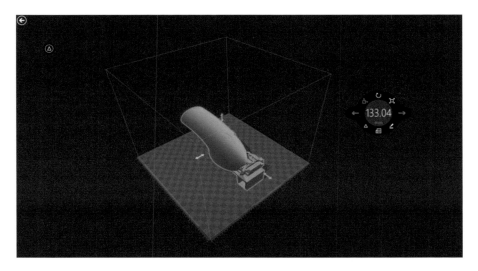

Figure 2-26. *The Microsoft Builder interface*

Microsoft 3D Builder is not the place to build a model; you will probably want to build it in Tinkercad or FreeCAD first. Like Tinkercad, Microsoft Builder will let you combine objects using Booleans to create more sophisticated geometries. What makes Microsoft 3D Builder stand out is its text-wrapping capabilities. In other applications, wrapping text around a three-dimensional object can be challenging, but with Microsoft 3D Builder, text wrapping and manipulation are easy operations.

FreeCAD

FreeCAD is an open source 3D CAD parametric solid modeler, which is great for designing mechanical objects. For designers interested in more sophisticated solid modelers, such as Solidworks, FreeCAD offers a great introduction to the world of solid modeling.

The FreeCAD modeling environment is divided into "workbenches" that have specific tools for specific tasks (see Figure 2-27). You begin sketching parts in 2D in the Part Design Workbench and then extrude them into 3D objects in the Part Workbench for further 3D editing. You can switch between workbenches at any time, and there is also a generic workbench (called the Complete Workbench) that combines the most commonly used tools in one place.

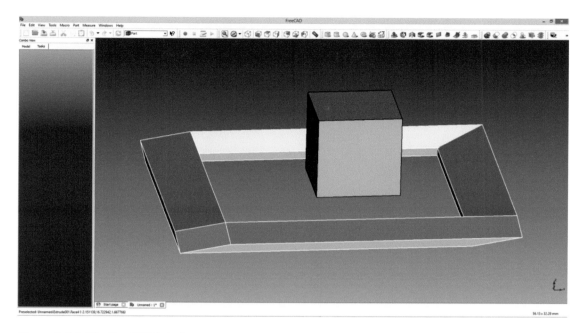

Figure 2-27. *The FreeCAD interface*

After getting familiar with Tinkercad and OpenSCAD, users should be ready to take on the greater complexities of FreeCAD, which will allow for the construction of intricate mechanical designs.

Autodesk 123D Design

Users of Tinkercad should feel comfortable in Autodesk 123D Design (Figure 2-28). While the interface of 123D Design looks similar to Tinkercad, this free tool is far more sophisticated.

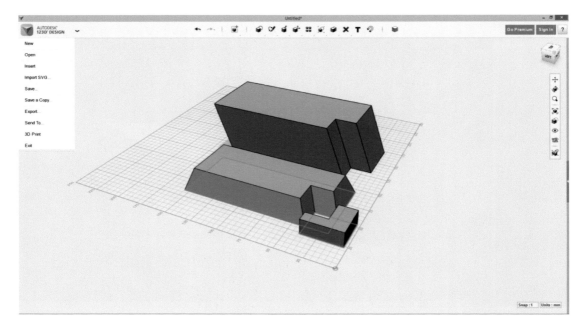

Figure 2-28. *The Autodesk 123D Design interface*

123D Design is similar to FreeCAD, in that users can begin with a 2D drawing that can be extruded into a 3D shape to be combined with other 3D objects and adjusted with a number of editing tools. While FreeCAD users may have more tools at their disposal, the 123D Design interface is far easier to get adjusted to, and many of the tools in 123D Design are self-explanatory. 123D Design works well with other 123D apps, and users of 123D Design (along with other 123D apps such 123D Catch, 123D Make, and 123D Sculpt+) can upload their models to the 123D Gallery where they can be accessed by Meshmixer for further editing.

123D Design is the perfect jumping-off point before learning more advanced Autodesk applications such as Maya and Fusion 360.

Pixologic Sculptris

One of best free options for organic modeling is Pixologic's Sculptris (Figure 2-29). If you are interested in learning ZBrush, Sculptris is the recommended place to begin; in many ways, Sculptris is a scaled-down version of ZBrush.

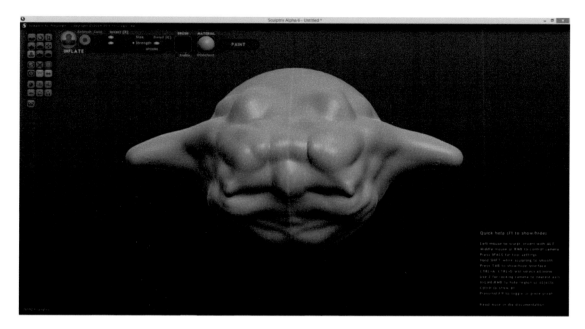

Figure 2-29. *The Pixologic Sculptris interface*

Users in Sculptris begin with a ball of digital clay that can be pushed, pulled, flattened, creased, inflated, and smoothed with a brush. The geometry in Sculptris naturally adjusts when the object is stretched disproportionally, with the resolution increasing when the ball of clay becomes unnaturally distorted.

Sculptris is the go-to tool when there is a need to add organic details to hard-edged models.

Autodesk Meshmixer

Autodesk Meshmixer (Figure 2-30) is similar to Pixologic's Sculptris in that it provides some great organic sculpting tools, but Meshmixer's main claim to fame is its ability to combine meshes. Meshmixer is a great place to finalize models and combine `.stl` parts imported from other programs. The merging algorithms used by Meshmixer are sophisticated, and parts flow together seamlessly when combined.

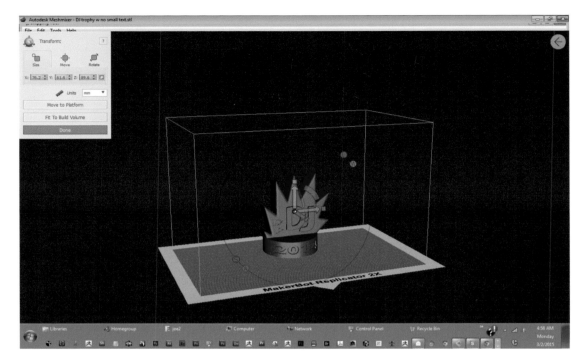

Figure 2-30. *The Autodesk Meshmixer interface*

The 3D-printing export function in Meshmixer will also repair any of the models in the 123D apps. It can also preview the digital model on a variety of 3D printer brands such as Stratasys, Makerbot, Type A Machines, Dremel 3D Idea Builder, and Autodesk's own Ember. Users can use Meshmixer to automate the process of creating supports and scale their models to ensure the most efficient fit on the 3D printer's build plate.

Blender

Blender (Figure 2-31) is a free, open source 3D modeling powerhouse. Blender users come in two groups: strong devotees who love the program and critics who disparage its challenging interface.

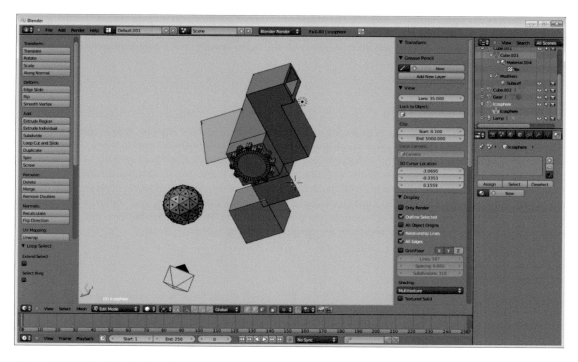

Figure 2-31. *The Blender interface*

Blender is intended for animation and has a number of functions that aren't applicable to 3D printing. But because of Blender's strong user base and continual development, Blender users have access to a broad range of tools that covers the full gamut of 3D design from hard-edged modeling to organic workflows.

Just about anything can be built in Blender with its diverse toolkit that combines meshes and curves. Blender users can combine objects using Booleans and turn low-resolution meshes into high-resolutions to enable digital sculpting techniques.

Blender's interface takes some time to get used to, but users who have already become familiar with tools such Tinkercad, FreeCAD, Sculptris, and 123D Design shouldn't have any trouble adjusting to the Blender environment.

Additional Skills Needed for 3D Printing

Being able to visualize objects in 3D is an essential skill and is learnable in time. As you dabble and learn the 3D applications mentioned, you will become more immersed in the functions and workflows, and your ability to visualize objects in 3D space will grow. As you advance, you will also acquire the aesthetic sensibility to distinguish good 3D designs from bad designs.

This desire to learn, along with the ability to visualize objects in 3D space, are two of the more essential skills necessary for getting started. What is also necessary is a good imagination and the creative desire to make 3D-printed objects of your own. 3D printing establishes a connection between the mind and the machine (in fact, some call this process the "mind to part" workflow). Therefore, the only barrier may be your own imagination. Don't be afraid to push your imagination to the limit. Pretend your imagination could be output as pixels and polygons. In a way, that is the most basic illustration of the design process for 3D printing. You imagine a new idea, design the idea in a 3D-modeling package, and then output that design as a final 3D-printed object.

As you let your imagination grow, don't be afraid to embrace the pioneering spirit that is sweeping the 3D-printing community and make a mark with a 3D-printed invention of your own. Throw away your 3D inhibitions by delving into the next chapters, where you will harness your creative desires and turn your imagination into reality.

Summary

With time and practice, anyone can acquire the necessary skills to model 3D objects. At first, many people may feel intimated since, early on, there was a level of complexity attributed to many CAD modeling software packages. Primarily used by architects, animators, and engineers, CAD packages had a reputation for intricate interfaces and multiple menus with many functions to learn, requiring a significant amount of training. There now exists a full spectrum of 3D-modeling software options for all levels of knowledge with simple tools that are freely available. These tools include Tinkercad, 123D Design, and Sculptris (and include many more). With these simplified 3D-modeling software tools, new designers can become familiar with the 3D space and learn the 3D process necessary for creating multidimensional objects.

CHAPTER 3

■ ■ ■

Begin with a Box

From this point forward you should now be familiar with the many design processes and modeling methods being used for 3D printing. You should also have a general understanding of the basic components that make up computer-generated 3D models, the differences between meshes and curves, and a range of 3D modeling workflows from precise to organic. We will now explore these concepts further through a series of lessons that will allow you to begin modeling 3D-printable objects of your very own.

To begin your exploration of 3D modeling, you will focus on a fundamental 3D design project: creating a hollow box with a lid. This hollow box concept can be used for a variety of things. The box you will create can act as a simple container, a jewelry box, or a desktop organizer. The design of this box is nothing more than a cube that has been made hollow with a Boolean operation. Ideally this simple design will lead to more elaborate ideas. For example, many of these hollow boxes can stacked and combined in interesting ways to create multicompartmental objects.

Autodesk's Tinkercad and OpenSCAD will be the featured software tools used in the creation of your box design. For beginners, these two software applications offer the quickest route to designing 3D models. Both programs are free and easy to comprehend, yet they present two different ways to create 3D content.

As you get started in these lessons, Tinkercad will be featured first, but at this point, the order in which you learn the following applications is not relevant. Tinkercad will be more appealing to artists and designers, while programmers may be more interested in OpenSCAD. If you already know Tinkercad, please skip that section and jump to the "Designing a Basic Box in OpenSCAD" section of this chapter.

The following exercises will take you through the design process step-by-step for each modeling application. The goal of the exercises is to help you learn how to design 3D-printable objects of your own while developing a diverse skill set. This will give even the most skilled 3D CAD artists and modelers some additional tools to add to their 3D design toolkits. But first, let's quickly review the tools you'll be using.

Tools of the Trade

Tinkercad is a free, web-based application that allows users to merge simple geometric objects to create more complicated structures. OpenSCAD is a free, downloadable application that uses input text (in other words, code) to generate 3D models. Both programs have their strengths and weaknesses. The Tinkercad interface is more visually compelling with colorful icons that can be dragged and dropped to quickly build complex forms. Tinkercad is also extremely easy to use, but this benefit can cause scenes to amass many geometric objects in a short amount of time, which can cause the program to perform slowly. Since OpenSCAD is installed on the end user's computer, it is not dependent on an online connection; therefore, large scenes in OpenSCAD can be more responsive than large scenes in Tinkercad. But because OpenSCAD is a coding environment, artists and designers who prefer more visually captivating tools often shun it.

If you are completely new to 3D modeling, it is recommended that you explore both Tinkercad and OpenSCAD. Exploring both tools will give you exposure to a wider range of 3D-modeling workflows, and this will help you build up confidence along with 3D visualization skills. On the other hand, if you are already skilled in a CAD or 3D design software program, Tinkercad can come in handy and shouldn't be ignored. Tinkercad can be a great tool to create quick, base shapes for other projects. Furthermore, Tinkercad can also be the means to sketch ideas using simple shapes. Likewise, OpenSCAD can be of additional interest to more experienced 3D modelers since it gives anyone the opportunity to learn how to use code to generate a 3D-printable model. Learning to code has its benefits since many more advanced modeling operations may require some sort of coding knowledge.

Beginning with Essential Building Blocks: Boxes, Spheres, and Cylinders

When thinking about how to build something for the first time, break that design down into its most basic components. Envisioning every object as a series of simple building blocks such as boxes, spheres, and cylinders will help plan out complex models, which is a great way to approach any 3D design project. Essentially, the act of using simple geometric shapes to create more complex forms is the design workflow behind most 3D solid modeling programs such as Tinkercad and OpenSCAD. Indeed, both Tinkercad and OpenSCAD use simple building blocks such as cubes, spheres, and cylinders to create more complex designs.

For new owners of 3D printers who lack design experience, starting off with a simple cube can be a great way to ease into the design process. For more advanced CAD users, the notion that everything in the world is built up from boxes and spheres may sound a bit far-fetched and a little simplistic, but as you explore the objects around you, you should be able to break down everything you see into simple geometric objects. Framed pictures on the wall are essentially flat boxes. Everyday furniture, such as tables and chairs, can easily be broken down into several boxes. A coffee cup is a hollow cylinder with a curved cylinder for a handle. The cars outside are boxes with cylinders for wheels. Buildings are nothing more than a series of large overlapping boxes. And the city around you is a huge jumble of boxes in a neatly organized pattern.

Even the most complicated objects can be broken down into boxes, cylinders, and spheres. A jet engine is a series of cylinders and overlapping boxes. This act of geometric reduction is something that fine artists have been practicing for decades. Many artists will study anatomy by breaking the human form into simpler geometric shapes. The human skull, for example, is a sphere overlapping a box.

The use of boxes, spheres, and cylinders is essential in making the modeling process as efficient as possible. In essence, most modeling software packages utilize this same method of combining simple geometric shapes to build more complex objects. Whether you use Tinkercad, Solidworks, or Fusion 360, the foundation and beginning stages of any project will be simple shapes, base geometric objects,. and curves.

To illustrate how basic geometric shapes are the foundation for most 3D modeling projects, let's begin with your first project, designing a basic box (with a lid) using Tinkercad.

Designing a Basic Box in Tinkercad

Autodesk's Tinkercad is a great way to get started with design for 3D printing. As a web-based application, Tinkercad is accessible to anyone with an Internet connection. Tinkercad is a cloud-based application that is part of the Autodesk family of 123D products. Projects created in Tinkercad are automatically saved to the cloud and accessible any time you log in to Tinkercad.

Tinkercad also acts a bit like a social network for 3D modelers. Designs created in Tinkercad can be made public. Such designs can be critiqued by the Tinkercad community, giving designers the opportunity to get feedback on their designs. To make a design public, users can click the properties in the design section listed on Tinkercad's main menu. Any designs created by Tinkercad users can be given copyright protections as designated by the Creative Commons licensing agreement. Users have several Creative Commons license options to choose from including Attribution-Share-Alike 3.0, Attribution 3.0, Attribution No-Derives 3.0, Attribution-NonCommercial 3.0, and Attribution-NonCommercial-ShareAlike 3.0.

Tinkercad artists can also send their creations directly to Thingiverse. In general, Tinkercad offers a nice platform for beginning designers to share their work with the greater 3D-printing community.

Tinkercad: Getting Started

To access Tinkercad, simply visit `https://www.tinkercad.com/`. Tinkercad is a web-based app that works in your browser and therefore can be accessed on both a Mac and Window PC. To get started, new users need to visit the Tinkercad web site and sign up for an account. Note that children younger than 13 need to get a parent's permission to join and must sign up using a parent's e-mail.

■ **Note** As an option, users can log in using their Facebook profile. (Since you must be 13 to use Facebook, this option will not work for younger Tinkercad users.)

Logging in to the Tinkercad site will give you access to a user account page (Figure 3-1), which provides access to all the Tinkercad models created by that user. Designs appear in the bottom half of the page and can be designated as private or public. Public designs will be viewable by other Tinkercad users. Previously created designs can be opened here and edited in the Tinkercad workspace environment.

Figure 3-1. *After logging in to Tinkercad, the user's account page will appear. Here users can access past Tinkercad models and create new projects*

By using the search bar in the upper-right corner, Tinkercad users can also search fellow Tinkercad artists and explore other Tinkercad designs. This is a great way to provide feedback on designs created by other users in the Tinkercad community.

To the left of the Tinkercad interface is a sidebar that provides the option to create a new project. Click the "Create project" link to begin a new model (Figure 3-2).

Figure 3-2. *Once on the main account page, users can click Create project" in the left sidebar to begin a new model*

By creating a new project, Tinkercad users will be presented with a simple interface with a sparse menu in the top bar and a window containing geometric objects to the right (Figure 3-3). To construct 3D designs, users can access the right menu of geometric shapes in order to build more complex objects. Also in the main window is a grid surface called the *work plane*, which serves as the interface for placing geometric shapes in the scene. This work plane grid is a common element found in most CAD programs (although in other programs it is simply called a *grid*) and is one of the universal features shared by almost all 3D-modeling software applications.

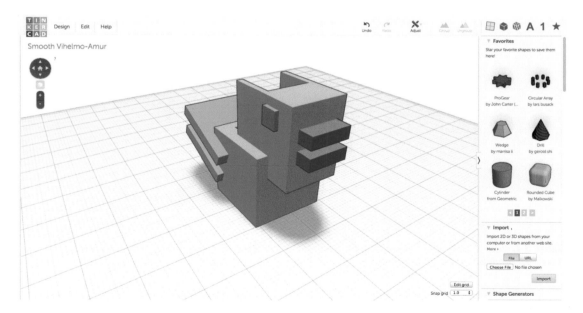

Figure 3-3. *The Tinkercad interface. The right sidebar contains the shapes that will be dragged onto the work plane. To the left are the navigation icons. The horizontal menu in the upper-right corner lists a number of modeling operations such as undo, redo, adjust, and group*

To the left are a few navigation icons (Figure 3-4). One icon resembles a compass, with triangle arrows pointing in the four cardinal directions and a small house icon in the center. Users can click these four arrows to navigate to various locations in the workspace. Clicking the home icon centers the whole view on the screen. Clicking the cube icon below the compass will focus on just the geometry in the scene. Below the cube are plus and minus sign icon, which let viewers zoom in to or zoom out of the scene.

Figure 3-4. *A close view of Tinkercad's navigation icons*

How to Use Tinkercad

The key to Tinkercad is simplicity. Tinkercad is meant to be straightforward and easy to use. This is evident by the short video on the Tinkercad home screen (before you log in). Essentially there are three main steps to using Tinkercad: (1) place, (2) adjust, and (3) combine.

1. *Place* simply means, while in the Tinkercad workspace, you can grab geometric shapes in the right-side menu and place them on the work plane. You can grab as many shapes as you want build a scene, but the more shapes that amass, the slower Tinkercad becomes.

2. *Adjust* means that once, shapes are placed on the work plane, they can be manipulated in a number ways. Shapes can be moved, scaled, and rotated as the designer sees fit.

3. Finally, users can *combine*, shapes by grouping them, or shapes can be cut out from other shapes to create entirely new forms.

Navigation in Tinkercad's 3D space is fairly straightforward and works entirely with a three-button, scroll-wheel mouse (or track pad). Middle-clicking allows you to move up, down, left, or right (also called *panning* in some applications), the scroll wheel lets you zoom in or out, and right-clicking lets you rotate in 3D space.

When learning the navigation of any 3D program for the first time, it's a good idea to practice the navigation controls for a bit to get used to them. In Tinkercad, drag a red cube from the right-side geometry window to the work plane and use the middle mouse, scroll wheel, and right mouse buttons to explore. In no time, navigating in Tinkercad will become natural to you.

Building the Box in Tinkercad

Here we will begin our first project, creating a simple box and lid in Tinkercad. The steps for this project take into consideration that you may be completely new to 3D modeling.

Drag a Cube onto the Work Plane

Follow these steps to get started:

1. A work plane will be the first thing you see. The default work plane is a grid consisting of 20 large units; these larger units are broken down into smaller units of 10. By default the larger units are in millimeters, but you can change this option to inches by clicking the "Edit grid" button the lower-right corner.

2. For the purposes of this tutorial, you will work in inches. Click the "Edit grid" button to open the grid properties dialog box. Here you can change the setting from millimeters to inches, which will create a grid consisting of 7.87 units in the X and Y directions.

3. On the right side of the interface is a scrollable window featuring geometric shapes in several categories. These shapes can be moved by right-clicking the shape in the right bar and then dragging it onto the work plane. Try dragging a red cube onto the work plane. As you drop the cube, it will "snap" to the gridlines of the work plane.

4. Below the "Edit grid" button is a "Snap grid" menu that will set a level of tolerance for the snapping function. For example, setting the snap grid to ½" will cause the cube to snap at larger increments on the grid (snapping to half the size of the larger grids). It's probably best (unless you decide to do more precise work) to keep the snap grid tolerance set to 1/8", which is the default. At a 1/8" setting, any object you drag to a work plane will snap at single grid increments.

5. Begin the modeling process by dragging the red cube you dropped from the Shape Generators panel onto the work plane (Figure 3-5). The cube will snap to the surface of the grid plane, and you will able to drag it in 1/8" increments.

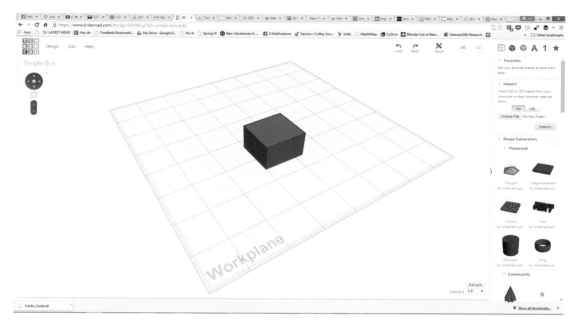

Figure 3-5. *A red cube has been dragged from the Shape Generators panel on the right and dropped on the work plane grid. The cube will snap to the grid*

Scale the Cube to the Proper Dimensions

Follow these steps:

1. For this tutorial, you want the cube (Figure 3-2) to be 4" in the X direction (4" wide) by 3" in the Z direction (3" long) by 2" in the Y direction (2" tall).

2. When you hover the cursor over the red cube, small icons will appear on various locations on the surface of the cube. Offset at the corners of the cube are small circular arrows; selecting these circular arrows will rotate the cube.

3. The small hollow rectangles and filled squares (appearing at the corners of cube, at the sides, and in the center) will let you scale the cube. The small upward-pointing cone will let you move the cube upward in the Y direction. Note that holding the Shift key constrains the various moving, scaling, and rotating operations. The small white square will turn red when selected, and the measurement line indictor will appear next to the cube indicating that it is now scalable (Figure 3-6). Scale the cube upward until it is 2" tall.

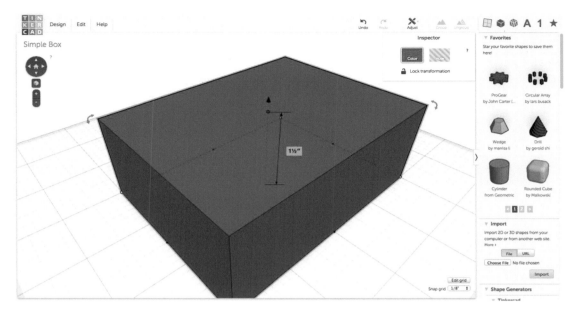

Figure 3-6. *The cube can be scaled by dragging the small, white square in the center of the cube. The small white cube will turn red when in scaling mode. Also, a measurement line will appear indicating the height of the box*

Duplicate the Cube to Create the Hollow Box

Follow these steps:

1. To create a hollow box, you can use a Boolean operation, but first you must create a duplicate and align it into position. This duplicate will represent the hollow portion of the box (Figure 3-7).

2. To create a duplicate box, grab the initial box while pressing the Option key (if you are using a Mac) or the Alt key (if you are using a Windows PC). The duplicated cube should overlap the initial cube, and you will align both cubes shortly.

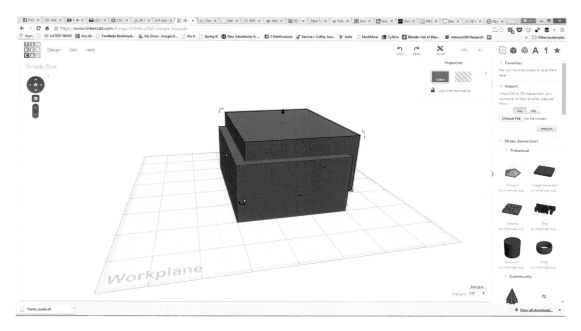

Figure 3-7. *The original box is duplicated by selecting and dragging the original with the Option/Alt key pressed*

Duplicate Objects in Tinkercad

Follow these steps:

1. To create a duplicate in Tinkercad, simply select the object you want to duplicate and click and drag while pressing the Option/Alt key.

2. Clicking and dragging will immediately create a duplicate or a whole series of duplicates if that is what you desire. This is an efficient way to create many duplicates in a short amount of time.

Scale Down and Align the Cubes

To scale down and align the objects, follow these steps:

1. To make the box hollow, first the red cube will be subtracted by the geometry of the second, duplicated red cube using Tinkercad's Hole function.

2. Scale the duplicated cube down and use the snapping function to make it a 1/4" smaller on all sides.

3. Move the smaller cube into place over the larger cube (Figure 3-8). With the tolerance set to 1/8" in the "Snap grid" menu, you should be able to do this manually. If you have trouble getting the two cubes to overlap properly, you can use the Align function in the Adjust menu (found in the menu bar in the upper-right corner).

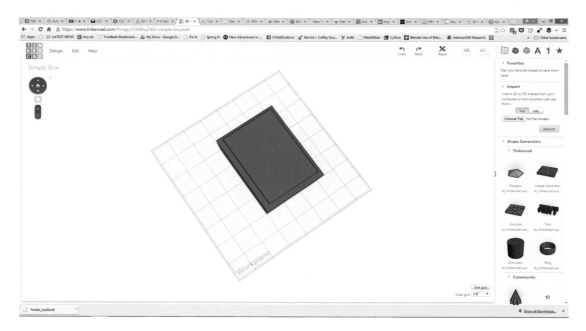

Figure 3-8. *The duplicated box is aligned with the original box*

4. To use Align, you must have two objects selected. When Align is activated, a series of black guides with dots at the intersections will appear. Clicking the various dots will cause one of the selected objects to be constrained to the other objects. For example, clicking the dot at the lower-left side of the larger cube will cause the smaller cube to be constrained and lie flush and centered against the left wall of the larger cube.

5. To center the smaller cube within the larger cube, click the dots appearing on the centers of both sides of the align guides. The smaller cube should then be centered within the larger cube.

6. Grab the small arrow/cone in the middle of the smaller cube and drag up to create an overlap between the bigger and smaller cubes. The two cubes must overlap for the Boolean difference operation to work (which will be discussed when we create the hollow box in the next exercise).

Create the Lid by Duplicating the Larger Cube

When you create any model, it is often a good idea to think ahead to determine the best order of operations. In this circumstance, you may be inclined to hollow out the box now that you have the two cubes overlapping. Making the box hollow at this stage wouldn't be too big of a problem, but the two cubes, in their unhallowed/solid state, can be a valuable asset for making another part of this model: the lid.

Therefore, before you use Tinkercad's Hole function to perform a Boolean difference operation to create the hollow box, let's first make a lid.

1. To make the lid, you can once again use the duplicate keyboard shortcut (Option/Alt+drag) (Figure 3-9). The lid should be the same length and width of the larger box. The bottom should also have an extruded inset surface (that way it will fit snuggly on the box below). You can create the inset portion of the lid by duplicating the smaller cube.

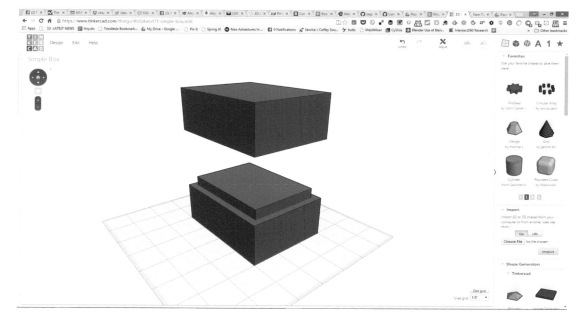

Figure 3-9. *Another box is duplicated in order to make a lid*

2. To proceed with making the lid, select the larger box and drag upward while keeping the Option/Alt key pressed. You now have a duplicate of the larger cube that can be scaled down to create the box's lid.

Scale Down the Larger Cube

Follow these steps:

1. Next, down the lid in the Y direction. Select the cube and grab the center white rectangle and drag downward (Figure 3-10).

2. Now that you have the basis of a nicely shaped lid, you can create an extruded inset on the bottom of the lid to ensure that it fits snugly on the box when closed.

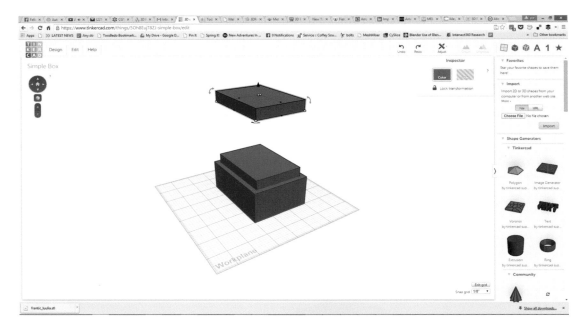

Figure 3-10. *A the second duplicate box is scaled down to make a lid*

A Note on Using Color Coding to Aid in Selecting/Identifying Parts of the Model

Before you continue with the lid, it may be a good idea to organize your scene.

At this stage, you now have three objects in the scene: a lid and the two boxes below. Three objects are not too much for you to handle at this current stage, but as you proceed to other projects, the number of objects in a scene can escalate quickly. As you advance to future projects, your models may consist of potentially hundreds or even thousands of independent geometric components.

Therefore, as your models grow in complexity with multiple components, it is always a good idea to name the objects in your scene as you create them. Naming the geometry in a scene is a good strategy in any modeling software application you may happen to use. Increasing the number of things you add to any computer-generated scene (geometry, components, shapes, and so on), regardless of the modeling software being used, will cause that scene to grow in complexity. The resulting multicomponent scenes will become visually complex with many shapes overlapping one another. Pinpointing and selecting specific objects in such multicomponent scenes can time-consuming, but if all the objects/components in a complex scene are appropriately named, it can be easier to locate them throughout the modeling process.

Unfortunately, Tinkercad won't allow you to name each object in the scene individually. Therefore, an alternative way to keep track of multiple objects on the Tinkercad work plane is through color-coding.

Color-coding is a common practice in many 3D-modeling applications as a means to distinguish parts in complex assemblies. It's a good practice to implement in any modeling package you use.

In Tinkercad, the geometric objects in the right-side menu have default colors. In Tinkercad, cubes are red by default; therefore, cube objects in your work plane will be the same red. But even in a simple scene, depending on how your box is positioned, it may be difficult to see the various cubes if they are on top of one another.

To make the process of locating and selecting objects easier in Tinkercad, change the color of the cube by selecting and then clicking the color swatch in the inspector window in the upper-right corner. The act of selecting the objects in your scene will be far more efficient if you use this color-coding technique consistently throughout your projects.

At this part of your process, the various components of your model can be defined with unique colors. In this particular exercise, the main box will be red, and the lid will be whatever color you have chosen (Figure 3-11).

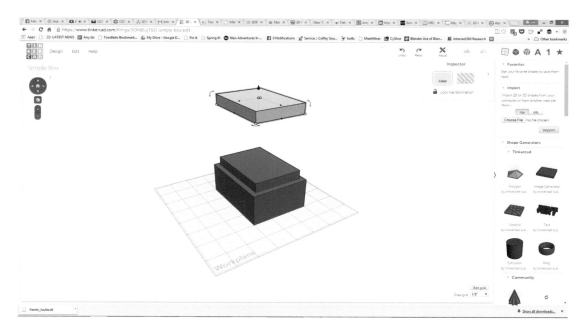

Figure 3-11. *Change the color of the lid to make it more easily identifiable during the modeling process*

Create an Inset on the Lid

To finalize the inset on the lid, duplicate the smaller, inner box by pressing the Option/Alt key, right-clicking, and dragging upward.

To ensure that the lid fits snugly, you will need to make it slightly smaller than the box opening below. To do this precisely, you will use the Ruler tool, which is found in the helper section of the shape generation toolbar.

1. Drag and drop the ruler onto the lower lid, and measurements will appear. Currently, the lower, inset lid is 3.5" long by 2.5" wide.

2. You want to adjust this slightly and reduce the size by .1" in each dimension. Clicking a measurement will allow you to adjust it. Change the length and width to 3.4" by 2.4", respectively (Figure 3-12).

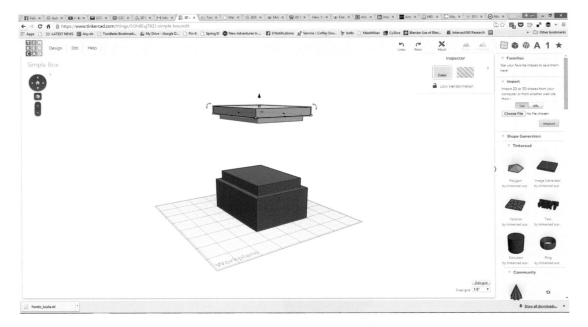

Figure 3-12. *The new for the box is now complete*

3. The inset lid part may now be slightly off-center. To bring the inset back in alignment with the top lid, use the Align function in the Adjust menu.

4. To finalize the lid, now that you have a lower inset created, go ahead and group the top lid part and lower part together. Select both pieces and then group them together using the Group function (the icon looks like two small triangles or a mini-mountain range) in the menu bar located in the upper right of the screen. Once the lid parts are grouped and in alignment, you can proceed to the next step and produce the hollow area inside the box.

Use Tinkercad's Hole Operation to Perform a Boolean Difference Operation

One of Tinkercad's more powerful functions is to create holes and cut away objects using the Boolean difference option. When using this Boolean operation, you can define geometric shapes as "holes" and use those holes to cut away and divide up other geometric shapes.

To create the hollow opening in the box (Figure 3-13), you will use Tinkercad's Hole function. Going back to the initial red boxes, the hole is defined by a smaller red box. In other words, the smaller box represents the negative space of the larger box.

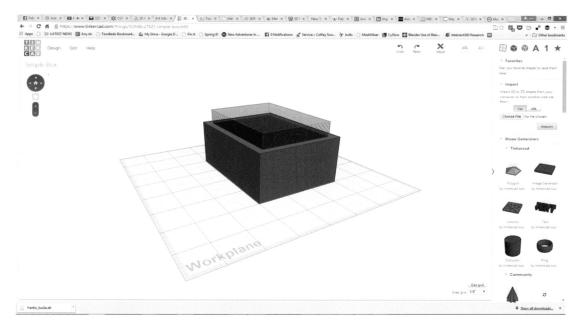

Figure 3-13. *A duplicate box is turned into a hole object*

1. To define the smaller box as a hole, select it (it will be highlighted with a soft blue outline) and then click Hole in the inspector window. The box will change from red to translucent gray. This color change indicates that you can now use the smaller box to cut into the larger box.

2. To make the larger box hollow, select both the larger box and the smaller, translucent box. Press the Shift key as you make both selections to keep both boxes selected simultaneously.

3. Once both boxes have been selected (again, they should be highlighted with a soft blue outline), group them together by clicking the group icon in the upper-right menu. Once grouped, the translucent smaller box will disappear, and you will have a final hollow, larger box (Figure 3-14).

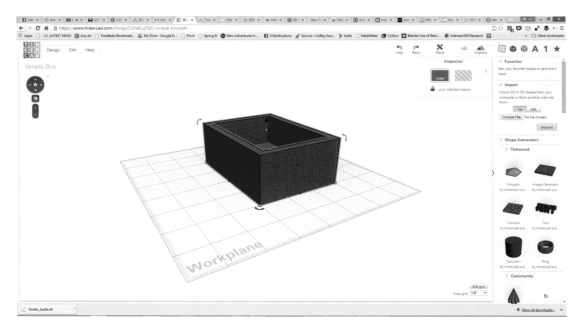

Figure 3-14. *Using the Group function on both the hole object and the main box "cuts out" the hole object from the box*

Add a Handle to the Lid

Now you have a nice hollow box with a lid. At this point, the lesson could be considered complete, but there is one final touch to add: a small handle for the lid.

1. Before proceeding, take a look at your competed box. Examine the box by zooming in and traveling around it using Tinkercad's navigation icons or the mouse button shortcuts.

■ **Note** Ideally, as you've been modeling, you've also been navigating around the model. Throughout the 3D design process, it's always a good idea to navigate around the model and look for any potential flaws in the design.

---

2. If anything appears to be off (maybe you improperly aligned or measured something during the design process), you can use the Undo function to go back to any previous stage in the design process. The Undo and Redo buttons have curved arrows and are in the upper-right menu. You can also use the shortcuts Command/Control+Z to undo and Command/Control+Z to redo. Also note that your models retain this undo/redo functionality even after they've been saved. In other words, you could walk away from a model and return to it months later and it would still undo to an earlier stage.

3. The lid will consist of two spheres. Drag a sphere from the right menu onto the lid and scale it down to a reasonable size.

4. Use the Align function in the Adjust menu and align the sphere to the center of the lid (Figure 3-15).

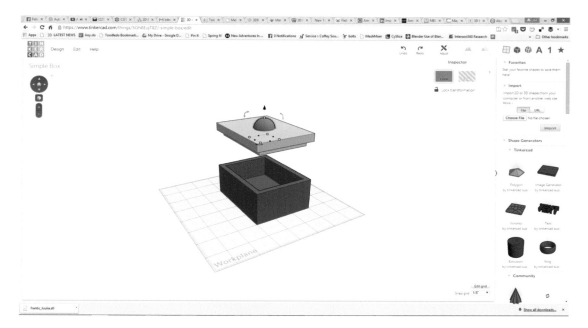

Figure 3-15. *A sphere is added and aligned to the lid to make a handle*

5. Drag another sphere to the top of the initial sphere.

6. Make this sphere slightly smaller than the first one.

7. Once again, use the Align function to make sure the smaller sphere is uniformly centered over the larger sphere.

8. To finish the lid, select the lid and two spheres one by one using Shift+right-click to select and group all three objects together (Figure 3-16).

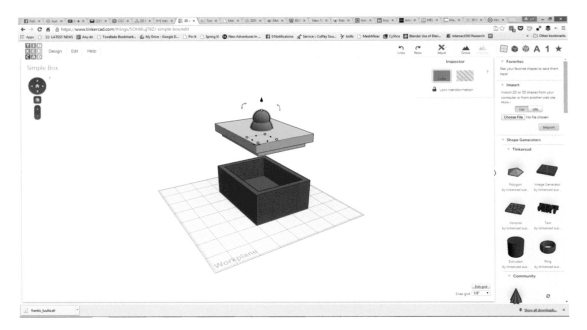

Figure 3-16. *The two spheres that make up the handle are aligned and grouped to the lid*

9. At this stage, the lid box is fully complete but not 100 percent ready for 3D printing. To ensure the box is printable, you want to validate that the file is "print-ready" using an additional software tool such as Meshmixer, Netfabb, or Cura. If you are eager to get your box 3D printed, please proceed to Chapter 4.

If you want to continue to build up your 3D modeling skills, let's continue to the next lesson where you will build another version of the box but in an entirely different way using OpenSCAD.

Designing a Basic Box in OpenSCAD

The introduction to 3D modeling with Tinkercad should make any beginning design feel more comfortable with the 3D-modeling process. Even experienced modelers should feel a bit of joy exploring Tinkercad's shapes. Interestingly, a simple tool such as Tinkercad can lead to some complex shapes and forms.

Behind Tinkercad and every other 3D-modeling program is the code. As you drag and drop shapes, complex algorithms are at work to calculate how the graphics will appear on the screen. It is entirely possible to create geometry directly with code. For those who are curious about code, OpenSCAD is the software tool to explore.

The following lesson will go through the same box-building steps as earlier but with OpenSCAD. Many may be apprehensive about coding, but going through this exercise is highly recommended. Coding enables artist, designers, and engineers to become more efficient in their design process. As you will see in the following lesson, using OpenSCAD is a more efficient and concise way to build your box.

OpenSCAD: Getting Started

Unlike Tinkercad, OpenSCAD is a not a web-based application. You will have to download it and install it on your PC in order to use it. OpenSCAD can be downloaded at www.openscad.org and is available for Windows, Mac OS X, and Linux.

The OpenSCAD interface is simple (Figure 3-17). In comparison to Tinkercad, the interface is sparse and consists of three windows. The window to the left is a text editor used for entering code.

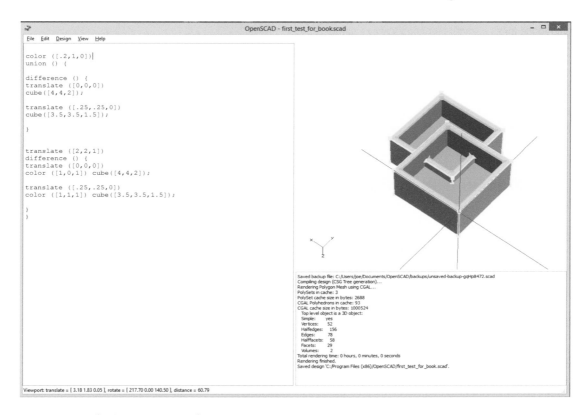

Figure 3-17. *The OpenSCAD interface*

How to Use OpenSCAD

With OpenSCAD, you are designing with code. If designing with code sounds a bit overwhelming, don't worry—writing code with Open SCAD is similar to using HTML on a web page.

The code to create objects in OpenSCAD is self-explanatory. For example, the cube command creates cubes, the sphere command creates spheres, and the cylinder command creates cylinders.

There are probably about 60 commands in OpenSCAD. Many of the commands will let you manipulate the geometry you create. With the commands in OpenSCAD you can move, rotate, scale, and use Boolean operations to combine objects.

There is a certain syntax to follow when using commands. To create a 3D cube that is 2 units wide by 3 units long by 4 units tall, you would use cube ([2,3,4]);.

> ■ **Note** The units in OpenSCAD are generic. There are no measurement systems in OpenSCAD; in other words, there is no designation for the units, and it is up to the designer to define the size of the object when setting up the file before 3D printing. Most likely a program such as Meshmixer, Cura, or Netfabb will be used to prepare the file for 3D printing. You can define your units at that stage. In the meantime, make a mental note of what the units could be as you work on your model and stick with those units for the duration of the modeling process. For example, if you begin the modeling process declaring that 1 OpenSCAD unit equals 1 inch, stay with those measurements for consistency's sake.

To see the cube, hit F6, which will render the cube in the larger window in the upper-right corner of the user interface.

Once the geometry is rendered, you can navigate and explore it. The navigation controls are similar to the navigation controls used in Tinkercad. The left mouse key rotates the object, the scroll wheel zooms in and out, and the right mouse key pans up, down, left, and right.

Once you are satisfied with the model, you can export it as an .stl using File ➤ Export.

Building the Box in OpenSCAD

As you will see, building the same open box in OpenSCAD is a far more efficient process when you use code. Using Tinkercad to create the box and lid took more than ten operations, consisting of dropping and dragging objects and aligning and grouping them to make the final forms. This process could easily take an hour or two. With OpenSCAD, you can create the same open box configuration with an inset lid in less than ten minutes by simply using code.

Type the following code into the text editor window. After you enter the code, hit F6 to see the final box come together in the render window.

```
difference () {
cube ([4,3,2], center=true);
translate ([0,0,1])
cube ([3.5,2.5,2], center=true);
}

union () {
translate ([0,0,2])
cube ([4,3,.4], center=true);
translate ([0,0,1.8])
cube ([3.49,2.49,.4], center=true);

translate ([0,0,2.2])
scale ([.1,.1,.1])
sphere (r=5, center=true);

translate ([0,0,2.7])
scale ([.07,.07,.07])
sphere (r=5, center=true);
}
```

The first section of code is used to create the hollow box (Figure 3-18). The command cube ([4,3,2], center=true); creates the initial box. The command center=true is used to ensure the box is perfectly centered in 3D space.

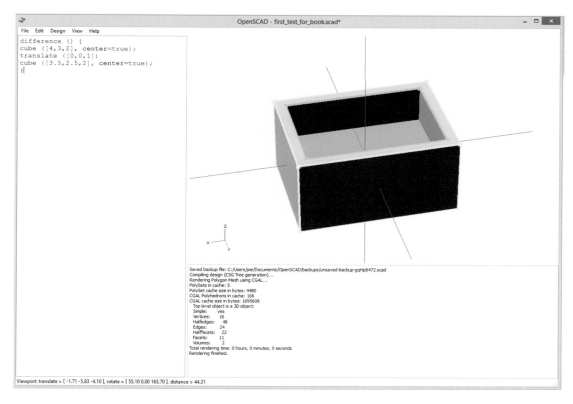

Figure 3-18. *Code in the left sidebar generates the box shapes in OpenSCAD's main window*

The next series of commands, translate ([0,0,1]) cube ([3.5,2.5,2], center=true);, is used to create a second, smaller box.

This second, smaller box is moved up 1 unit in the Z direction using the translate command and will be used in the Boolean operation to create the hollow box.

The difference command is used to subtract the smaller box for the large box and is a Boolean operation. Any shape commands such as cube, sphere, and cylinder found within the curly brackets preceding the difference command will be used in the Boolean operation. The first object listed in the brackets will be the base shape, and the preceding objects listed will be "cutter objects" and will subtract the geometry from the base.

The next set of commands, translate ([0,0,2]) cube ([4,3,.4], center=true); translate ([0,0,1.8])cube ([3.49,2.49,.4], center=true);, creates the upper lid (Figure 3-19).

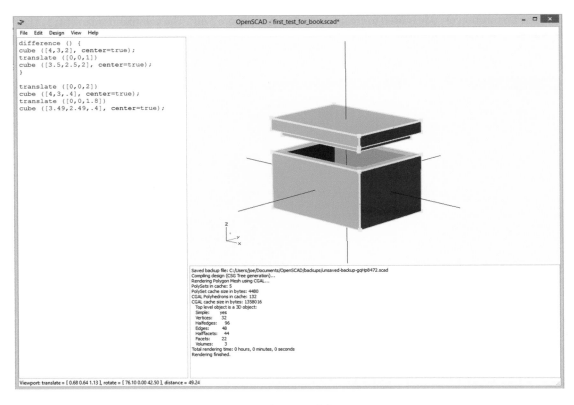

Figure 3-19. *The cube command is used to create the upper lid*

The final two sets of commands create the spherical handle for the top of the lid (Figure 3-20).

```
translate ([0,0,2.2])
scale ([.1,.1,.1])
sphere (r=5, center=true);

translate ([0,0,2.7])
scale ([.07,.07,.07])
sphere (r=5, center=true);
```

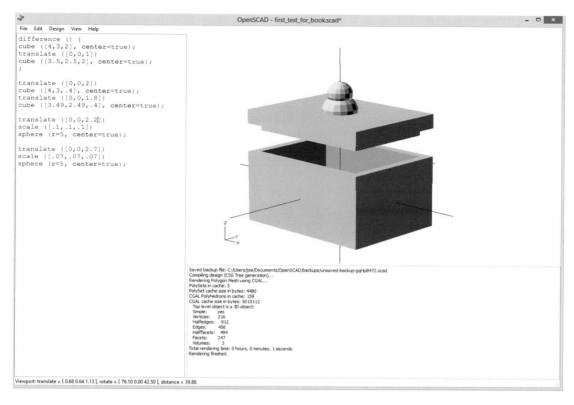

Figure 3-20. *The spherical handle is added to the top of the box's lid using the sphere command*

Finally, the `union` command is used to combine all the lid elements together.

Summary

Simple geometric shapes are the building blocks of more complex objects. A building block is nothing more than a simple box or sphere. From simple boxes and spheres, more complicated forms emerge. Both Tinkercad and OpenSCAD are easily accessible 3D-modeling applications that will let you build more complex objects. Using the example of a hollow box with a lid, both Tinkercad and OpenSCAD users can be introduced to the 3D-modeling process to learn how simple base shapes can lead to more complex designs.

CHAPTER 4

■ ■ ■

Preparing the Box for 3D Printing

Now that the step-by-step process of modeling the simple box with a lid is complete, the next step is to prepare the model for 3D printing and final 3D-printing output.

Remember, the box exercise in the previous chapter was just a warm-up. In later chapters, you will investigate the design process even further to create more sophisticated 3D-printable objects. As previously mentioned, every complex object design will be built from (or can be broken down into) simpler building blocks. Knowing how to construct simple objects will give you the confidence to explore more complex designs as you proceed.

But to truly master the 3D-printing process, from initial design to final 3D-printed product, knowing how to send .stl files to the 3D printer will be essential. This chapter will describe the process of preparing, correcting errors, and validating 3D models for final 3D-printed output. The lessons provided here will apply to every remaining chapter in this book.

If you are using your own 3D printer, this book assumes you are already familiar with the technical details of operating that particular machine. But, regardless of the 3D printer being used, this chapter will provide several avenues to prepare the box for 3D printing. Featured here are five software programs used to prepare .stl files for 3D printing to ensure a successful final printed product: Meshmixer, Netfabb, Cura, MatterControl, and Slic3r. Like the other software programs used for designing the models throughout this book, the applications mentioned here are free and easily accessible to anyone with online access.

Meshmixer, Netfabb, Cura, MatterControl, and Slic3r are known for their mesh repair, error checking, 3D printing preparation, and validating functions and are essential tools for getting models ready for 3D printing. This chapter will focus on most important validation and error-checking functions in these programs, specifically the ability add supports, the methods to fix nonmanifold meshes, and the workflows to properly pack parts on the 3D printer's build plate. This chapter will also explore the important design considerations that should be made prior to preparing .stl files to ensure the best outcome for 3D printing. Also, there will be mention of how these mesh correction tools can be used in combination as a fail-safe method to ensure that 3D models are free of errors.

3D DESIGN SOFTWARE VS. 3D-PRINTING ERROR CORRECTION/VALIDATION SOFTWARE

Now is a good time to make the distinction between 3D design (modeling) software and 3D-printing error correction/validation software. Many software tools enable designers to create 3D-printable geometry, from the free tools mentioned in Chapter 2 to the more professional-level CAD and animation packages, such as Maya, Inventor, Fusion 360, SketchUp, Rhino, Cinema4D, Modo, ZBrush, and many more. While these tools can be used to create any 3D model imagined, it is easy to create designs that are not 3D-printable (that is, nonmanifold objects). While many of these 3D-modeling applications offer error correction and mesh cleanup tools, they still lack some of the functions necessary to properly prepare files for 3D printing. One feature, in particular, that is missing from many 3D-modeling applications is the ability to generate g-code for 3D printing.

■ **Note** G-code (Figure 4-1) is a computer language that gives a machine a type of action to perform. A number of manufacturing tools such as CNC machines, laser cutters, water jet cutters, lathes, and (of course) 3D printers must use g-code in order to function. Software (such as Cura) is used to translate a CAD file into g-code, and generated g-code script is used by the tool in question (in this case a 3D printer) to construct the part outlined by the initial CAD file.

```
;Generated with Cura_SteamEngine 13.11.2
M109 T0 S227.000000
T0
;Sliced ?filename? at: Tue 26-11-2013 17:33:05
;Basic settings: Layer height: 0.2 Walls: 0.8 Fill: 20
;Print time: #P_TIME#
;Filament used: #F_AMNT#m #F_WGHT#g
;Filament cost: #F_COST#
G21        ;metric values
G90        ;absolute positioning
M107       ;start with the fan off
G28 X0 Y0  ;move X/Y to min endstops
G28 Z0     ;move Z to min endstops
G1 Z15.0 F?max_z_speed? ;move the platform down 15mm
G92 E0             ;zero the extruded length
G1 F200 E3             ;extrude 3mm of feed stock
G92 E0             ;zero the extruded length again
G1 F9000
M117 Printing...
;Layer count: 179
;LAYER:0
M107
G0 F3600 X87.90 Y78.23 Z0.30
;TYPE:SKIRT
G1 F2400 E0.00000
G1 F1200 X88.75 Y77.39 E0.02183
G1 X89.28 Y77.04 E0.03342
G1 X90.12 Y76.69 E0.05004
G1 X90.43 Y76.63 E0.05591
G1 X91.06 Y76.37 E0.06834
```

Figure 4-1. *An example of a g-code script*

To ensure 3D models can be translated into g-code, several new software tools have been developed to create the proper g-code for 3D printing. In addition to generating g-code, tools such as Meshmixer, Cura, Netfabb, Slic3r, MatterControl, and more, have the ability to create supports, check for nonmanifold geometry, and fix errors that may prohibiting the model from printing. Note some of these tools do have 3D-modeling functions, but not at the same level as a more dedicated 3D-modeling application, and they are meant to be used in conjunction with preexisting 3D-modeling tools. Therefore, most 3D-printing pipelines will consist of two or more software tools in the beginning design stage: a dedicated 3D software tool application for creating the geometry and one or two of the applications mentioned previously to validate and prepare the files for 3D printing.

The 3D-Printing Production Pipeline

From the initial preparation to design to the final 3D-printed output, Chapters 3 and 4 combined will take you through every stage of the 3D-printing pipeline. Conceptualizing and designing the box in Chapter 3 was just the first stage in the 3D-printing pipeline, and as mentioned, this chapter will guide you through the steps to turn the virtual 3D box into the final 3D-printed object.

A typical workflow begins with an intial sketch or draft followed by the design stage, which was presented in Chapter 3. The stages that will now be covered in Chapter 4 are are preparing the box for 3D printing and outputting the g-code, which will be necessary for final the 3D-printing output (Figure 4-2).

Figure 4-2. *An example of a 3D printing pipeline from initial concept development to final 3D-printed product*

Four Paths to 3D Printer Access

Since the goal of this book is to ensure that you can get your designs 3D printed, regardless of whether you have personal access to a 3D printer, this chapter will guide you through those crucial final steps. The knowledge provided here applies to every lesson offered in the later chapters and will help establish design guidelines for future 3D-printing projects.

Remember, owning a 3D printer is not a requirement to create 3D-printable designs. This book places 3D-print designers into four basic categories.

- You own a 3D printer.

- You have access to a 3D printer at school, at work, or at a local maker space.

- You created the model for a client or friend, and they will be responsible for getting the model 3D printed.

- You will send the file to a service bureau for 3D printing.

If you own a 3D printer, the steps in this book will help you get that file ready for printing regardless of the 3D printer owned. Most likely, first-time 3D-printer owners are using FDM desktop machines. Therefore, the 3D-printing validation workflows provided in this chapter will mostly focus on outputting from FDM 3D printers. Possibly there are a few SLA 3D printers owners reading this book as well. For those in that category, Meshmixer and Netfabb can be used to validate and fix 3D models, but most SLA printers, such as FormLab Form1+ and SprintRay's MoonRay DLP SLA printer will have theiir own specialized software tools for correcting meshes and creating supports.

Ensuring That 3D Models Are 3D Print Ready

If you don't own your own printer and intend on sending your `.stl` files to a service bureau, it is still recommended that you follow the mesh validation procedures provided in this chapter. As a designer, ensuring that the `.stl` files are "3D print ready" is proper etiquette, and having knowledge of how Meshmixer, MatterControl, Netfabb, Cura, and Slic3r can correct and validate files will help ensure that `.stl` files are "3D print ready" and error free. This chapter offers a sampling of tools; most likely you will not use all five, but using two in combination (such as using both Meshmixer and Cura to prepare files) is a surefire way to double-check your creations and spot potential errors. This due diligence to double-check files will help you create a positive relationship (and successful 3D print) with the service bureau providing the final output. Possibly, the `.stl` files will be uploaded to an online database for either sale or free download, and in this circumstance, `.stl` files should be print ready as well.

■ **Note**   A 3D print-ready `.stl` is a 3D design file that has been properly prepared and optimized for 3D-printing success. A print-ready file should be free from manifold errors (no holes or breaks in the mesh) and should be a watertight mesh. The geometry should be organized and "packed" properly on the print bed. Unless the `.stl` file is going to be sent to a multimaterial printer, intersecting geometry should be avoided, and the final file should be a single enclosed mesh. If you are sending the file to a service bureau, supports will be generated at the service bureau.

Software Preconfigured (Plug and Play) to Work with 3D Printers

Some of the programs mentioned in this chapter have preset print configurations that can be used with a number of 3D printers. For example, Autodesk has worked closely with Stratasys and Type A Machines to allow designers to print directly from Meshmixer to a Makerbot or Series 1 printer (and a number of other select 3D printer brands). These established relationships between the software and hardware manufacturers are a means to make the 3D-printing experience plug and play. But with so many 3D printers now available on the market, plug and play for all 3D printers has yet to become a reality.

If you own a printer brand that is not supported directly by the validation software that you are using, you should have the option to add your 3D printer configuration manually. The parameters for a 3D printer's configuration will most likely be found on the manufacturer's web site for the 3D printer you are using. These print parameters need to be input into the application to ensure that the `.stl` fie can be output properly using g-code.

■ **Note**   The 3D printer's configuration parameters include such settings as build volume, nozzle diameter, and extrusion. This information should be available on the 3D printer's manufacturer's web site. Some 3D printer manufacturers offer an `.ini` or configuration file that can be downloaded and then imported into programs such as Cura or Slic3r.

If you are sending a file to a friend or client to get printed, you may be totally unaware of the printer being used. The best guidelines are to prepare the files based on a generic standard printer configuration (such as a Makerbot) and validate those files using both Meshmixer and Netfabb. By validating the model in two applications, you can ensure that the file is as print ready as possible. Nevertheless, it will be up to the person who is 3D printing the files to ensure final printability.

Finally, for those designers using a service bureau, the service bureau will provide proper guidelines for delivering the .stl file. Oftentimes, if those parameters are not followed, the files will be returned to the designer who will be responsible for correcting the .stl file.

Regardless of what category you are in, the steps in this chapter will get your box ready for 3D printing. Once again, five different methods (Meshmixer, Cura, MatterControl, Netfabb, and Slic3r) will be covered in this chapter, and since they are all free, there is no harm in trying all five for maximum exposure to a range of 3D-printing preparation techniques. Eventually you will settle on the one or two software tools that work best for you.

Final Design Considerations to Ensure 3D Printing Success

There are additional design considerations to ensure that the print job is run as efficiently as possible. For example, if there are multiple objects being printed, those files should be packed and oriented properly on the printer bed.

Based on all the necessary criteria for ensuring successful prints, you should realize that a design is not complete until it has been properly formatted for successful 3D printing. While much time has been spent building the virtual box in Chapter 3, the job is only half done, and the design is not complete until it's properly prepared for 3D printing. The following sections cover the steps and considerations that should be taken to prep the box for 3D printing. As mentioned, these considerations should also be factored into the projects presented in later chapters (and all 3D-printing projects for that matter).

Consideration 1: What Type of 3D Printing Process Will Be Used?

One of the first decisions (and probably most obvious) that you will need to make is to choose the type of 3D-printing process will be used to 3D print your design. Knowing what type of 3D printer is being used on any project could have an important impact on the design of the object being created. If you own a 3D printer, you are probably familiar with the device, but if you design a 3D-printable object for someone else, it will necessary to know how the object will be printed.

If you aren't printing models with your own personal 3D printer, there are three potential 3D-printing methods that could be used to output your design. Not all 3D-printing methods are the same and the ability to 3D print certain aesthetic features, such as fine details, small text, interconnecting parts, and hollow recesses will depend on the 3D-printing method being used. Since the audience for this book may be new to the 3D-printing experience, the general assumption is that they will be using either a service bureau or a desktop FDM 3D printer. If the mode of production is through an FDM 3D printer, then the material being utilized will be either an ABS or PLA filament. (Note that the majority of the workflows presented in this chapter will focus on output using FDM 3D printers.)

Conversely, if you are submitting your file to a service bureau for final output, you may be printing using any number of 3D-printing processes, and those printing processes could use any number of possible materials (ceramics, gypsum, plastic, resin, metal, and more).

Service bureaus will be able to assist you with the necessary techniques for ensuring printing success. In order to not waste valuable printing time on failed jobs, it is in the service bureau's best interest to ensure that customer files are properly formatted for 3D printing. For this reason, service bureaus most likely will not accept unprepared .stl files. If the .stl file is not properly formatted, a technician at the service bureau will guide you through the necessary steps.

Generally, there are three different 3D-printing methods that will be accessible to most designers: FDM, SLA, and SLS. Certain design considerations should be made depending on the method being used.

Fused Deposition Modeling (FDM)

The most likely 3D printer being used by readers of this book will be an FDM desktop machine. The proliferation of FDM machines has recently been marked by a number of "mini" machines that have brought FDM printers into an affordable price range. Regardless of whether you own a $40,000 FDM 3D printer or a $400 FDM 3D printer, all FDM printers operate the some way, using plastic filament as the material for constructing the final product. Filament is extruded through a "hot end," producing layer heights ranging from 50 to 300 microns (.05mm to .3mm). Even at 50 microns, the layering resulting from the fused deposition modeling processing will be an obvious feature viewable to anyone examining the final 3D-printed part. Layering will appear as slight stair-stepping on the final object, giving the output 3D print a subtle texture. This layering will be impossible to avoid. Because of the layering of material from the FDM process, fine details will be possible only on larger objects. If you are designing smaller objects, it would be fruitless to spend time modeling detailed features around 200 microns in depth (.2mm).

With FDM 3D printing, thin walls and narrow parts should also be avoided; again, parts less than .3 mm in thickness may not print properly.

Stereolithography (SLA)

While the first 3D printer in existence developed by Chuck Hull was an SLA machine, only just recently have SLA printers entered the market place for everyday consumers. The most popular printer in this category is the Form1+, which uses an ultraviolet laser to solidify (the processing is also known as *curing*) a liquid photopolymer resin layer by layer. Some SLA printers use ultraviolet light from a DLP projector to solidify the resin as well. With the concentrated, more-precise light used in the SLA process layer, heights of just 10 microns are achievable in some circumstances. Artists and designers who require highly detailed prints will be happy with the SLA output. While layering stills exists in a 3D object produced by the SLA process, it is barely perceptible (the output of an SLA 3D printer will look smooth). Fine details at 100 microns are possible with an SLA printer.

Selective Laser Sintering (SLS)

SLS printers used a laser (or an electron beam for some additive metal processes) to fuse together metal dust, ceramic material, or gypsum powder. Owning an SLS 3D printer will most likely be out of the price range for most everyday consumers, and the only accessible way to take advantage of SLS technology is through a service bureau or online service such as Shapeways, Sculpteo, or i.materialise.

SLS 3D prints tend to have a grainy, rough surface finish and have resolutions around 100 microns. The graininess of an SLS 3D print tends to hide any perceivable layering. But again, fine details and thin parts can be challenging on small SLS prints; therefore, if a highly detailed final print is desired, it is best to work at a larger scale.

One distinct advantage that SLS 3D printers have over FDM and SLA 3D printers is the range of materials available. Also, SLS printers that use gypsum powder can print objects in full CMYK color.

Another big advantage is that most SLS processes don't require support structures. Objects printed using an SLS process will be naturally supported by the powder material in the print bed. Fully enclosed designs must be avoided since powder will accumulate in the final 3D-printed object.

Consideration 2: Final Output Size

The scale of the objects being designed is arbitrary; scale can be changed at the time of printing in the software being used. The two factors that will affect the scale of a 3D print are the bed size of the 3D printer being used and the desired final quality of the 3D print. Even though the process of designing the box in Chapter 3 asked for specific measurements, these measurements may have to change if the build size of your printer is too small. The 3D printer's build plate dimensions will dictate the build size of a 3D printer.

If you don't know the build size of a particular 3D printer, that information should be available on the 3D printer manufacturer's web site. Service bureaus will provide final output sizes on their web sites as well.

Also, certain details will dictate the scale of your final object. The minimum detail size of any feature on a design will be dictated by the layer height achievable with the 3D printer used. Most 3D printers print using layer heights ranging for 50 to 300 microns (.05mm to .3mm). Small details should be at least two to three times larger than minimal layer height. Scaling anything downward with small details will go beyond what is possible for the layer height achievable for the printer and should be avoided.

Two more important considerations that will be applied to the scale of your 3D-printed object are material cost and availability.

Consideration 3: Orientation of the Parts on the Print Bed

Designing the box in Chapter 3 completes one stage in the 3D-printing production pipeline. At this point, there should be an `.stl` file consisting of two separate meshes: a bottom box and the upper lid. To complete the design for 3D printing, the parts must be properly arranged on the printer bed.

Therefore, the orientation of the parts must be carefully considered while preparing the model for the build plate. Carelessly placing an object on the build plate can result in longer printer time, aesthetically unappealing prints, and even failed print jobs. All of the software mentioned in this chapter will have a virtual representation of the build space that will allow designers to visualize the orientation of their parts. Some software packages have sorting algorithms that will automatically arrange print jobs in the 3D printer's build space for maximum efficiently to ensure parts are printed correctly. Unfortunately, some of the 3D-printing packages mentioned here lack this auto-arranging capability. (auto-arranging is considered to be a premium feature in some software packages). Meshmixer has the ability to pack and orient geometry, but oftentimes the designer must manually adjust the results.

■ **Note**   *Packing* is the term used to describe how the models are organized on the printer bed. If multiple files are being printed at once, the files can be organized for maximum efficiency. Models should be flush on the printer bed and spaced out evenly without touching one another. Some of the programs mentioned here have functions to allow models to lie flush on the surface of the print bed. Other programs have algorithms to pack and organize files on the print bed for maximum efficiency. Oftentimes the models will have to be adjusted manually.

When manually orienting designs in the build space, you should consider three factors.

- *Durability*: The stress of any 3D-printed object flows with the deposition of material (that is, layering direction). A tube printed upright will be composed of more lateral layers, and each layer is a stress point that can break if enough pressure is applied.

- *Aesthetics*: Layers can be unappealing but are unavoidable. Angular and flat objects tend to show off layers more than highly textured, visually complex objects and designs with curvy, organic features. If the surface of the designed object is flat, the layers will be more noticeable. Figurines and highly detailed tools will look best when printed upright (standing tall).

- *Printability*: Even with brims and rafts, thin parts will be hard to print. Thin supports may collapse as well. Make sure you have sufficient supports to ensure that the previous one supports the next layer printed. If you can't create sufficient supports, then the best way to avoid problems is to print the object with its widest dimension lying flat on the print bed.

Consideration 4: Supports

After the parts have been sized and orientated in the build space, the next consideration to be made is how to support overhangs. Overhangs are areas of a design that can extrude from a surface with no material below. Unsupported overhangs can create a mess; filament will fall to the surface of the build plate in a random tangle. Technically, nothing is stopping a designer from sending a design to a printer without supports, but if the proper precautions are not taken, most likely the 3D print fail (or at the least improperly print in some areas). For example, while the box form in Chapter 3 is a fairly simple design, there are overhangs in the lid, and some issues may occur if the parts aren't lying flush on the build plate and if the lid is printed without supports. As a general rule, any design element that is parallel to and elevated from the build plate is considered to be an overhang. Without adding proper supports, overhangs are impossible to print and will result in a mess of filament being produced.

■ **Note**   Overhangs are any feature in the design that would run parallel to the 3D printer's build plate, within a variance of roughly 50 degrees in the positive or negative direction.

Unless you are using an SLS printer through a service bureau, supports will be a necessity in your 3D-printable design project. As mentioned earlier, any designs featuring overhangs with a variance of about 50 degrees in either direction should have supports to ensure that the layers being 3D printed do not collapse while the object is being printed.

When using an FDM 3D printer, many third-party software tools can help generate supports. Meshmixer, MatterControl, Slic3r, and Cura (all explained in further detail in this chapter) are capable of support generation. Typically, support generation is an automatic process enabled by the software. Each software will have its own method of generating supports. MatterControl, Slicer, and Cura tend to generate tall upright supports that act as "planks" to hold up the overhanging material. Meshmixer generates treelike branching structures that are thinner than most other support generators, but this thinness is compensated by branching algorithms that allow Meshmixer provide maximum support using a minimal amount of material. MatterControl, Slicer, and Cura supports tend to be more difficult to remove. Meshmixer's supports are easier to remove but may appear in unwanted areas.

■ **Tip**   Removing supports can be a challenging and time-consuming process. Supports should snap off naturally, but it can be a little tricky doing it by hand. The easiest way to remove supports is to use needle-nose pliers to grasp supports and then twist back and forth. After several twists, the supports should snap off. To avoid personal injury, do not use sharp, pointy devices (such as an X-acto knife or screwdriver) for support removal.

Any software that can create supports should provide the opportunity to manually adjust support parameters. If the generated supports are too difficult to remove or are causing parts of the 3D-printed object to break away, it will be necessary to adjust the supports manually within the software (see the following sections for each of the software tools discussed in this chapter). The best way to evaluate whether supports are working as they should is to run a test print to examine the generated supports. A test print will help determine whether the supports are too difficult to remove. Test prints can also help identify thin structures that may break upon support removal. Sometimes it will be necessary to correct the automatically generated supports by adjusting supports until the best optimal support structure is achieved.

Other Supportlike Structures

Here are a few additional support-like structures that can help stabilize a part while it is being printed.

Skirts

With FDM 3D printers, skirts are first strands of filament to get applied to the build plate and are an outline representation of the object being printed. The skirt can give a quick indication if a print is going to be successful. The skirt is usually offset 3mm to 4mm from the part being printed. It may have one to two layers, may have one to two outlines, and may surround the supports.

Brims

Brims can be used to stabilize narrow parts and help thin parts. They will typically be one or two layers in height and extend for 2mm to 3mm from the part being produced.

Rafts

A raft is a horizontal lattice of filament that is located underneath your part. Rafts are primarily used with ABS to help with bed adhesion. Rafts are similar to brims in that they can help stabilize narrow parts as well.

Consideration 5: Material Type

I am assuming you are new to 3D printing, and if that is the case, most likely you will be working with an FDM machine. With FDM 3D printing, the two most common material types you will be using will be PLA and ABS. Each material type has unique properties that lend themselves to either more detailed designs or more durable parts.

PLA

For beginning designers using FDM 3D printers, PLA is the recommended material to use. PLA is an accommodating thermoplastic that is used by every FDM 3D printer on the market. PLA is an easy material to work with and will adhere to the build plate on contact. Having parts adhere to the printer bed is important since it will ensure that the 3D object being printed remains stable.

The PLA material has more consistent quality when outputted from the extruder; it rarely bubbles or warps during the printing stage, making it ideal for more detailed objects.

PLA is made from natural materials such as cornstarch; biodegradable material is endorsed by designers who promote sustainability.

While PLA is less susceptible to warping during the 3D-printing stage, it is acceptable to heat and may melt if the right considerations present themselves (such as keeping a PLA-printed part in the back seat of a car on a hot summer day).

ABS

ABS has a higher melting point and longer life span than PLA. ABS is also stronger than PLA and is a better choice for 3D-printed parts that need to be durable.

ABS can be difficult to work with as well and requires a heated bed to ensure that objects being printed properly adhere to the build platform. ABS is not recommended for highly detailed designs since it can be prone to bubbling during the extrusion stage.

Unlike PLA, ABS is not environmentally friendly because of its oil-based plastic composition.

Testing, Exploration, and Experimentation

Even when all considerations have been taken into account, 3D prints may run into problems. Therefore, 3D-printing success comes from repeated testing, practice, and experimentation.

If you are doing the 3D printing yourself and you don't own a top-of-the-line printer, you may find that even the most perfectly-planned model will occasionally fail. Sometimes prints will fail halfway through a job for any number of reasons. Many reasons are beyond your control (for example, the power goes out while the model is being printed); other reasons may be the results of a of a executed design.

Running a test print should also be considered, since at the end of day, even that most well-concieved design can run into problems. A 3D printed test is usually the first 3D print to be outputted from the printer for a particular design job. That intital test must first gain approval by the designer and client before additional 3D prints are made. This first run 3D print should be thouroghly examined by the designer to ensure that the proper specifications are followed. These a first-runt tests are also called proofs. Graphic designers work in a similar way, reviewing initial proofs for errors before a design or publication is sent to press.

The part-testing process includes calibrating the 3D printer, which may involve some tinkering with settings such as bed temperature, layer height, and speed of the printer.

If you are working with a surface bureau, you will have to ensure that the file you provide is thoroughly devoid of errors. If the final product is going to be expensive to output, try to find a local maker space or school that will let you run a test 3D print for proofing purposes.

Besides being a means of finding possible errors, testing is a great way to explore creative variations of a design. Using the box as a base object, spend time creating variations in Tinkercad and OpenSCAD. Explore variations in the design, play with scale, add geometry to the box, and combine boxes together. Increased creative exploration in the virtual environments of Tinkercad and OpenSCAD (and any other 3D design program for that matter) can uncover a multitude of complex structures and visually pleasing geometric forms. Eventually, through this mastery, the virtual construction of digital geometry will give birth many more 3D-printed constructs. The 3D-printed box is one of the countless examples, and later chapters will provide the necessary workflows to 3D print your many design explorations.

Software Tools to Validate 3D Models for Printability

The remainder of this chapter will review the steps to format the box designed in Chapter 3 using Meshmixer, Cura, MatterControl, Slic3r, and Netfabb. While the support structures in the box are minimal, the information presented will still focus on the generation of supports, and it will be up to you to determine which software tool will work best for you.

Getting the Box Ready to 3D Print in Meshmixer

As part of your 3D-modeling toolkit, Meshmixer is a great tool to have handy. The features in Meshmixer will allow you to create supports, correct nonmanifold geometry errors, and organize geometry on the print bed to ensure objects print correctly and in an efficient manner.

Of the five packages mentioned in this chapter, Meshmixer by far has the most features for adjusting the geometry of an imported model. Not only can Meshmixer validate models for 3D printability, it has a number of features that can be used to modify geometry. Meshmixer comes with a number of preloaded mesh parts and also allows for the import of mesh geometry that can be combined in an unlimited number of ways. The power of Meshmixer lies in how it merges parts together, allowing designers to combine parts seamlessly in order to create watertight solids. Meshmixer can also handle fairly complex models and is a great tool to use to examine 3D models more closely.

Using Meshmixer

Meshmixer, like Tinkercad, belongs to the Autodesk family of 123D apps. In fact, most of the apps in the123D family are capable of directly exporting 3D designs into Meshmixer for error checking and final 3D print setup.

As mentioned, Meshmixer can also stand on its own as a 3D design application. A number of features in Meshmixer can be used to combined 3D objects, add features to 3D objects, and sculpt 3D geometry.

Meshmixer is also outstanding when it comes to correcting errors in geometry, adding support structures, and preparing .stl files for 3D printing. The following sections will help you prepare the box you created in Chapter 3 for 3D printing. These same steps can be applied to any model you will design from the lessons in this book.

Meshmixer is available to download at www.meshmixer.com/download.html and www.123dapp.com/meshmixer. Since Meshmixer is free, it is a highly recommended multifunctional tool for any 3D-print designer's tool kit.

Navigating in Meshmixer

The navigation controls using a scroll wheel are similar to Tinkercad. The middle mouse pans, the scroll wheel zooms in and out (pressing Option/Control will zoom in and out as well), and the left mouse bottom rotates around the object in the scene.

Hitting the spacebar in Meshmixer brings up a pop-up menu with the navigational tools, along with some other functions (Figure 4-3).

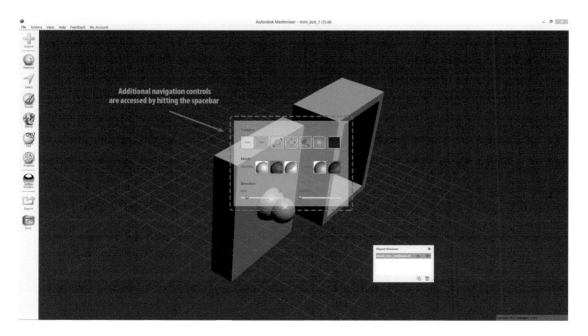

Figure 4-3. *The pop-up menu pictured here (overlapping the box) gives access to the navigation controls. Hitting the spacebar opens this pop-up menu*

Preparing the Box .stl File for 3D Printing with Meshmixer

Upon opening Meshmixer for the first time, you will be greeted with small window (Figure 4-4) with a number of icons arranged in a grid. These icons in the top row (beginning with the plus sign icon) from left to right will import geometry (.obj or .stl files), open Meshmixer documents, and access the 123D cloud service to access a number of precreated 3D models. The bottom row of icons opens a base mesh (a rabbit, sphere, and cube, respectively). The last icon in the bottom gives access to Meshmixer's list of keyboard shortcuts. Through this interface you can open 3D files in Meshmixer, and this is where you will open your box model created in the previous chapter.

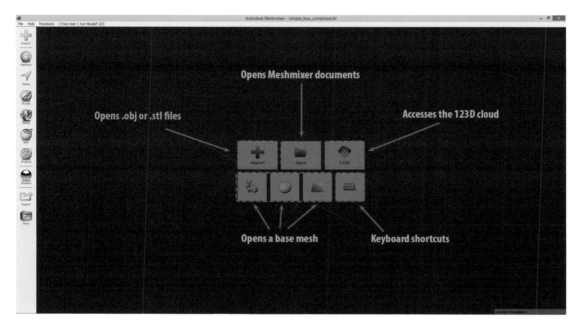

Figure 4-4. *The window grid of icons that appears when you first open Meshmixer*

■ **Note**   Meshmixer can open both .obj and .stl files.

Follow these steps:

1. Click the big plus sign icon to search for and open the .stl file that you created in OpenSCAD or Tinkercad in Chapter 3. Note that in Meshmixer the y-axis faces up. In many 3D modeling applications, the z-axis faces up. Therefore, when .stl and .obj files are imported from other programs, they may be facing the wrong direction in Meshmixer.

2. To ensure the geometry is properly oriented in Meshmixer, click Flip Z-Y on import.

3. Upon clicking the Flip Z-Y on Import option, the box should appear as you designed it in Tinkercad or OpenSCAD, with the lid floating above the main box. If you hit W, you can view the box in wireframe mode, which will display the tessellated faces (that is, the individual polygons) of the box mesh (Figure 4-5).

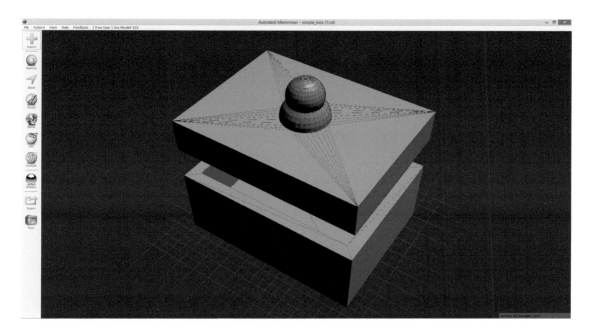

Figure 4-5. *The box you created in Chapter 3 as it appears in Meshmixer in wireframe mode*

■ **Note** One nice feature in Meshmixer is its compatibility with other 123D apps. Hitting the 123D button in the upper row of icons will give access to Autodesk's 123D cloud service. Signing into the 123D cloud feature allows artists to save their files in the cloud and access them in any of the 123D programs (see Figure 4-6).

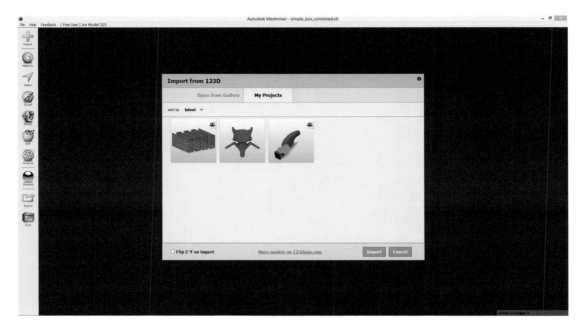

Figure 4-6. Meshmixer allows designers to import 3D models saved to the Autodesk 123D cloud

Properly Orienting the Parts of the Box Using the Select Tool

Follow these steps:

1. With the box imported into Meshmixer, now is the time to organize the various parts (the lid and the main box) properly on the printer bed. You can use the Select tool to grab individual polygons, parts, or whole designs. (The Select tool is third icon from the top in the row of icons on the right side of Meshmixer interface.)

2. Use the Select tool to select the lid of the box. Right-click the lid several times to select all the faces. The lid will change color once it has been fully selected to a darker brown (Figure 4-7).

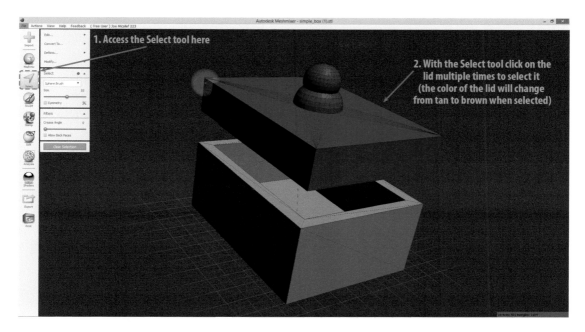

Figure 4-7. *With the Select tool, clicking the lid once will select one polygon. Clicking multiple times will grow the region of the selection and eventually select the whole lid.*

3. You may want to navigate around the lid using the left mouse key to ensure that every face has been selected.

4. An alternative way to create a selection in Meshmixer is clicking and dragging with the right mouse button to create a red lasso around the object you want to select.

5. Right-clicking multiple times and dragging after each click will create a lasso with straight lines (Figure 4-8). Keeping the right mouse button depressed as you drag creates a circular selection.

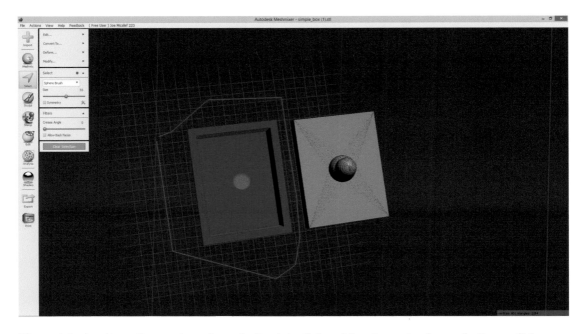

Figure 4-8. *An alternative way to make a selection is to click and drag to create a lasso selection or click repeatedly to create a hard-edged lasso selection*

6. If the wrong faces are inadvertently selected, hit Clear Selection and start the selection process over again.

Moving the Lid to the Base of the Build Plate Using the Move Tool

Follow these steps:

1. Hit T to access the Transform tool. Click the red and green arrows to move the lid in the x- and y-axes, respectively.

2. Once the lid is lying flat on the grid, hit Accept in the Transform dialog in the upper-left handle corner to complete the transformation process (Figure 4-9).

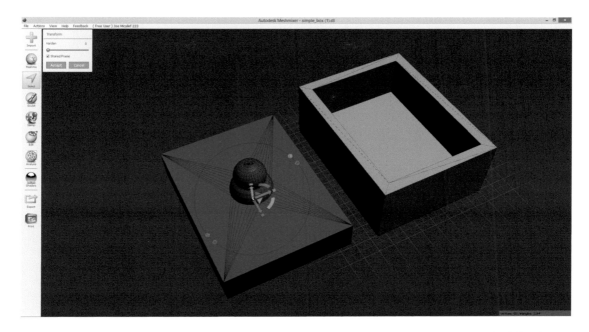

Figure 4-9. *While the box is still selected, hit T to access the Transform tool and use it to move the lid to the base of the build plate next to the bottom of the box*

■ **Note**   In many 3D design applications, the transform tools are red, green, and blue. This color-coding correlates to X, Y, and Z. Therefore, if you grab the green arrow, you know you are moving an object in the Y direction.

Exporting to the Printer

Once the lid and box bottom both lie flush on the build plate grid, it's time to prepare the box model for 3D printing.

1. To make the final preparations for 3D printing in Meshmixer, hit the last icon (the printer icon) in the row of icons on the right side of the Meshmixer UI. The interface will change, giving you access to all the commands necessary for 3D printing (see Figure 4-10).

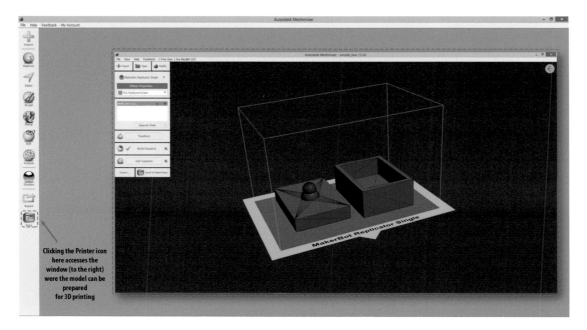

Figure 4-10. *Hitting the printer icon changes the interface and provides a new series of functions to prepare the model for 3D printing*

2. Find the printer you are using in the print settings. If the printer you are sending to is not on the list, you can add it by hitting the Printer Properties button.

3. In the print properties window, click the Choose Printer button, and on the Printer tab click Add New Printer (Figure 4-11).

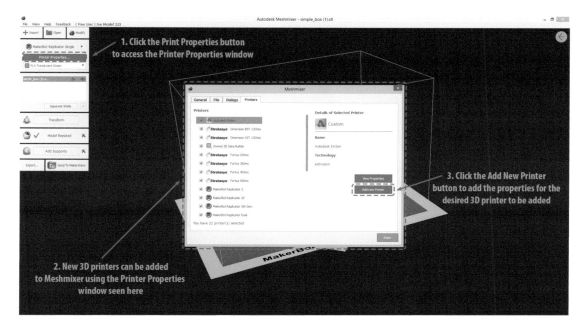

Figure 4-11. *You can add your own 3D printer to Meshmixer using the print properties window*

If you want to send the box file to a service bureau, you can access Shapeways, Sculpteo, and i.materialise.

Adjusting the Size of the .stl File

Note that if you adjust the build size by adding your own personal 3D printer to Meshmixer's list of preconfigured 3D printers, the build size representation may be too small for your 3D-printed design. If that is a case, you can adjust the scale of your object by hitting the transform button in the right-side menu.

In the New Transform menu that appears, you have three options to adjust the size of the model. First, the model can be adjusted manually using the controls for size, move, and rotate. Second, the Move to Platform button will cause the model to lie flush in the bottom of the build space. And, third, if the model exceeds the size of the build space or if you want the model to scale up to fit the build space, you can click the Fit to Build Volume button. Hitting Done will complete the size adjustment.

Repairing the Model

Repairing is a one-click option, but be sure to examine the model after running the repair. Hit W to go into wireframe mode, and rotate around the model to make sure the geometry looks correct.

Adding Supports

Follow these steps:

1. The Add Support button in Meshmixer is a one-click option as well. Click the Add Support button in the menu on the right side of the Meshmixer interface, and Meshmixer will automatically add supports to any overhangs in the box model design (Figure 4-12).

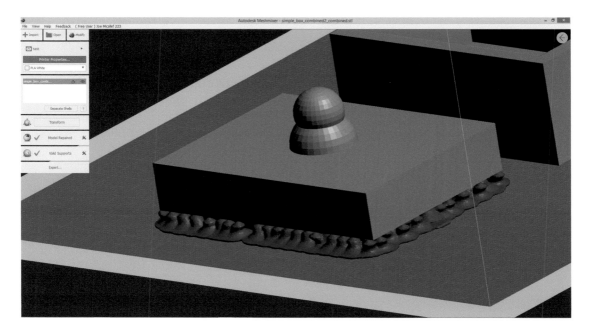

Figure 4-12. *Showing the resulting supports to the lid after clicking the Add Support button*

■ **Note** Adding supports in Meshmixer can take a few minutes depending on the complexity of the model. Occasionally, Meshmixer adds too many supports, which may be difficult to break off.

2. To adjust the supports, click the small icon to the right of the Valid Support button. This will open the Overhangs menu where you can manually adjust supports, support density, and support thickness (Figure 4-13).

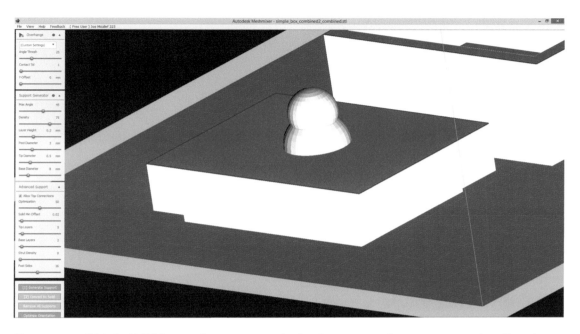

Figure 4-13. *Click the Valid Support button to enter the Overhang menu where supports can be adjusted manually*

3. Adjusting the sliders will create a new configuration of supports. Hitting the Generate Support button will regenerate the supports (Figure 4-14). Here you can click any support to manually add a new branch or Option/Control+click any branching support to delete it.

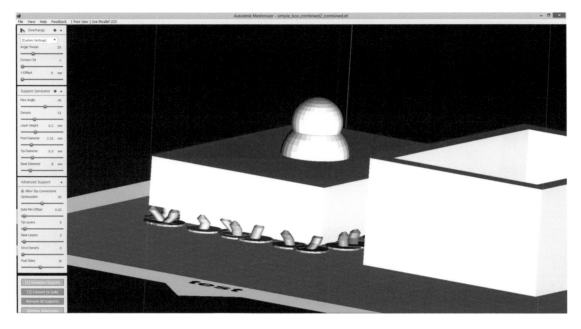

Figure 4-14. *Newly generated supports after being adjusted manually*

Sending to Printer, Exporting, or Sending to a Service Bureau

Once the supports are generated, it is time to send the model directly to a 3D printer or export the `.stl` file. Autodesk has collaborated with several 3D-printing manufacturers to give designers the opportunity to send files to a 3D printer directly. If you are using a 3D printer listed in the print settings, you should be to send directly to your 3D printer. If you don't own a printer that is in Meshmixer's list of printers, you can export the `.stl` and then generate the g-code or send to your printer using Cura, MatterControl, or Netfabb.

You also have the option of sending the model to a service bureau such as Shapeways, Sculpteo, or Materialize to be printed. This will bring up a shopping cart window where you can place an order for the model (Figure 4-15).

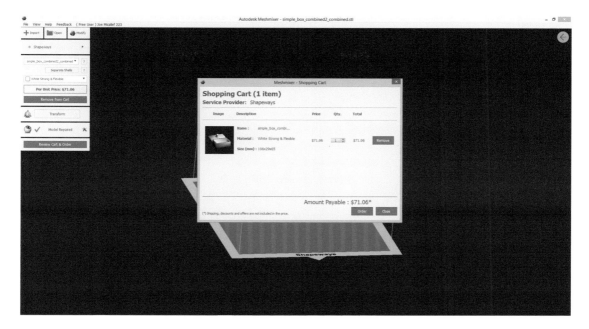

Figure 4-15. *The model can be sent to a service provider, such as Shapeways, for 3D printing*

Getting the Box Ready to 3D Print in Cura

Cura is great to use as a backup program to double-check `.stl` files that have been validated using Meshmixer. The Cura interface environment is similar to Meshmixer. A virtual representation of the 3D printer's build space shows the orientation of the model. To the right is a menu that lets users adjust various printing parameters (Figure 4-16).

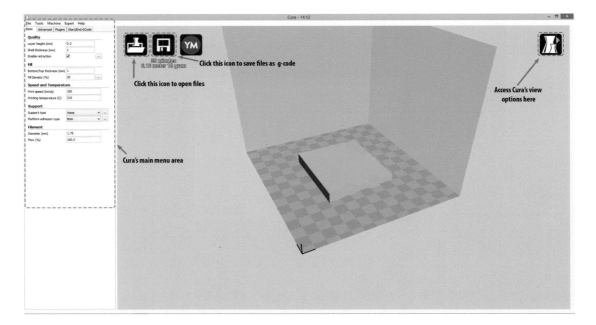

Figure 4-16. *Cura shows a virtual representation of the 3D printer's build space. To the left is the main menu*

Cura is an open source 3D-print preparation software developed by Ultimaker and can be downloaded at `www.ultimaker.com/pages/our-software`. While designed to be used with the Ultimaker line of 3D printers, Cura can be used with any 3D printer. Cura is Windows, Mac, and Linux compatible.

New users opening Cura for the first time will be introduced with configuration pop-up window. The wizard will ask new users a series of questions regarding the 3D printer being used. Cura comes with a list of predefined 3D printers to make setup easy. Not every 3D printer is on Cura's list of predefined 3D printers, and some of the information may have to be entered by setting up a custom profile. Some 3D-printer manufacturers will provide an `.ini` file that will contain their 3D printer's profile information. This `.ini` file can be opened in Cura by using File ➤ Open File. Additional information can be entered by using the Add New Machine function in the machine menu.

Navigating in Cura

In Cura, hold the right mouse button to rotate the around the 3D object. Use the scroll wheel to zoom in and out. Holding both the right and left mouse buttons simultaneously will allow you to zoom in and out as well. Hold the Shift key and the right mouse button to pan the 3D view.

Opening the Box .stl in Cura

Cura can import a variety of files including `.obj`, `.sla`, `.dae`, and `.amf`. When you load your model into Cura, you will see an indication of how long it will take the model to print in the upper-left corner of the viewport (Figure 4-17). This number will update automatically if you change the quality settings or rescale the model.

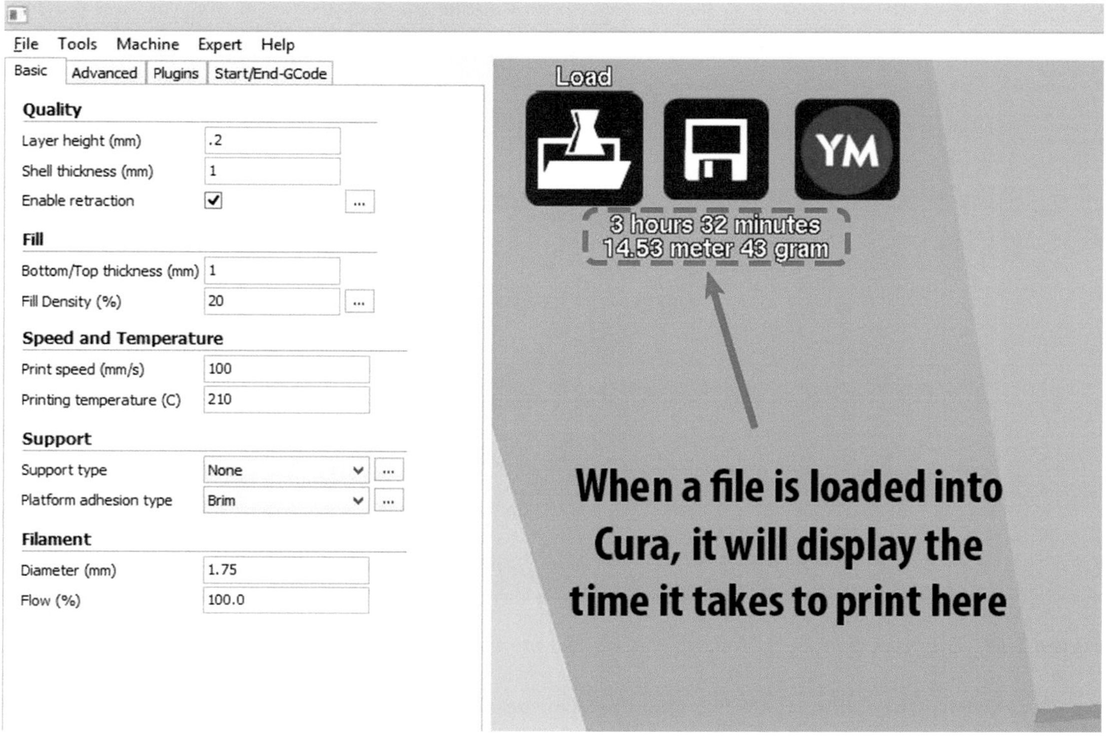

Figure 4-17. *Cura displays the time it takes an object to print*

The file in Cura will appear exactly as it did in Meshmixer (Figure 4-18). If you are satisfied with the placement of the file, you can generate the g-code and finalize the model for 3D printing.

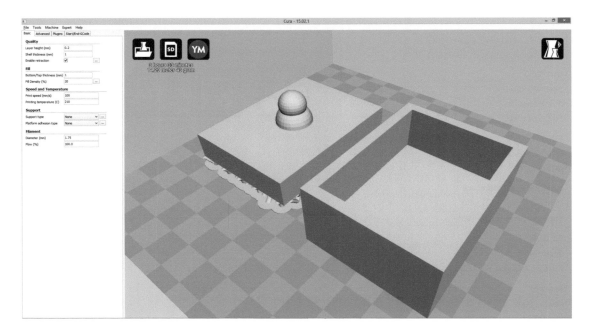

Figure 4-18. *The box model from Meshmixer is loaded into Cura*

Cura also has the ability to view files after they have been sliced for 3D printing by allowing users to view the files layer by layer (Figure 4-19). To access this capability, click the icon in the upper-right corner of the interface (it looks like two hour glasses side by side), which will open a menu of smaller icons; click the last icon, named Layers.

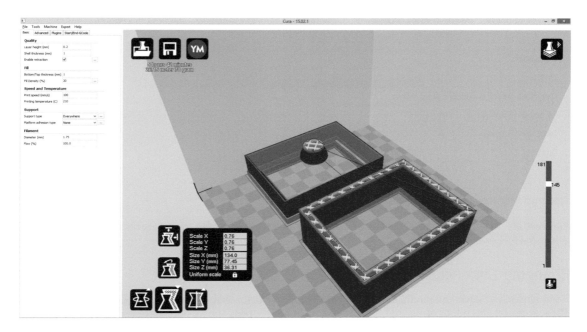

Figure 4-19. *Cura shows the slices of the model. Using the scroll slider to the right, designers can show the slicing of a model layer by layer*

Creating Supports in Cura

If you bring in an `.stl` file from Meshmixer, you may already have supports and can leave the support type set to None. (The option to choose supports is found in the Basic tab in the left-side menu.)

If you load a model with overhangs into Cura and need supports, choose either Touching Build Plate or Everywhere in the support type. The touching build plate option will only create supports with support structures touching the build plate. The Everywhere option will create supports anywhere there are overhangs.

You can adjust supports further by clicking the button with three dots next to the Ssupport Type menu. Here you have a variety of options to help customize supports and can change the structure type from Grid to Line (Figure 4-20). Grid supports are designed to come off the model in one piece and can be a bit challenging to remove. Line supports break off one at a time and are more time-consuming to remove but are better for more complicated objects.

Expert config		✕
Support		
Structure type	Grid	⌄
Overhang angle for support (deg)	60	
Fill amount (%)	15	
Distance X/Y (mm)	0.7	
Distance Z (mm)	0.15	
Ok		

Figure 4-20. *The "Expert config" dialog for supports allows users to further customize the support structures generated by Cura*

Changing Dimensions and Orientation in Cura

Right-clicking to select the model in Cura will bring up three icons in the lower-left corner of the screen. These icons let you rotate, scale, and mirror objects (in other words, flip an object's orientation), respectively (Figure 4-21). Clicking the middle icon, users can automatically have objects fit in the build plate (the uppermost icon) or scale the object using a specific measurement or percentage. The middle icon will also reset the object to its original position.

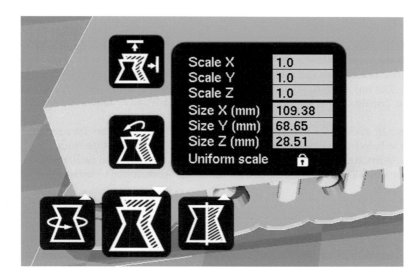

Figure 4-21. *Clicking a model in Cura gives access to three icons in the lower-left corner that allows users to rotate, scale, and mirror their models*

Right-clicking the model in the Cura viewport brings up a menu with additional options for object placement. Users have the choice to center their models on the platform, delete objects, and multiply objects. The multiply option will enable users to create duplicates of the model on the build plate (Figure 4-22). Users can create as many duplicates as possible based on the amount of build plate space available.

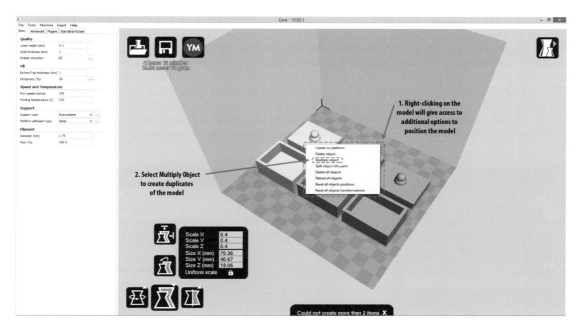

Figure 4-22. *Right-clicking the model in Cura gives access to additional positioning options. The multiply object option will allow designers to fit multiple duplicates of a model on the build plate*

Generating G-Code in Cura

Once you are satisfied with the model in Cura and it has been properly scaled with supports, it is ready to be printed. Cura can print directly via USB using the Print command, but it is recommended that you print using g-code saved to a mini-SD card. If you load an SD card, the disk icon in the upper-left corner of viewport will change to the letters *SD*. Clicking the SD icon will automatically save the g-code for your model to the SD card. You can now print the model directly from the mini-SD card. If you do not have a mini-SD card handy, clicking the disk icon will save the g-code directly to your hard drive. If your printer lacks the capability to load mini-SD cards, then MatterControl (see the next section) is the best option to print directly to your 3D printer.

■ **Note**   If the mini-SD card is inserted into a 3D printer and the g-code file is renamed to `autoo.g`, that file will print automatically when the 3D printer is turned on.

Getting the Box Ready to 3D Print in MatterControl

MatterControl is another great option to help prepare files for 3D printing. Available for Windows, Mac OS X, and Linux, MatterControl is a free application with a powerful feature set that will help create, organize, and prepare .stl files for 3D printing.

MatterControl is designed to work directly in your 3D printer and has an Add Printer feature that lets you connect to a number of pre-installed 3D printer configurations. Out of the five software tools featured in this chapter, MatterControl comes preconfigured with the broadest range of 3D printers. Adding a 3D printer to MatterControl is an easy process. To add a 3D printer, simply select Add Printer in the File menu. In the window that appears, click the Add icon in the lower-left corner, and a Select Make menu will appear (Figure 4-23). Choose the model of your 3D printer here. If your model is not in list, choose Other. After selecting your printer, hit Save and Continue. After saving, the dialog may ask you to install a driver. Clicking Install Driver will allow MatterControl to install a driver for your particular machine. If you choose the option Other, MatterControl will ask a series of questions to help configure your machine.

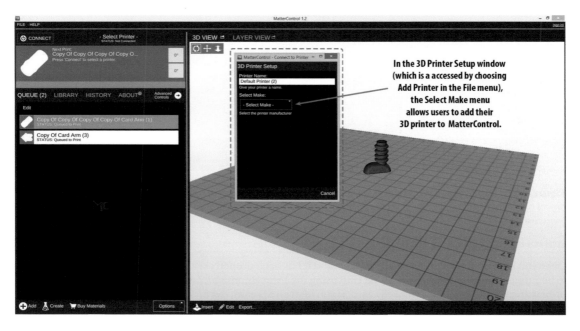

Figure 4-23. *Select Make menu*

■ **Note**   If your 3D printer lacks an option to use a mini-SD card, MatterControl will allow you to print directly to your 3D printer.

Navigating in MatterControl

In MatterContol, either the left or right mouse button will rotate around the 3D object. The scroll wheel will zoom in and out. Clicking Option/Control and the left mouse button will zoom in and out as well. The middle mouse button will allow you to pan.

Loading the Box .stl File into MatterControl

You can load the box .stl file into MatterControl by selecting File ➤ Add File.

A nice feature of MatterControl is the part queue. MatterControl lets you load multiple .stl files, and they will appear as a list on the left side of interface (Figure 4-24). The model that is ready to print will appear as the main item on the top of the other items in the print queue.

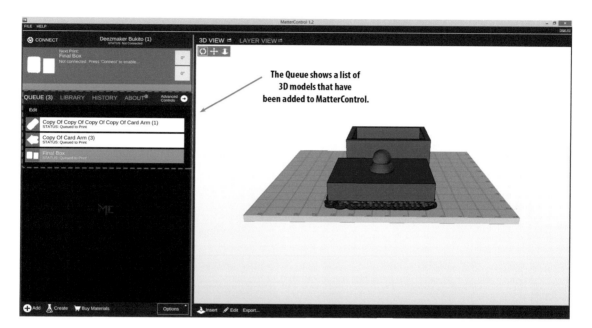

Figure 4-24. *The list to the left in the MatterControl interface shows a list of 3D models that have been loaded into MatterControl*

Resizing and Organizing Models in MatterControl

In the main viewport, click Edit in the lower menu to adjust the scale and rotation of the model. These options will appear on the right side of the viewport. Here you can click auto-arrange to allow MatterControl to automatically place the model on the print bed.

Creating Supports

To generate supports in MatterControl, click the Advanced Controls option in the queue and then click Settings. In Settings, simply clicking Generate Support Material will create supports. Click the Intermediate option to adjust the supports further. Here you can choose between Grid and Lines for the support time (similar to the support options offered in Cura). Clicking the Advanced option gives access to more support options.

Generating G-Code in MatterContol

Before you can generate g-code, you will be asked to select a printer. You can generate g-code by clicking the Option button in the lower menu and then selecting GCode ➤ Export to Folder.

Printing Directly to a 3D Printer from MatterControl

MatterControl will let you print directly to your 3D printer as well. Once a 3D printer is connected to MatterControl and a model has been uploaded, hitting the Print button located in the MatterConrol interface will 3D print model featured the top of print queue.

Getting the Box Ready to 3D Print in Slic3r

Slic3r likes many of user interface features found in MatterControl and Cura. The interface is simple, intuitive, and easy to use (Figure 4-25).

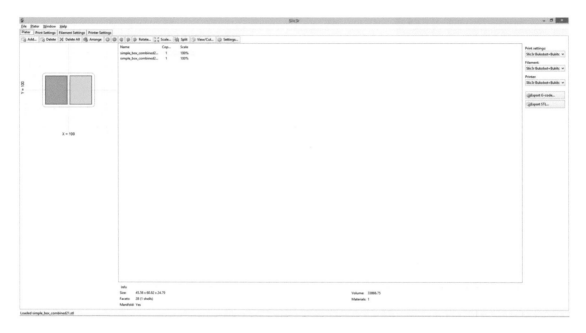

Figure 4-25. *The main interface for Slic3r*

Slic3r is available to download at `http://slic3r.org/`.

Slicer will need a config file for the 3D printer being used. Config files will have a `.ini` extension and can be found at the 3D printer manufacturer's web site.

Navigating in Slic3r

To navigate around a 3D model in Slic3r, you must first click View/Cut, which is found on the Plate tab in Slic3r's main menu (Figure 4-26). In the View/Cut window, the left mouse button rotates around the 3D model, the scroll wheel zooms in and out, and the right mouse button pans the direction.

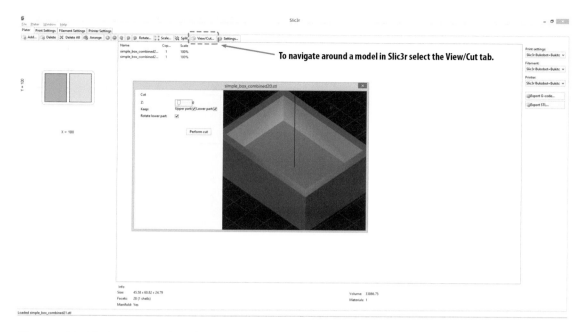

Figure 4-26. *Navigate around models using the view/cut window in Slic3r.*

Adding the Box .stl File to Slic3r

Hitting the Add button in the upper-right corner of the main interface allows you to add files. Slic3r allows you to import .sla, .obj, and .amf files.

Scaling and Organizing Files on the Printer Bed with Slic3r

To scale objects in Slic3r, click the Scale button in the Plate tab, and a dialog box will appear asking for a scale percentage. You can rotate objects here as well as using the Rotate button.

Hitting the green plus icon will multiply the model and create duplicates on the printer bed.

Creating Support Material

Click Print Settings to generate support material using Slic3r. You can find the option to generate support material in the "Support material" settings (Figure 4-27). Slic3r offers some additional pattern options for support material that is not offered by other applications such as "honeycomb" and "rectilinear grid."

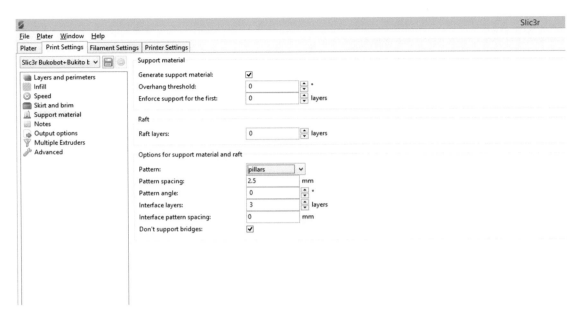

Figure 4-27. *The settings generate support material in Slic3r*

Generating G-Code in Slic3r

To generate g-code for the box model, click the Export G-code button in the right-side menu. There is no option to print directly from Slic3r.

Using Netfabb to Correct Mesh Errors

This section features the basic version of Netfabb, which is free to download. The basic version of Netfabb will not generate g-code or print directly to your 3D printer, but it does feature a number of .stl error-correcting tools that can be helpful.

You can download Netfabb at www.netfabb.com; it is available for Windows, Mac OS X, and Linux.

Navigating in Netfabb

In Netfabb, using the middle mouse pans in the viewport, the right mouse rotates around the 3D model, and the scroll wheel zooms in and out. Holding down Option/Control and right-clicking will zoom in and out as well.

Loading the Box File into Netfabb

Load the box .stl by going to the part in the main menu and selecting Add File. The model will appear gray, lying flush on the yellow grid (in other words, the print bed in Netfabb). Objects in Netfabb can be selected using the left mouse button. Selected objects will turn green (Figure 4-28).

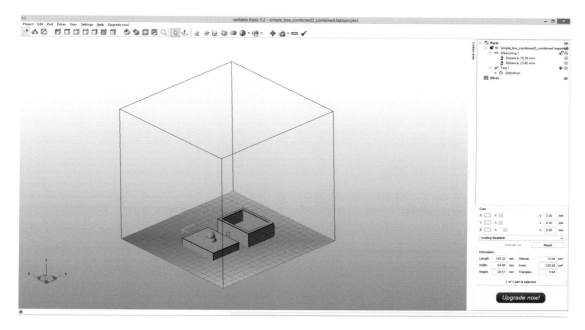

Figure 4-28. *The box model selected in Netfabb*

Correcting Mesh Errors Using Netfabb

Netfabb is a good tool to fix an `.stl` file that may have errors. Clicking the plus sign in the upper menu will enter error-checking mode. In error-checking mode, the model will turn blue (Figure 4-29). If there are errors in the mesh (that is, nonmanifold geometry), a red triangle with an exclamation point will appear in the lower-right corner of the viewport. To fix any errors on the mesh, click Automatic Repair in the lower-right corner of the interface, and in the window that appears, click the Execute button (the default repair options should suffice). Once the mesh has been repaired, click the Apply Repair button in the lower-right corner of the interface and then click Remove Old Part in the window that appears.

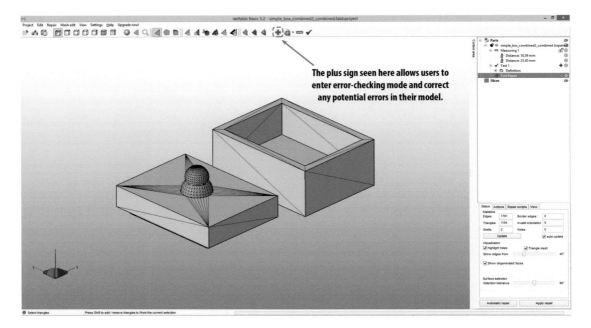

Figure 4-29. *The box model appears blue in error-checking mode in Netfabb*

Configuring Netfabb for Your 3D Printer

To have the print build configured in Netfabb for your 3D printing, you have to manually add that information in the Settings dialog under "default platform size" (Figure 4-30).

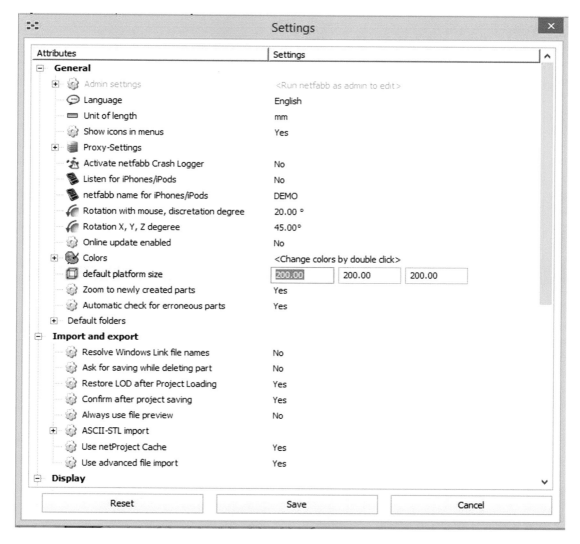

Figure 4-30. *The Settings dialog is where you can change the build size in Netfabb*

Summary

This chapter answered the most important question designers may ask: how do I prepare and print my 3D designs? With the information provided, you are now ready to tackle more complicated designs, knowing you have the necessary knowledge to get those designs 3D printed.

You should now know how to prepare models for 3D printing, correct nonmanifold geometry, and generate supports. The chapter featured five of the most common software tools used to validate and prepare files for 3D printing: Meshmixer, Cura, MatterControl, Netfabb, and Slic3r. While this chapter cannot cover each software tool in full detail, enough information was provided to help you generate the g-code necessary to get your .stl files 3D printed. Also, the information provided in both Chapters 3 and 4 encompasses the whole production pipeline for 3D printing, giving you the necessary knowledge to undertake every step of the 3D-printing process.

■■■

CHAPTER 5

Creative Applications for Simple Shapes

With Chapters 3 and 4 complete, the whole 3D-printing pipeline has been explored, from the initial design and file preparation for 3D-printing production to the final 3D-printed output. At this stage, you should be familiar with the entire design process for 3D printing, including creating a simple box in either Tinkercad or OpenSCAD, generating supports in Meshmixer, and creating the final g-code to make the box printable. Ideally, you also have access to a 3D printer and, with your newly attained knowledge, are now 3D printing boxes of your own (Figure 5-1).

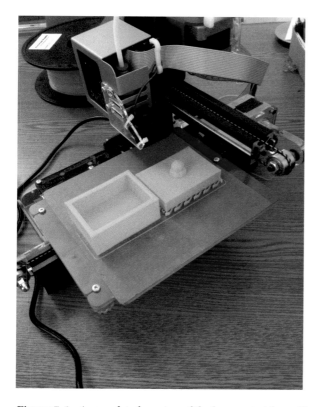

Figure 5-1. *A completed version of the box project from Chapter 3 printed on a Deezmaker Bukito 3D printer*

In this chapter, you will begin to investigate how you can combine simple geometric forms in Tinkercad to create more complex objects. The goal in this chapter is to get your creative juices flowing and show the diversity of what can be created when working with basic shapes and shape generators.

Tinkercad is a great repository of base shapes that can lead to more complex designs. In fact, as you explore alternative modeling applications in later chapters, you may find yourself wanting to return to Tinkercad to access the simple tools and geometric objects that are not available in other applications.

In this chapter, you will build complex objects by taking advantage of Tinkercad's vast library of 3D geometry and shape generation tools. As part of this process I will introduce you to parametric design, which is a fundamental concept of many 3D design applications. Herein you will find many more projects to create such as 3D-printable mini-wall shelves, key chains, bracelets, and custom wall hooks.

Begin with Base Shapes

Every design in this chapter will begin with a base shape, since, as I mentioned in previous chapters, the best way to tackle the design of a multi-part object is to break it down into base shapes and simpler forms. Most of time, it's possible to break down a design into elemental primitives such as boxes, cylinders, and spheres, but occasionally a more complex geometric form is needed. Thankfully, Tinkercad has a vast, growing library of shapes to choose from, giving designers the opportunity to explore a wide range of geometries in order to come up with more elaborate designs and complex assemblies.

■ **Note**   Primitives, or specifically geometric primitives, are considered to be the building blocks of more complex objects and are represented by simple three-dimensional forms. The more common primitive geometric forms to be found in most 3D design programs are spheres, cubes (or boxes), toroids, cylinders, and pyramids.

Within Tinkercad's sidebar creation menu, there are a number of additional geometric shapes, numbers, letters, and shape generators that should be investigated during your design explorations. While Tinkercad may lack many of the more advanced functions found in higher-end design programs, it excels in providing a vast library of building blocks that lead to countless design possibilities. Don't be afraid to group, duplicate, and combine geometries in unexpected ways; you may be surprised by the novel 3D-printable ideas you discover.

These additional geometric building blocks in Tinkercad are detailed throughout the rest of the chapter.

Letters, Numbers, Symbols, and Extras

Beyond the standard geometric shapes provided in Tinkercad, there is a full alphabet of 3D letters, numbers, symbols, and a few extra unique shapes that don't fall into any other particular category. The 3D letters, numbers, and symbols can be used to help customize designs, or they can stand entirely on their own (Figure 5-2).

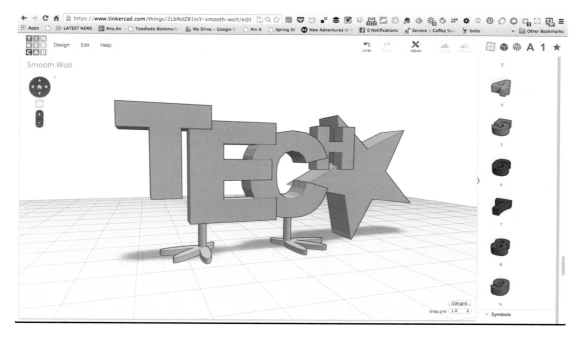

Figure 5-2. *Combine shapes, letters, and numbers to create unique designs*

Since other 3D applications may lack access to singular shapes and letters, Tinkercad is a great resource if you need to add a quick 3D letter/number to any project you are working on. (Other packages may have text capacities, but it may be a hassle to go through the process of 3D text generation in those software applications if you need only one letter or number shape for a project.)

When using the singular letterform shapes in Tinkercad you are unfortunately limited with access to just one font (which resembles Arial or Helvetica), but that limitation can easily overcome by accessing Tinkercad's Text Shape Generator, which provides additional text-editing capabilities, along with several fonts. The Text Shape Generator is detailed later in this chapter.

The 3D numbers, letters, and symbols geometries found in Tinkercad can come in handy and, with a bit of inventive imagination, lead to some interesting design possibilities. While it can be tedious to write long names using the single number and letter shapes provided, when a job calls for a single letter, initial, monogram, or short number combination, these three-dimensional letter/number shapes can be useful.

The following exercises will explore several 3D-printable designs using Tinkercad's letter, numbers, and symbol shape libraries. Included here are lessons on how to create custom wall hooks, business card holders, mini-shelves, and jewelry.

CUSTOM WALL HOOKS

Here is a quick project to create a wall custom hook to hang your hat. This project is a clever way to take advantage of TInkercad's shape alphabet. Simply attach an angled cylinder to a letter shape to create a personalized wall hook (Figure 5-3). This sidebar outlines the steps in greater detail.

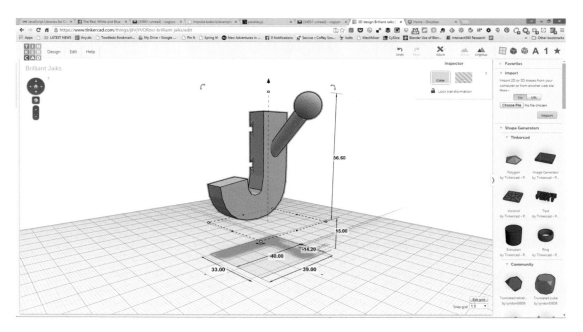

Figure 5-3. *Use single letter shapes to create personalized wall hooks*

1. Drag and drop the preferred letterform to be used from the Letter section of the Geometric shape library (Figure 5-4).

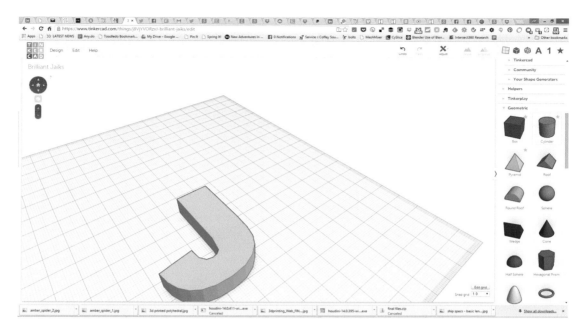

Figure 5-4. *Drag your preferred letterform from the Letter section of the Geometric shape library to the grid*

2. Drag a cylinder onto the letterform that is already on the grid (Figure 5-5).

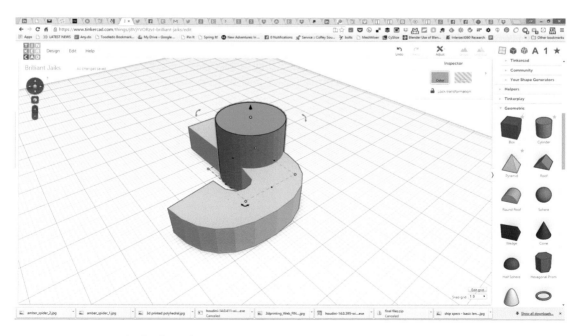

Figure 5-5. *Drag a cylinder from the Geometric section of the shape library onto the letterform that has been placed on the grid. The cylinder will become the hook for the wall hook*

3. Scale the cylinder down by Shift+dragging the corner square inward (it will be highlighted red when selected). Then heighten the cylinder by dragging the central square upward (Figure 5-6).

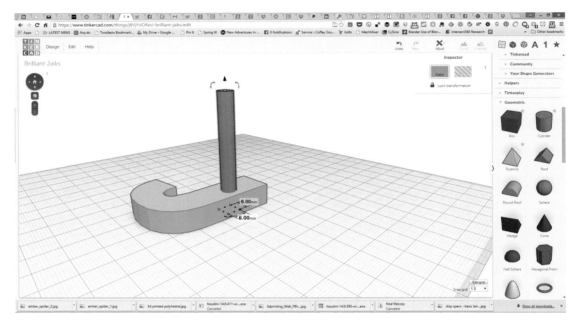

Figure 5-6. *Narrow the cylinder by scaling it inward while holding down the Shift key. Then drag the central white box upward to increase the height of the cylinder*

4. Drag a sphere into the scene and place it at the top of the cylinder (Figure 5-7). Scale it down by Shift+selecting a corner square and dragging inward.

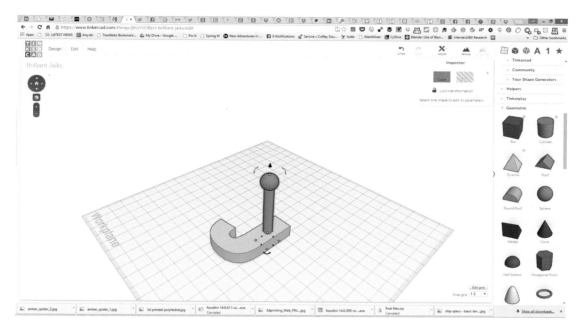

Figure 5-7. *Add a sphere to the top of cylinder*

5. Select both the sphere and the cylinder. In the main menu, select Align option in the Adjust menu. Click the small central dots to center align the cylinder and sphere. (Once the cylinder and sphere are aligned, the word "*aligned*" will appear indicating the alignment was successful.)

6. Click the Group icon in the main toolbar to combine the sphere with the cylinder.

7. Rotate the cylinder/sphere (the hook) 45 degrees. To make the letterform and hook a single object, select them both and then click the Group button in the upper-right corner of the interface (Figure 5-8).

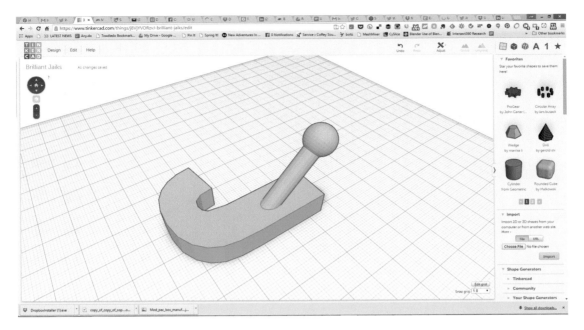

Figure 5-8. *The final letterform hook assembly after all the parts have been grouped*

8. If you want make the hooks wall-mountable, one option is to add recesses to
    the back of the letterforms that can latch onto wall screws. The recesses can be
    designed to slide over a Phillips-angled screw. You can create the recesses on the
    back of the letterforms using a Roof object (Figure 5-9).

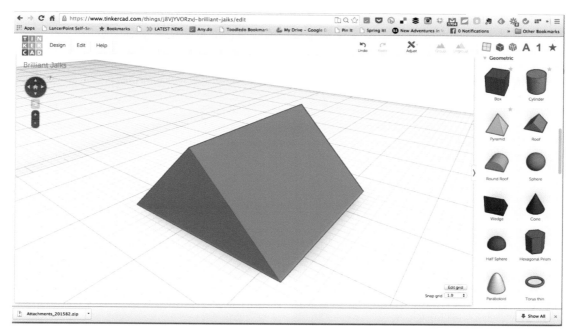

Figure 5-9. *The Roof object can conveniently be used to cut recesses into the back of the letterform hook for wall-mounting purposes*

9.   Rotate the roof 90 degrees around the y-axis; then flip it so the tip of the roof is facing downward by rotating it 180 degrees along the z-axis (Figure 5-10).

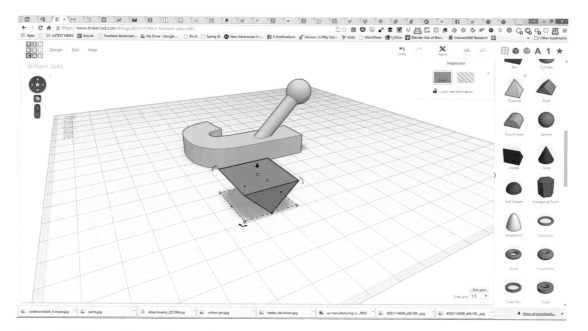

Figure 5-10. *Rotate the Roof object to have the peak point downward*

10. Scale the Roof object proportionally by grabbing one of the small squares in the corner and, while holding the Shift key, drag inward to 9mm in both the height and the width. Then select the small square at the tip of the roof and drag outward to about 28mm. In the next step, you will use this long roof piece to cut away from the back of the wall hook, which will create an angled inset that can latch onto a flat-angled Phillips screw (Figure 5-11).

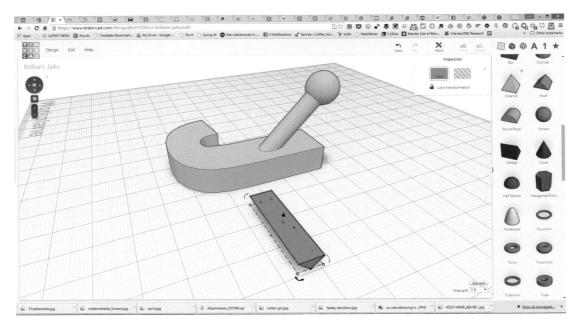

Figure 5-11. *Shift+select a corner square and drag inward to reduce the size of the Roof object. Then grab a central square and drag outward*

11. Cut and paste the Roof object. Move the duplicate about 10mm back behind the original and then move both Roof objects to underneath the hook and have them intersect with the back of the hook. Select the Roof objects and then turn them into Hole objects by clicking the Hole object icon (Figure 5-12).

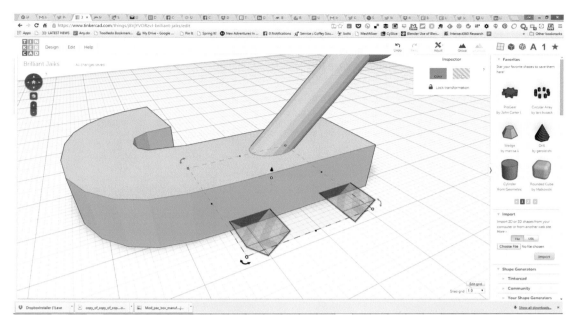

Figure 5-12. *Duplicate the Roof object using copy and paste. Drag it away from the initial Roof object, keeping it in position beneath the letterform hook. There should be two now running parallel beneath the wall hook*

12. Group the main hook and the Roof objects together to create the back slots that will be used to hang the hook (Figure 5-13). This step will finalize the hook's wall mounts.

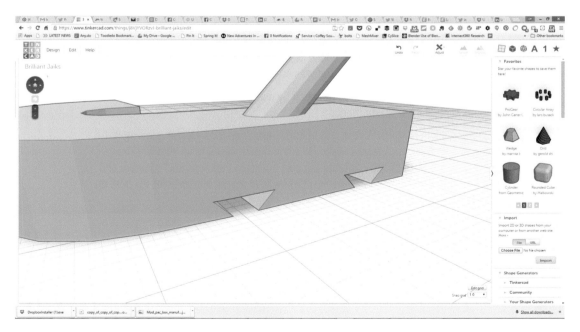

Figure 5-13. *Group the Hole objects with the main hook to create the recesses*

13. Save the model as an `.stl` that will be imported, and then finalized in Meshmixer for output to a 3D printer. To save this as an `.stl` file, select Design in the main menu and then select "Download for 3D Printing" (Figure 5-14). In the window that appears click the .stl button to save the hook as an .stl file.

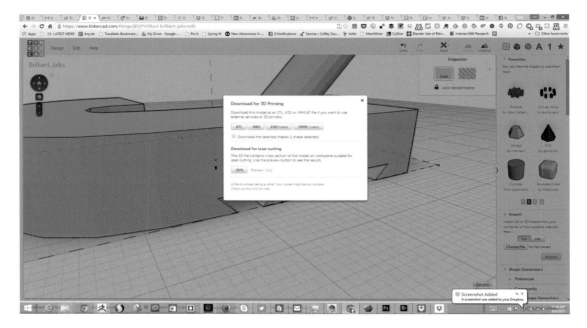

Figure 5-14. *In the Design menu, select Download for 3D Printing to save the hook as an .stl file*

14. You can now import the hook `.stl` into Meshmixer to create the necessary supports needed for 3D printing.Launch Meshmixer and click the "plus sign" icon that appears to import the .stl file that was created in step 13.

15. Adjust the rotation and location of the hook by using the Transform function, which is found in Meshmixer's Edit menu.

16. Once the hook is lying flat on the grid in Meshmixer, supports can be generated. To create supports, in the Analysis menu (found in Meshmixer's main side-bar menu)_ select Overhangs. Click the Generate Support button in the menu that appears and then hit Done (Figure 5-15). The hook will now have proper supports for 3D printing as seen in Figure 5-16.

Figure 5-15. *Prepare the hook for 3D printing by adding supports in Meshmixer by clicking on the Overhangs button that is found in the Analysis menu*

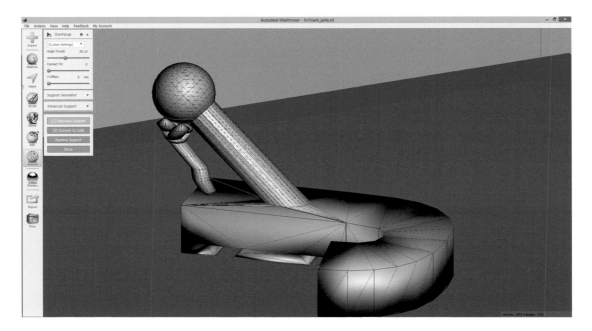

Figure 5-16. *Here is the hook in Meshmixer with the generated supports*

17. With the support added, hit Export in left side-bar menu (Figure 5-17) to save an .stl version of the hook with the generated supports.

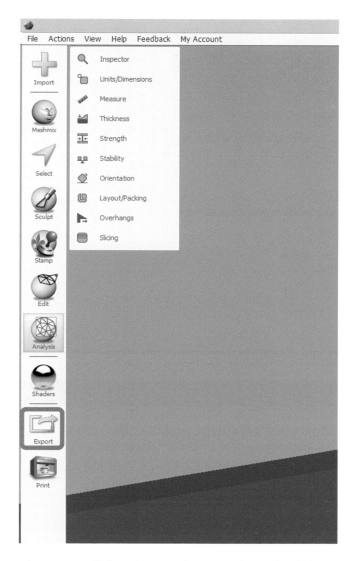

Figure 5-17. *Click on the export button Meshmixer's side-bar menu to save the .stl that has supports*

18. Now, the .stl version of the hook with supports, can imported into the slicer program of your choice (such as Cura or MatterControl) to generate G-code for your 3D printer. Figure 5-18 shows a 3D printed version of the file with supports removed.

Figure 5-18. *Here is a 3D printed version of the hook*

PERSONALIZED BUSINESS CARD/DOCUMENTS HOLDER

Create a personalized letter, document, and business card holder using a person's initials, or use a single 3D letter to represent a specific category. (For example, use a letter *R* to hold receipts or use the letter *F* for financial information.)

1. A flat box base can act as a stand. Drag a Box object from the shape library onto the workplane grid.

2. Create the stand by scaling the Box object downward to about 9mm and outward to 80mm (Figure 5-19).

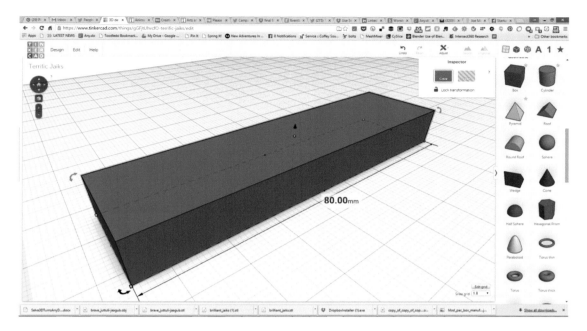

Figure 5-19. *Scale a box shape to create a base for the letterforms. Make the base wide and thick enough to ensure stability*

3. From the Letters section of the shape library, drag the 3D letterforms you prefer onto the workplane.

4. Rotate the letters so they are standing upright and scale them up to a preferred size. Place the letterforms onto the base object.

5. Group the letterforms and align them to the base. Move the letterforms downward, allowing the letters to slightly intersect with the surface of the stand (Figure 5-20).

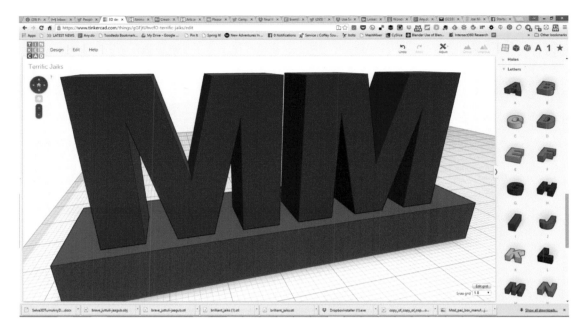

Figure 5-20. *Letters are added to the base object*

6. To hold the business cards or documents, create a slit in the top of the 3D letters using a thin, rectangular Hole object. To create the Hole object, use a stretched-out box. Scale the width of box to 4mm and elongate it to a width that exceeds the width of the letterforms. Place the box within the letters to create a slit, and while the elongated box is selected, click the Hole option in the Inspector window (Figure 5-21).

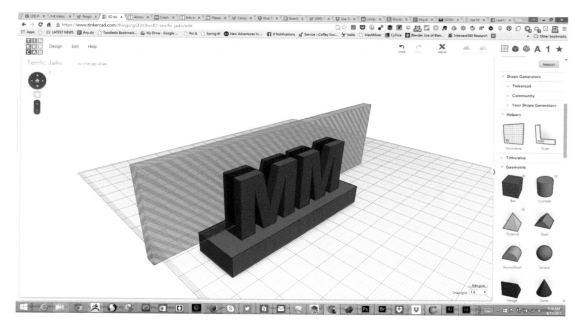

Figure 5-21. *A slit is added to the letters by intersecting the top of the letterforms with a flattened box that has been converted to a Hole object*

7. Select the letters; then Shift+select the Hole object and then group them to create the final personalized document/business card holder (Figure 5-22), which is now ready to exported as an `.stl` and then imported into Meshmixer for support generation. At this stage, you should be familiar with importing geometry into Meshmixer to generate supports, so I will leave those final steps up to you. Note that some models may have not require supports and can be imported directly into Cura or MatterControl to create the G-code for 3D printing. For example, the two letter M's used in the project here did not require supports. Figure 5-23 shows the 3D printed version of the project (this was printed without supports).

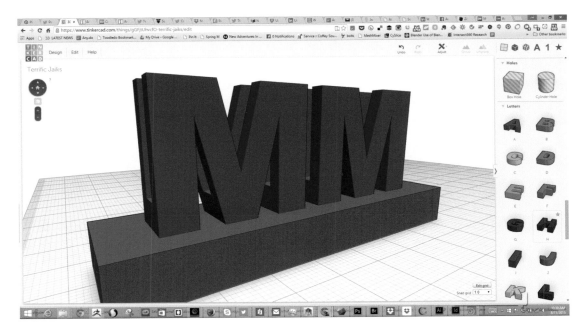

Figure 5-22. *The final personalized document holder*

Figure 5-23. *The 3D printed version of the document holder*

USE 3D NUMBERS FOR LABELS AND AGE INDICATORS

The 3D printed numbers and letterforms can come in handy as cake toppers (to designating a person's age) and can be used for a number of additional purposes. Having a set of 3D-printable numbers and letters at your disposal makes it unnecessary to purchase plastic display type.

Extra Shapes

The extra shapes included are fun and whimsical but may have limited usefulness. For a wider range of extra shapes, the shape generators are worth exploring (which are also detailed later in this chapter). In this grouping of shapes is a pair of chicken legs that can be used as an interesting stand for a small box, vase, or cup. The Egg object can be fun to play with as well. Use the Egg object in combination with the Hollow Egg object to create small egg containers (or even an egg holder or egg carton).

Hole Shapes

Two "premade" hole shapes are Box Hole and Cylinder Hole (Figure 5-24); you can use them as alternatives to the Hole function in the Inspector window. Grabbing a Hole object from the shape library can be a quick way to build a box, a series of mini-shelves, or a simple vase.

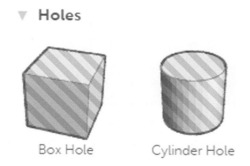

Figure 5-24. *You can find the Box Hole and Cylinder Hole shapes in the shape library*

Shape Generators

One of the most useful aspects of Tinkercad is the addition of shape generators, which are adjustable shape tools that can help speed up the design process (Figure 5-25). Shape generators are parametric geometric forms that have adjustable parameters. The parameters provided are unique for each shape generator. For instance, users can adjust these parameters to create and explore variations in shape design, change dimensions, add sides to a shape, or change a shape's profile.

Figure 5-25. *The shape generators greatly expand the library of shapes in Tinkercad*

■ **Note**   A *parametric model* is a general term to describe any type of geometric model that has adjustable parameters. Some parametric modeling applications will let you adjust the model by changing parameters at any time during the model process. For most applications, if a model is significantly changed (by using Booleans, for example), the model loses its parametric capabilities and can no longer be adjusted.

Dragging a shape generator to the work pane gives access to the parameters, which appear in a pop-up Inspector window on the right side of the interface. As long as you don't modify the shapes using the Combine function, you can always return to the generated shape to change its various properties using the Inspector window.

Text Generator

Not only do Tinkercad users have access to singular letter and number shapes, they can use Tinkercad's handy 3D text editor (Figure 5-26). The 3D text generator in the shape generator section gives access to a range of fonts that are provided by the Tinkercad application (users can't import their own fonts). Users can adjust the length of extruded and the text size. The text generator acts as a text editor, and users can enter long strings of text as needed.

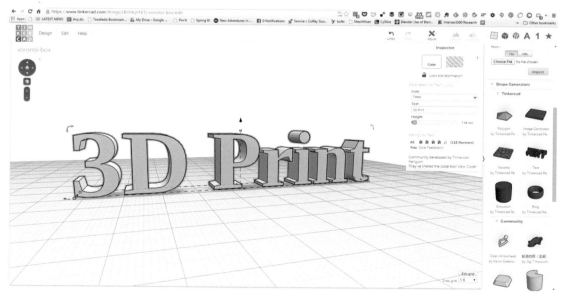

Figure 5-26. *Tinkercad's text-generating shape generator can be used for long strings of text*

For small embossed signs, the text generator is indispensable, allowing any 3D printer owner to become a sign shop. Add a rectangle to any string of text to create a quick, wall-mountable sign.

■ **Note**   An easy way to mount a 3D-printed sign or picture frame to a surface is with nondestructible wall-mounting tape. The weight of the PLA or ABS materials should be light enough and will stay adhered to the surface to which they are mounted. The company 3M creates wall-mounting tape under the Command brand, and it is nondestructive (it can peel off of drywall without damaging it) and is available at most hardware stores.

Voronoi Shape Generator

The Voronoi Shape Generator creates an interesting pattern reminiscent of cracks found in drying mud (Figure 5-27). Use this shape generator to come up with interesting patterns for miniature shelves, cups, and vases. You can also use the Voronoi editor to create interesting art panels to hang as wall decorations.

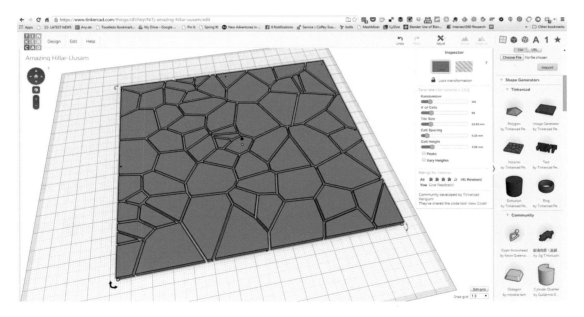

Figure 5-27. *The Voronoi generator can create interesting random patterns*

CREATE A MINI-SHELF/COMPARTMENTS USING THE VORONI SHAPE EDITOR

You can use the Voronoi Shape Generator to come up with a number of interesting designs. The celluar patterns created in the Voronoi Editor can be used as compartments or shelves.

1. First generate the Voronoi pattern by dragging the Voronoi shape generator to the workplane.

2. The Inspector window that appears(Figure 5-28) will allow you to change parameters for the Voronoi pattern such as the number of cells, cell spacing and cell height. The defaults should work just fine but, if desired, smaller shelves can be creaed by increasing the "number of cells" parameter.

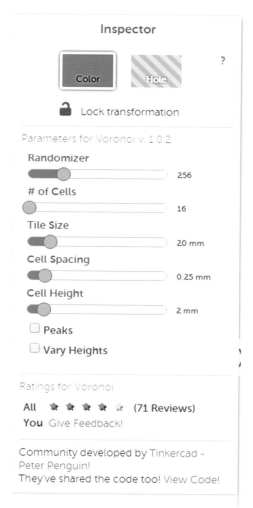

Figure 5-28. *After the Voronoi object is dragged to the Workplane, the Inspector window will appear, allowing for the adjustment of various Voronoi parameters*

3. Add a box to the base of the Voronoi pattern (the pattern will be cut from a box to create the shelves).

4. Scale the box so it surpasses the length and width of the Voronoi pattern. Make sure the Voronoi pattern extends beyond the top and bottom of the box.

5. Select the Voronoi geometry pattern on the workplane. Then click the Hole button in the Voronoi Inspector window to turn the Voronoi pattern into a Hole object (Figure 5-29).

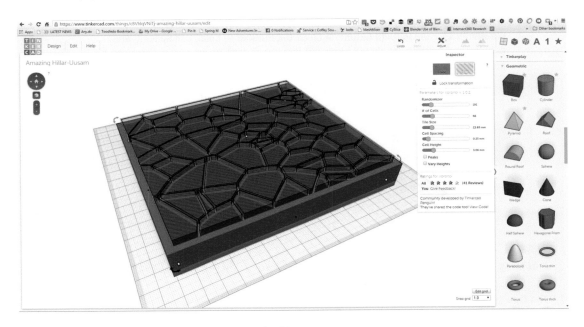

Figure 5-29. *Turn the Voronoi pattern into a Hole object*

6. Finally, combine the Hole object and the box using the Combine function (Figure 5-30). The final product is the completed mini-shelf. Note that supports are not necessary if the shelf is printed flat on the printer bed as designed. Figure 5-31 shows the final 3D printed version of the Vornonoi pattern.

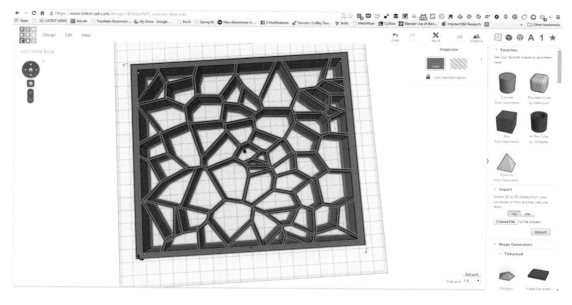

Figure 5-30. *The final Voronoi mini-shelf after the box and Voronoi hole have been combined*

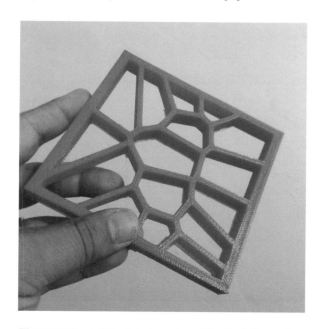

Figure 5-31. *A 3D printed version of the final Voronoi pattern*

Image Embossing Generator

Another interesting shape generator is the image generator (Figure 5-32). The image generator allows users to import black-and-white images, which are then used to create an embossing or relief on a planar-slab of geometry. You can then combine this embossing/relief with other objects.

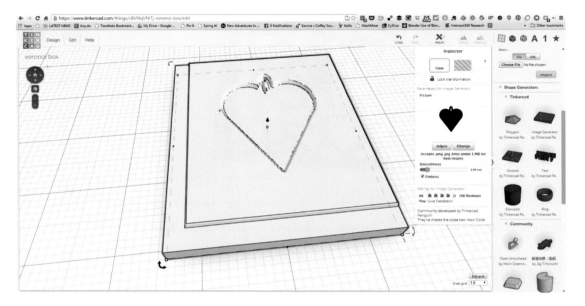

Figure 5-32. *The Image shape generator allows users to import black-and-white images to create an embossed surface*

Extrusion Generator

The Extrusion shape generator can create organic and curvy shapes. The extrusion is controlled by an editable shape profile that is found in the Inspector window (Figure 5-33). You can combine extrusions in interesting ways to create highly organic, 3D-printable sculptures.

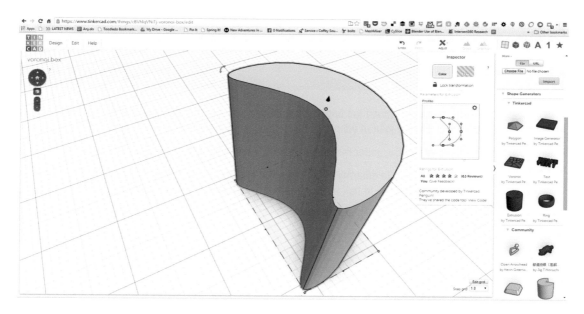

Figure 5-33. *Extrusions can be used to create interesting organic forms*

Ring Generator

The Ring shape generator is perfect for creating quick rings and bracelets (Figure 5-34). Combine rings and bracelets with other shapes to create quick customized jewelry.

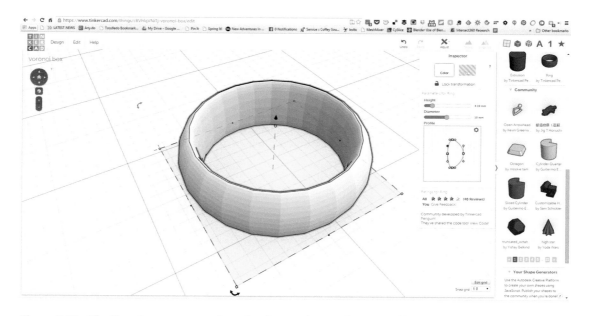

Figure 5-34. *The Ring shape generator is perfect for creating quick rings and bracelets*

If you want to measure your ring size, wrap a small strip of paper around the finger you are designing the ring for and follow the steps in "Measuring Ring Size."

MEASURING RING SIZE

1. Wrap a strip of paper around the finger you are designing the ring for. Make sure the paper is below the joint of your finger and close to your knuckle.

2. Mark the spot where the paper meets and measure the distance with your ruler.

3. Use the following chart to determine your ring size (be sure to not make the ring too tight). Rings also come in half sizes, and the measurements will fall somewhere between the whole sizes.

    - *Size 4*: 1 13/16 inches

    - *Size 5*: 1 15/16 inches

    - *Size 6*: 2 1/16 inches

    - *Size 7*: 2 1/8 inches

    - *Size 8*: 2 1/4 inches

    - *Size 9*: 2 5/16 inches

    - *Size 10*: 2 7/16 inches

    - *Size 11*: 2 9/16 inches

    - *Size 12*: 2 5/8 inches

    - *Size 13*: 2 3/4 inches

    - *Size 14*: 2 7/8 inches

Creating Your Own Shape Generators

Finally, Tinkercad provides the means to create your own shape generators. The process of creating a shape generator requires a bit of coding knowledge and is similar to the process of creating geometry using OpenSCAD (Figure 5-35).

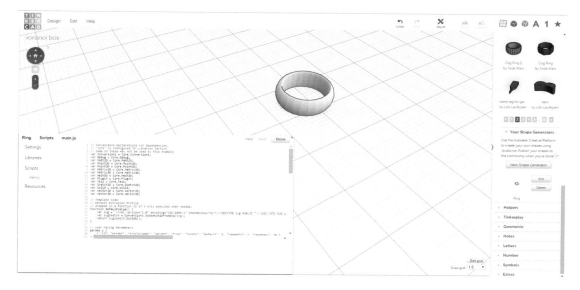

Figure 5-35. *Clicking New Shape Generator will open a code editor, allowing for the creation of custom shape generators*

Favorites

If you hover over the right corner of any shape in shape sidebar menu, you will see a small gray star appear. Clicking the gray star will change its color to orange and designate that shape as a favorite shape. Favorite shapes appear in the Favorites section of the shape sidebar menu.

Using the favorite feature is a great way to make some shapes (especially shapes in the shape generator menu) more easily accessible. If you tend to make the same shapes repeatedly, keep those shapes in the Favorites section to speed up the modeling process.

Tinkerplay

One cool new feature of Tinkercad is called Tinkerplay. Tinkerplay provides a number of connector parts that interlock to create articulated robot action figures. These various parts can be used to create connectors, which can be used for other projects.

Importing Your Own Shapes

You can also import your own .stl (.stl files are the standard file format for 3D-printed objects and were explained in greater detail in Chapter 1) and .svg shapes into Tinkercad using the import option in the shape menu on the right. The option Import .svg Files allows designers to import profile curves created in a vector-editing program such as Adobe Illustrator or Inkscape. (Inkscape is an open source vector art–editing program that is available at inkscape.org.) When the .svg file profile curve is imported, you have the option of extruding the curve using the Height option in the Import section of the shape panel. Giving the .svg profile a height in millimeters will create a 3D object based on that profile curve. In this example, a radiating vector graphic design (Figure 5-36) is imported as an .svg file and then turned into a geometric object in Tinkercad (Figure 5-37).

Figure 5-36. *This vector graphic was created in a program such as Adobe Illustrator or Inkscape and exported as an .svg file for Tinkercad*

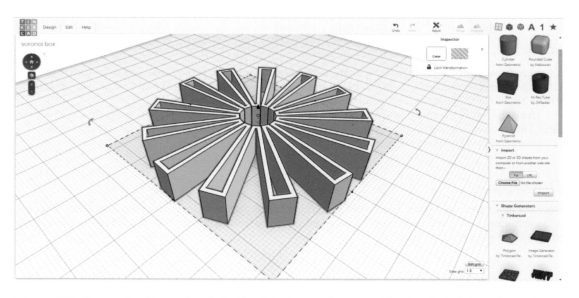

Figure 5-37. *The results of increasing the height of the imported .svg graphic using the Height option in the Import section of the shape panel*

■ **Note** SVG is a common format used for web-based vector images and stands for Scalable Vector Graphics. Both Adobe Illustrator and Inkscape can export vector graphics as .svg files.

Remember: Simple Shapes Are Your Friends

It can be easy to ignore the more common 3D boxes and spheres in favor of exotic geometries such as pyramids, hexagons, and cones. But remember, simple shapes in combination can lead to interesting design possibilities.

Working with simple shapes is a great way to exercise your imagination. In Tinkercad, give yourself a design constraint of working only with a 3D box shape. Test your design skills by seeing how many objects and animal shapes can be created using just a simple box. The results will be surprising (Figure 5-38). Many times what appears on the screen may not look too interesting, but the final 3D-printed results can be quite captivating (Figure 5-39). (If you have ever played Minecraft, building objects up with only boxes can be an engaging experience.)

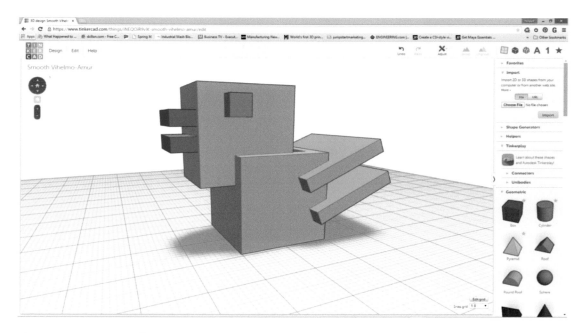

Figure 5-38. *For example, to create Minecraft-inspired art, start with a simple box and duplicate it several times by using the Option/Alt+drag shortcut*

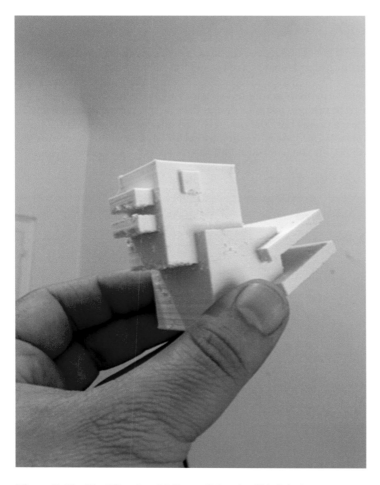

Figure 5-39. *The 3D-printed Minecraft-inspired bird design*

Quick Ideas Using Tinkercad's Vast Library of Shapes

Here are some more interesting ideas to explore using some of Tinkercad's shape generators and extra shapes. The following lessons will investigate how to create guitar picks, jewelry, and a USB cable holder.

PERSONALIZED GUITAR PICKS

Here is a quick way to create a guitar pick using the Egg object, which is found in the Extras section of the shape library:

1. Drag an Egg object from the Extras section in the shape library onto the workplane.
   The contour of the egg will serve as the basis for the guitar pick shape (Figure 5-40).

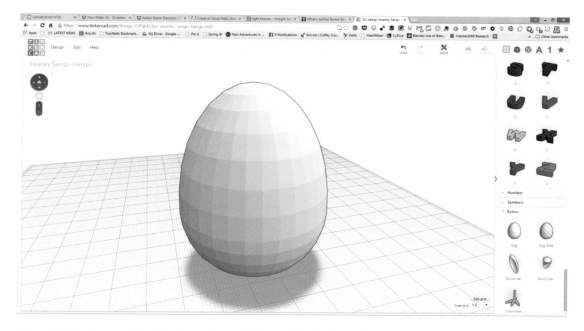

Figure 5-40. *Drag an Egg object onto the workplane to be the design for the guitar pick*

2. Use two Box Hole shapes to slice off the top and bottom of the Egg object to create the guitar pick shape (Figure 5-41).

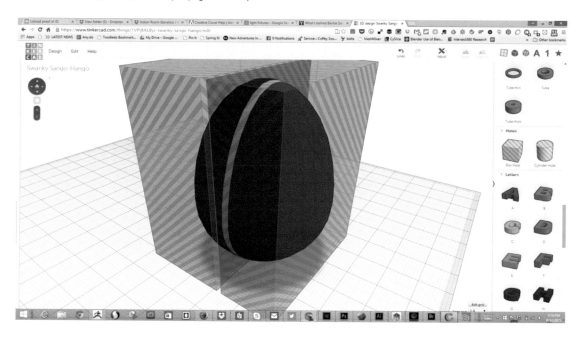

Figure 5-41. *Drag two Hole objects to the grid and have them intersect the front and the back of the Egg object. Only a thin slice of the Egg object should be revealed*

3. Group the Hole object and the Egg object together (click the Group icon in the main menu) to perform the Boolean operation that will remove the front and back sections of the egg.

4. Rotate the guitar pick so it is lying flat on the workplane.

5. Scale down the pick by Shift+selecting a corner handle and dragging inward. The pick should be 30mm long (Figure 5-42).

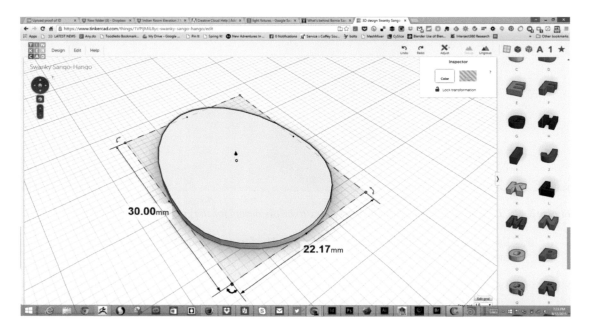

Figure 5-42. *Scale down the guitar pick to its proper dimensions*

6. Add text shapes to personalize the guitar pick with the guitar player's initials or the name of the band (Figure 5-43).

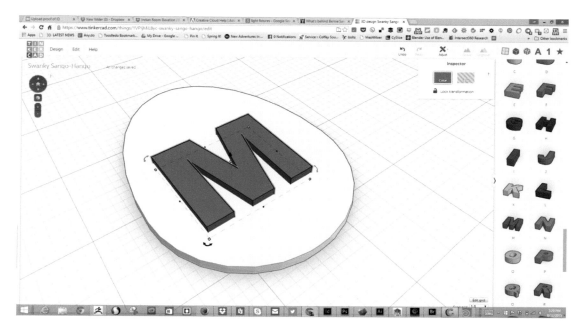

Figure 5-43. *Personalize the guitar pick with a letterform from the Letter section of the shape library*

7. Now that the guitar pick design is complete, it can be downloaded from Tinkercad for 3D printing and then imported into Cura, MatterControl, or the program of your choice to generate the g-code. Note that since the guitar picks will lie flat on the print bed without significant overhangs, they will not require supports. Figure 5-44 shows several 3D-printed guitar picks designed using the previous steps.

Figure 5-44. *An example of the final 3D-printed guitar picks*

PET TAGS, KEY CHAINS

Key chains and pet tags are easy to create; just follow these steps:

1. Use any shape you prefer to create the main pet tag or key chain. Explore exotic and interesting shapes to create the main base shape.

2. Flatten the shape you selected using the same method in the previous "Personalized Guitar Picks" exercise.

3. Add letter shapes to customize to represent the name of the pet or key owner.

4. Group a Cylinder Hole object with the main tag/key chain to create the final object.

QUICK PERSONALIZED RINGS AND BRACLETS

The Ring shape generator will allow you to create an interesting assortment of personalized jewelry.

1. Use the Ring shape generator (refer to the "Rign Generator" section earlier in this chapter to learn about Tinkercad's Ring Shape Generator) to create a ring or bracelet.

2. If necessary, scale up the ring to create a bracelet.

3. Combine the ring or bracelet with symbols from the Symbol section of the shape menu, or you can use a shape generator to create a gem stone to create costume jewelry.

USB CABLE HOLDER

You can use a Torus object to create a USB cable holder.

1. Drag a box to the workplane and make it about 100mm long, 15mm tall, and 8mm thick (Figure 5-45).

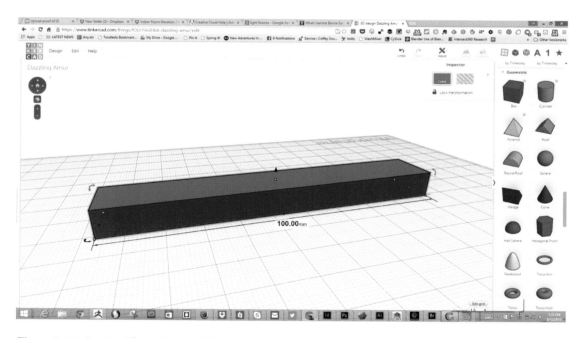

Figure 5-45. *Begin with an elongated box*

2. Create a ring by dragging a Torus object onto the workplane. Make the ring 20mm wide (Figure 5-46).

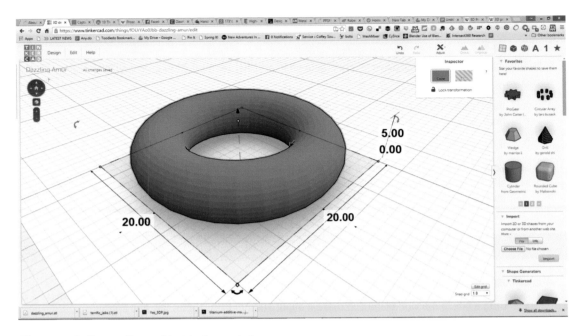

Figure 5-46. *Drag a Torus object to the workplane*

3. Use a small Box Hole object to subtract the front of the ring. Scale down the width of the Box Hole object and cut away a small section of the ring (Figure 5-47).

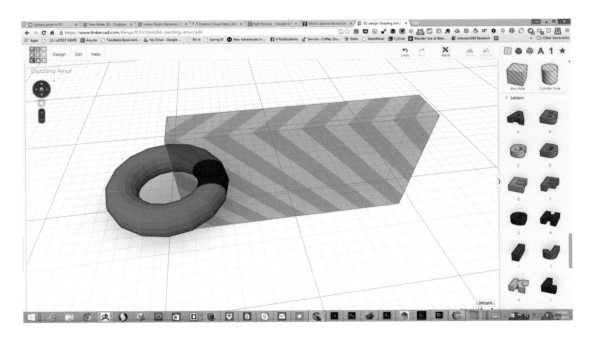

Figure 5-47. *Remove a section of the torus with a Hole object*

4.   Group the Hole object and the ring to create a gap in the ring (Figure 5-48).

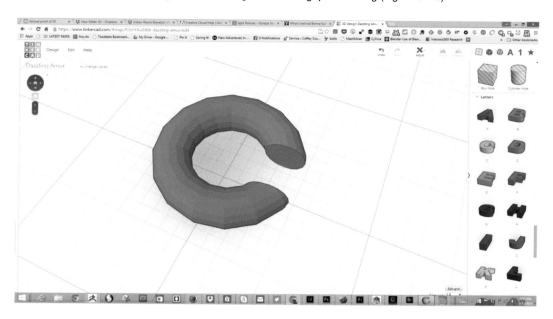

Figure 5-48. *The new shape should resemble the letter C*

5.   Rotate the ring so the gap is facing upright.

6.   Move the ring to the top of the box base. Embed the ring into the box base (Figure 5-49).

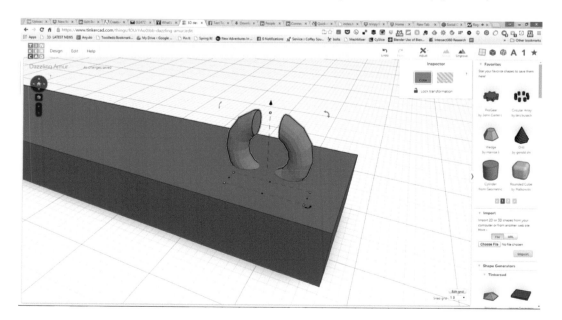

Figure 5-49. *Move the C shape onto the elongated base*

7. Duplicate the ring three times using Option/Alt+drag and evenly space the rings across the 100mm box.

8. Use Align in the top menu and the Ruler tool from the shape library to ensure the rings are precisely placed on the base box (Figure 5-50).

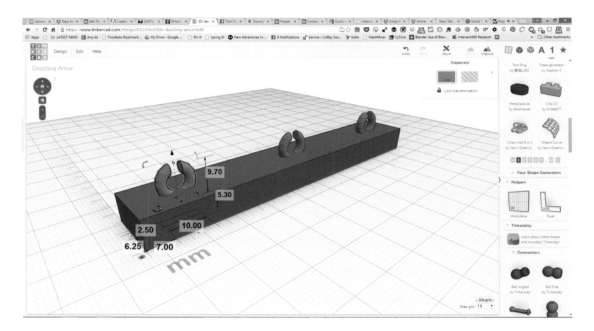

Figure 5-50. *Duplicate the C shapes along the length of the base*

9. Combine the rings and boxes together to make the final USB cable holder. As with some of the earlier projects in this chapter, supports will not be needed for the cable holder. Once the cable hold is complete, export the file as an .stl (select "Download for 3D Printing" in Tinkercad's Design menu) and generate G-code for the file using Cura or MatterControl. Figure 5-51 shows the 3D printed version of the cable holder.

Figure 5-51. *The final 3D printed usb cable holder*

Additional Ideas

Put your design skills to the test and try to come up with your own variations of the following ideas. These are just a few more examples of the nearly limitless ideas to explore with Tinkercad's vast library of shapes.

- Group any number of shapes together for your own holiday ornaments (Figure 5-52).

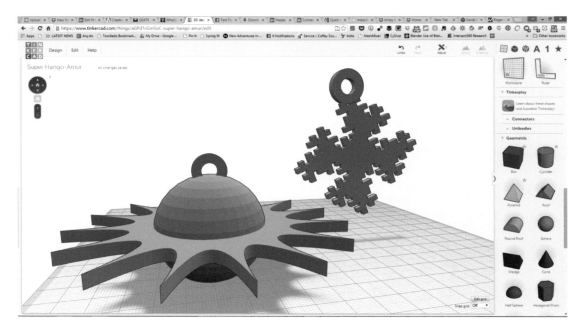

Figure 5-52. Combine shapes to create holiday ornaments

- Once you become a master of using Hole objects, you can develop some intricate designs, such as the doorknob sign in Figure 5-53.

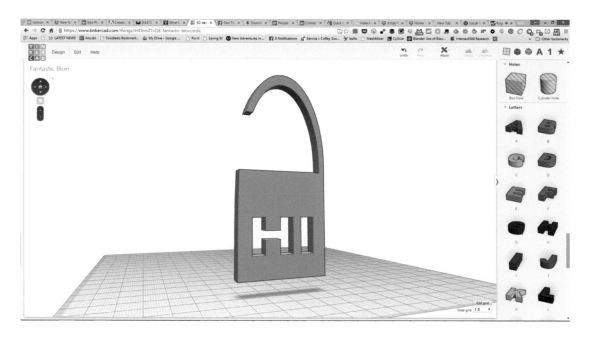

Figure 5-53. Group Hole objects together to create a hanging doorknob sign

- Coasters are easy to make and useful when you have guests. You can combine flat shapes in interesting ways to create a wide variety of coasters (Figure 5-54).

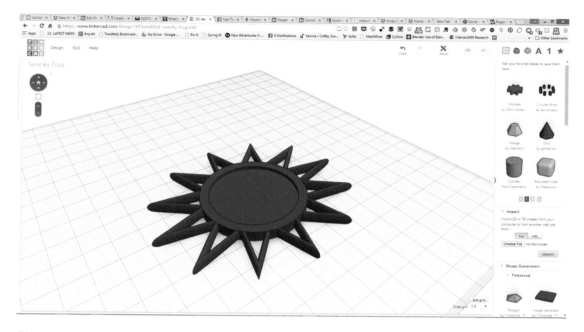

Figure 5-54. *A wide range of coasters can be designed by grouping together flat shapes*

Summary

It may be easy to dismiss Tinkercad as a 3D-modeling tool for kids, but its usefulness as a library of geometric shapes can't be understated. Take the time to explore the various shape generators and to combine shapes with letters to create personalized objects. Also use Tinkercad as a go-to tool when exporting simple shapes for projects in other 3D-modeling applications.

CHAPTER 6

■ ■ ■

Design Strategies for 3D Printing

At this stage you have explored a wide range of design possibilities using simple geometric forms. If you have gone through every step in the 3D-printing pipeline, from the initial design to the final 3D-printed product, you should have the confidence to begin working on more complicated designs for 3D printing.

Possibly, during one of the stages in the 3D-printing pipeline, a problem may have occurred. If you were able to fix it, please congratulate yourself—troubleshooting is part of the process. But potentially something happened that caused the design to fail entirely and you were unable to find a solution. Maybe the supports were too dense and upon removal of those supports your part got damaged. Or maybe the software crashed repeatedly when you attempted to use a certain function. The potential for problems can arise from a number of factors: the design was too thin, too large, or full of nonmanifold errors. Whatever is the case, the 3D-printing pipeline is a complex system that combines a number of software tools in collaboration 3D-printing hardware (in other words, the 3D printer). This complex system is an open doorway to many unknown variables that may cause a variety of unanticipated issues. The magic that makes 3D printing possible (from the digital design to the final output) has been cobbled together with a broad range of complex technologies, and with an increasing number of new 3D printers being released into the marketplace, oftentimes it is the user of the 3D printer who will discover faults unseen by the 3D printer's manufacturer. Whatever the case, the design process for 3D printing brings designers and engineers into uncharted territories. Add to this a human's natural inclination to make mistakes, and unforeseen issues will be inevitable.

The most frustrating challenge of 3D printing is that when problems do unveil themselves, it often occurs during the final stages of production when the part is almost fully printed. Having an error occur during the final stage of the 3D-printing process can be disheartening since a great deal of time and effort has been placed into the design's early development. Some problems are often out of the designer's control such as mechanical defects in the 3D printer and bugs in the software used to prepare and design the 3D models. But many problems can be managed by the designer if smart decisions are made during the initial design stages. Oftentimes, it is a design feature that causes the 3D print to fail. Therefore, making the right design decisions up front can help ensure that valuable time put into a project isn't wasted. With that in mind, this chapter will focus on design decisions that will help ensure that jobs will print properly. This chapter will provide useful design considerations and guidelines that will help limit problems during the final 3D-printing stage. Making a part thicker, designing an element at a certain angle, and having supports in just the right places are just a sampling of the design techniques that will be featured in this chapter.

The guidelines included here will focus on part thickness, design orientation, and workflows for dealing with overhangs to ensure parts print properly. Also provided will be methods used to hollow out parts, along with instructions on how to divide objects into smaller pieces when size becomes an issue. All the methods discussed will help make the 3D-printing process more efficient and error-free.

In presenting these tips, Tinkercad will be the used predominantly, but these rules can be followed within any 3D-modeling software. Meshmixer will also be discussed in this chapter (Autodesk's Meshmixer software is an excellent companion to Tinkercad and the other software tools in Autodesk's 123D family of 3D design tools.)

Design Guidelines for Successful 3D Printing

Design decisions made at the earliest stages of a project will impact a project's success during the final stage of output. In other words, making the right design decisions up front is essential. During the initial design stages, 3D print designers must strike a balance between aesthetics and practicality. This balance can be influenced by many factors such as the build size of the printer, the type of printer being used, and the materials used for final output. The designer must take all of these factors into consideration to determine the size of the part being produced, along with features such as part thickness and design orientation.

Since many readers will be first-time 3D print designers, most likely the type of printer being used is a fused deposition, filament-based 3D printer (such as a Makerbot), and the biggest challenge to deal with (when designing objects for FDM 3D printing) will be managing support structures. In some projects, smart design decisions can be made to allow for minimal supports, and the easiest way to avoid supports is to design objects without overhangs. Unfortunately, designing objects without overhangs not only is an engineering challenge but can compromise the aesthetics of the part being produced. Many times a designer will want to create a highly intricate object or an object with features such as bevels, bridges, and inset features. If the designer is outputting to an FDM printer, any elaborate, intricate, and highly detailed designs will most likely have many overhanging features that will require an abundance of supports to print properly. But this presents another challenge since too many supports, when removed, can scar the part and even cause structural damage to the design. Therefore, many design strategies need to be taken into account in order to design complex and intricate parts with properly placed supports.

With this in mind, the majority of tips listed here focus on design strategies to limit supports without sacrificing design. Some of these tips deal with the limitations of the machines themselves, focusing on the structural integrity of the 3D-printed parts. As stated earlier, these rules will apply more to fused deposition modeling (FDM) methods. If you are printing to an SLS machine, support structures are a nonissue, and many of the design tips will be less applicable. If you are printing to an SLA machine, most SLA machines will have their own tools to create proper supports, but following the rules in this chapter will still be helpful in ensuring successful prints.

Part Heights

If you need to create precisely measured parts, remember that all methods of 3D printing use a layer-by-layer process, and this layering has an impact on the level of precision you may want to achieve. Each layer will have a minimal thickness. Most FDM printers will have a minimal layer thickness between .05 mm and .2 mm (equivalent to between 50 and 200 microns); therefore, parts thinner than 50 microns will be impossible. As mentioned in previous chapters, the information on the minimal layer thickness achievable by any particular printer can be found on that 3D printer manufacturer's web site. If you are using Cura, Slic3r, or MatterControl as your slicing software, the layer thickness should already have been set by you within those program's print parameters.

When designing parts with precise measurements, the layer height needs to be taken into account. If you are printing with a layer of 200 mm and are looking to print parts with precise measurements, then all measurements of the printed part must be in multiples of 2. In other words, you will not be able to print a part with a length of 10.35 mm (you will have to either round up or round down to 10.2 or 10.4 mm). When taking precision into account, think in terms of the number of layers that are being produced for the object being printed. For example, if your layer height is 0.2 mm and your print is ten layers, then you would use the following equation: 0.2 mm x 8 layers = 1.6 mm layer. In other words, if the layer thickness is set at .2 mm, an 8-layer object will have a thickness of 1.6 mm, as illustrated in Figure 6-1.

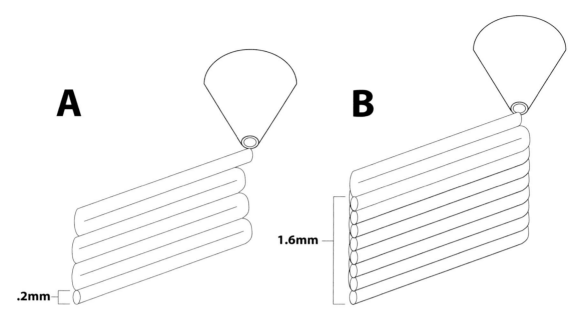

Figure 6-1. *In illustration A, the hot end is emitting a stream of filament with a layer height of 2 mm. All measurements will be in multiples of 2 based on this .2 mm layer height, as shown in illustration B where 8 layers of filament have created a wall 1.6 mm (a wall of 1.5 mm would be impossible)*

Build Orientation

When printing your own parts, build orientation will affect print times because a part's orientation will have an impact on support distribution. Build orientation will have an impact on the strength of a part as well. Both of these factors will be dependent upon the size and complexity of the part, and most of the time, build orientation will be a matter of common sense. For example, an object designed horizontally with many overhangs may need less support if printed vertically. In Figure 6-2, the space shuttle model was designed to be resting on the stand at a slight angle, but this produces one big overhang, requiring many supports. In Figure 6-3, the part has been placed on the build plate vertically, resulting in far fewer supports.

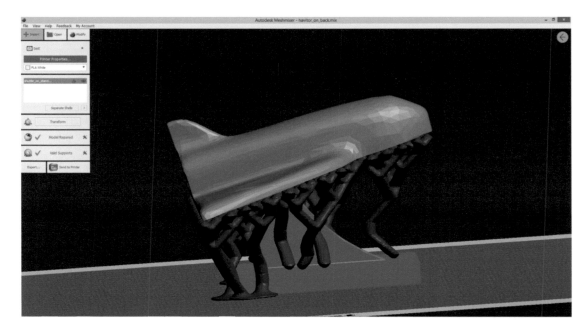

Figure 6-2. *The shuttle, when printed horizontally, produces a large overhang that results in many supports being added to the part*

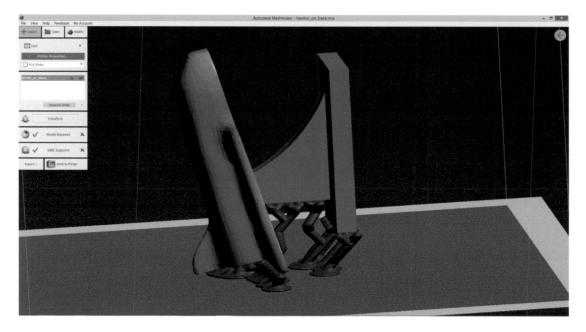

Figure 6-3. *When printed upright, the shuttle requires far fewer supports, but the layers of material may be more noticeable in the final 3D-printed output*

One trade-off caused by switching the orientation of the part will be the final quality of the print. In the previous example, the layering of material may be more noticeable on the shuttle that is printed vertically upright. While it may add time to the process, a good practice is to print a test part to help determine the most effective and efficient way to print a part.

Finally, consider the contact area of the part being printed. The contact area is where the part touches the build plate. If the contact area is small in relation to the overall size of the part being printed, there is also a risk of the part being unstable and collapsing during the 3D-printing process. For parts with narrow bases, consider adding a flat stand to the final 3D-printed part or printing the part on its side along the widest length.

Overhangs and Angled Geometry (the 45-Degree Rule)

Printing overhangs at an angle may lessen the number of supports that are applied to your model (especially if you're using Meshmixer to help generate supports).

As a general rule, parts that overhang at 0 to 90 degrees will require supports. The number of supports needed diminishes as the angle between the base of the object and the overhang increases (see Figure 6-4). Note, for the purposes of this book, parts printed at 90 degrees are be printed perpendicular to the build plate, or in other words "straight-up," and no longer could be considered an overhang.

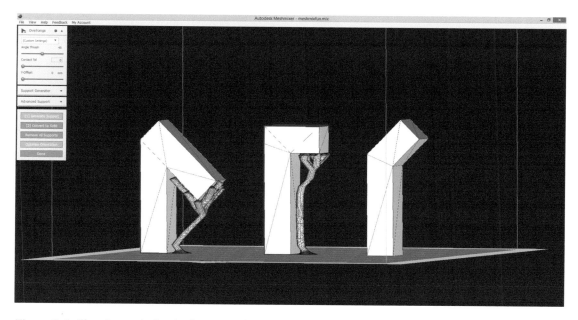

Figure 6-4. *Showing variation in sloping angles of an angle and the supports that can result in Meshmixer. When an overhang slopes at a greater angle from the base, supports will be minimal and even completely unnecessary*

Again, how you design for supports is a balance between practicality and aesthetics. It will be possible to print slight overhangs that reach out a few millimeters from the base without supports. Oftentimes the software generating supports will create supports for all overhangs regardless of how far they protrude from the base of the part.

Figure 6-5 demonstrates a range of support configurations applied to a robot arm model that has been posed at various angles. As shown in example D, even when the arm is posed upright, the smaller details of the arm design—the bevels of the joints and inward angles of pincer claw—have small overhanging features that have been augmented with supports using Meshmixer's support-generating algorithms. Some of these supports may not be necessary and can be eliminated in Meshmixer before printing.

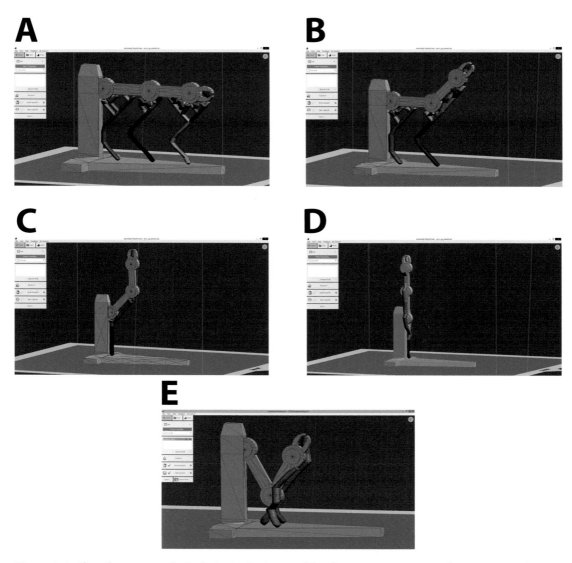

Figure 6-5. *If you have an aesthetic choice in the design of the object you are creating, then certain angles will produce more supports than others. In this example, a robot arm in a variety of poses shows variations in support distribution*

■ **Note**   In Meshmixer new supports can be added by right-clicking a preexisting support. Supports can be removed by Ctrl+right-clicking.

Repeated Overhangs

If an overhang needs to be repeated in a design, keep those overhangs as close together as possible. Examples of repeated overhangs include designs that have multiple ridges, treads, and deep recessed textures.

For example, if an artist designs corrugated tube, having big gaps in between the overhanging corrugations (as in example A in Figure 6-6) will necessitate many small supports to ensure the printability of the overhanging features (Figure 6-7). These small overhangs will be difficult and time-consuming to remove. It would probably be best to bring the corrugations closer together, as in example B in Figure 6-6, in order to limit the supports needed.

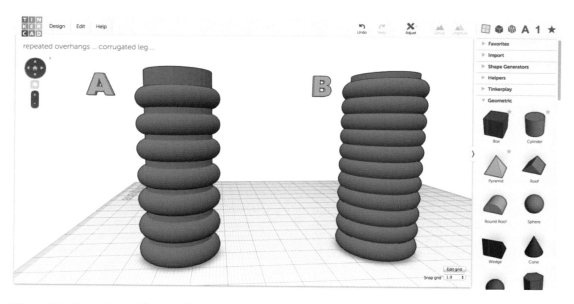

Figure 6-6.   *Part A has wider gaps between the overhanging layers, raising the possibility of difficult-to-remove overhangs between gaps. In part B, the gaps have been removed, lessening the number of overhangs needed*

Figure 6-7. *Shows the results of adding supports to a part with gaps between overhangs. These supports will be difficult to remove*

Part Thickness

Part thickness is also dependent on layer height. Parts thinner than the layer height capabilities of the printer will be impossible. As discussed earlier, parts can be made in widths that are multiples of the layer height of the 3D printer being used. While thin parts are possible, they have widths greater than the 3D printer's layer height capabilities, and any thin part that requires supports may not survive the process of support removal.

When designing objects with thin features, good design sense should prevail. It may take a bit of trial and error to determine how thin parts can survive support removal, and much of this will depend on the scale of your model. If thin parts are absolutely necessary, try changing the orientation of the object being printed. Try to have thin parts run parallel and flush to the printer bed. Also, because of the layering of material, long, thin parts will break more easily when the longer length of the part runs perpendicular to the printed layers. As a general rule, consider each layer to be a point of possible breakage for any part printed. When parts are printed tall and thin, there will be more layers running along the height of the part, and each layer is a stress point that can increase the chance of a part breaking. In Figure 6-8, part A has more layers along the height of the part and therefore more stress points that may lead to breakage. Part B is printed with the longest length parallel and flush to the build plate. The odds of part B breaking are reduced since there are few stress points (in other words, layers) along the height of the part.

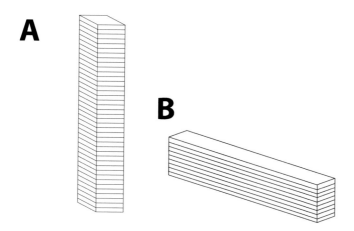

Figure 6-8. *Part B is stronger than part A since the layers run across the longest length of part B*

If, because of the orientation of the part on the build plate, thin parts will have to be printed upright, try to thicken and shorten the parts as much as possible (Figure 6-9).

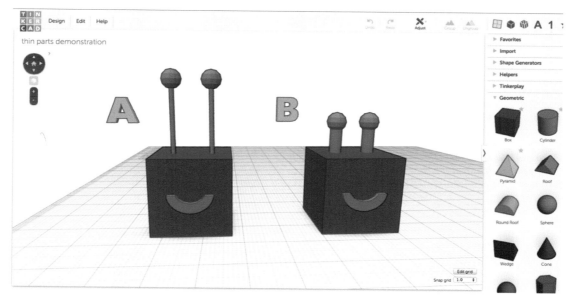

Figure 6-9. *A case where, if thin parts, as in example A, are absolutely necessary, then they should be thickened and shortened to ensure printability, as in example B*

Connected Parts

When connecting parts, the part will be weakness at the point of the connection. If a connected part is also an overhang, it could potentially break when the support structures are removed. The temptation may be to create a connecting piece that is smaller (maybe for aesthetic purposes) than the pieces that are being connected (Figure 6-10). If possible, have the two larger parts intersect slightly (don't use a smaller part to connect them) and then fuse all the pieces together by using a grouping/combine Boolean function (Figure 6-11).

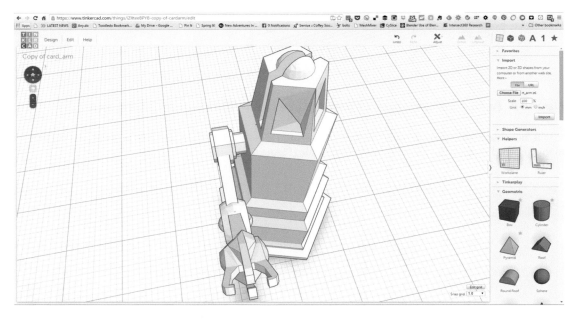

Figure 6-10. *The arm of the robot is connected to the base of the robot's body with an small cylinder "connector part." Most likely, since the arm will be an overhang, supports will be required, and because of the thinness of the connecting cylinder, the arm may break of the body during support removal*

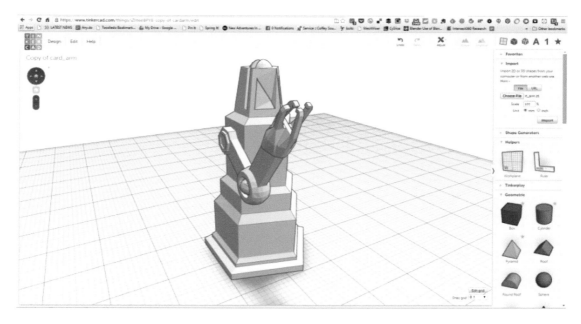

Figure 6-11. *Instead of using a cylinder to connect the arm to the body, the arm has been embedded into the body itself, making a stronger connection and helping to ensure it will not break off during support removal*

Fine Details

Because of the layer-by-layer process of 3D printing, fine details will be impossible on small objects. For any fine details to be viewable, they should be at least four to five times larger than the layer height used for the printer. For example, details such as an engraved line on a part that is being printed using a .2 mm layer height should be at least .4 to .5 mm wide.

This same rule also holds true for text on objects. Small text less than a millimeter in height may not print legibly.

Chamfers

Chamfers are a type of bevel that can be added to the corners of objects to flatten out edges (Figure 6-12). Fillets are another type of bevel used to round out corners (Figure 6-13). Applying chamfers to overhanging corners not only can help reduce the number of supports needed but may add some style to your design.

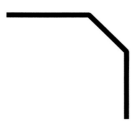

Figure 6-12. *A chamfer is used to create a hard-edge bevel for corners*

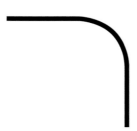

Figure 6-13. *A fillet is a rounded corner used as a bevel for sharp edges*

Chamfers can be applied to both interior (Figure 6-14) and exterior angles of geometry. Most often the chamfer is applied to geometry that is angled at 90 degrees. To add a chamfer to the corner of an object, some applications, such as Autodesk's 123D Design, have an Add Chamfer function. Unfortunately, Tinkercad lacks this functionality; instead, you can use Tinkercad's Grouping and Hole functions to create chamfers just as easily.

Figure 6-14. *Chamfers can be applied to interior or exterior corners of geometry*

ADD A CHAMFER TO A DESIGN USING TINKERCAD

1. Determine the areas of the model where you would like to add the chamfers. Drag a box onto the workplane, which will be used to add or subtract from the preexisting geometry.

2. Rotate the box to a 45-degree or greater angle. The greater the angle of the chamfer, the less likely supports will be needed for the chamfered geometry, as in Figure 6-15. (In this example, the chamfering geometry is blue.)

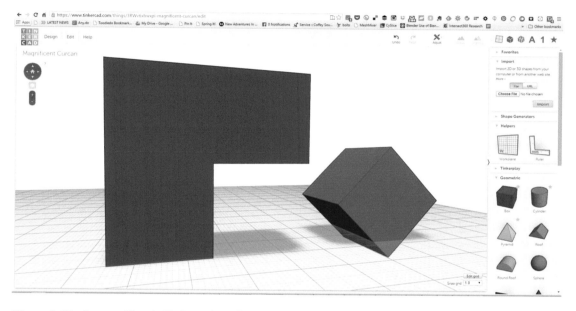

Figure 6-15. *A rotated box in Tinkercad can be used to create the geometry for the bevel*

3. To add a chamfer to an interior angle (inset angle), move, group, and align the "chamfering box" with the geometry (see Figure 6-16).

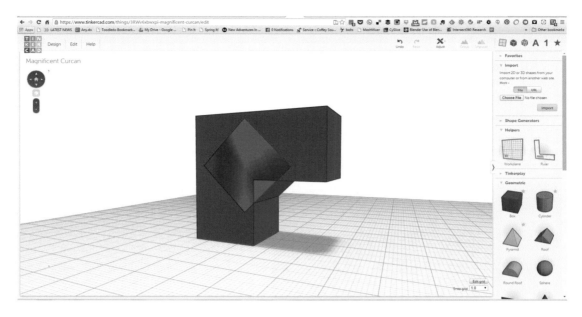

Figure 6-16. *The rotated box is aligned to the geometry to create a chamfer for an interior angle*

4. To add a chamfer to an exterior angel, turn the box into a Hole object (click the Hole icon in the Inspector window) and then move, align, and group the box to the geometry (see Figure 6-17).

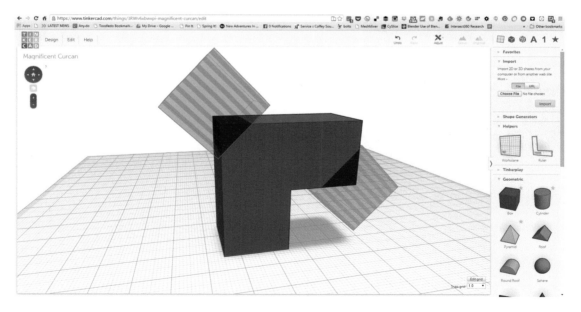

Figure 6-17. *The rotated box is turned into a Hole object and aligned with exterior angles. Grouping the Hole objects with the main geometry will create chamfers in the desired areas*

Recesses and Holes

Sometimes recesses are unavoidable. Deep recesses can be challenging since the resulting supports can be formed deep within the object. Such deeply recessed supports can be difficult to remove. If you have an important need for a deep recess, print the object with the recesses exposed upright toward the extruder if possible (Figure 6-18). Otherwise, don't make recesses too deep. Also, ensure that the recess is wide enough to enable support removal if necessary. Examples of a deep recesses include an open mouth on a toy character, a deep hole in a part, or a slit that is added into the geometry, as shown in Figure 6-19.

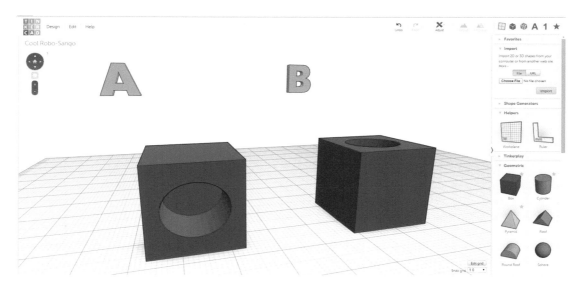

Figure 6-18. *Objects with holes and recesses should be printed with the hole face upright, as in example B*

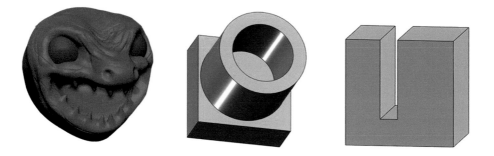

Figure 6-19. *Examples of objects with deep recesses*

Even though shallow recesses may print fine without supports, it is always a good idea to perform a test print to determine whether supports are necessary.

Work with Gravity, Bridges, and Arc

Bridges are entirely possible without supports, and shorter bridges will be easier to print than longer bridges. The post ends of the bridge are in fact supports; generally, support material in between will be unnecessary if the distance between posts is short.

Longer bridges will sag because the filament will droop between supports. One way to keep supports minimal is to use chamfers, fillets, and arcs in the bridge design. Figure 6-20 shows three bridges. The shorter bridge was the one that printed with the least amount of sagging.

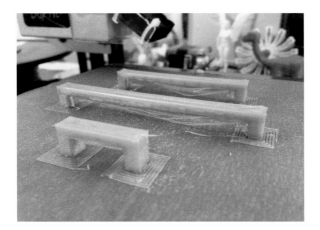

Figure 6-20. *Short bridges are possible without additional supports. With longer bridges, filament will droop across the span of the bridge*

Designing bridges using arcs, chamfers, and fillets to help connect the post supports with the bridge can also help reduce drooping filament. If the design of the bridge is well thought out, then supports may be avoided entirely.

Pinnacles

If you are printing a pyramid, pinnacle, or inverted cone (basically anything that ends with the point upward), level off the top point. If the top of the pointed object is not leveled, the filament sometimes will bundle up at the tip of the object and leave a thin strand of plastic. Such bits of string filament may not be a big deal, but sometimes leveling off the tip of pinnacle can lead to cleaner results (see Figure 6-21). Use a Boolean operation (or, in Tinkercad, a Hole object can be the grouped tip of the pinnacle) to level off the point. For best results, when creating the Boolean to level off the point, make the diameter of the flat tip wider than the 3D printer's layer height.

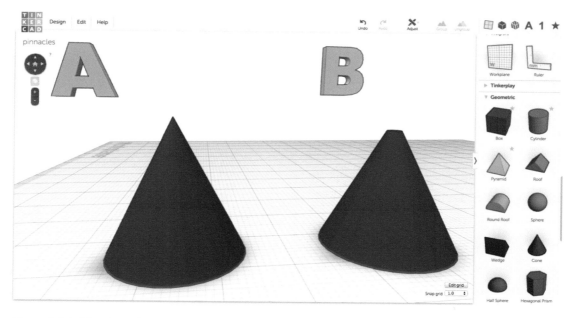

Figure 6-21. *The pinnacle in example A has been leveled in example B using a Hole object in Tinkercad*

Dividing Objects Into Pieces and Creating Assemblies for Best Outcomes

Sometimes it's necessary to break large or complicated objects into a number of pieces.

In Tinkercad, parts can be divided into smaller components (in other words, separate pieces) using the Hole and Grouping workflow that was featured in Chapter 3 and in the earlier sections of this chapter. Another way to split up a model into smaller pieces is with Autodesk Meshmixer. Meshmixer has two specific functions for dividing objects: the Plane Cut tool and the Separate Shells function. You can find the Plane Cut and Separate Shells functions in Meshmixer's Edit menu, as shown in Figure 6-22.

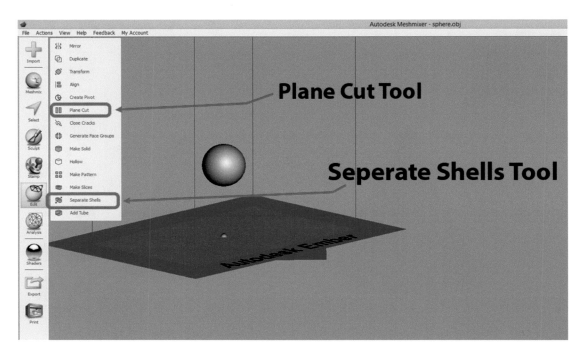

Figure 6-22. *You can use the Plane Cut and Separate Shells tools in Meshmixer to divide models into separate pieces*

In the example featured in the following exercise, you will be splitting up a model of a dinosaur (Figure 6-23). The particular dinosaur you are going to divide into pieces has a long, elevated neck and tail, which may provide challenges for 3D printing. One reason to divide this model into individual pieces is to isolate and protect delicate parts, such as the neck and tail, that may break off during the process of support removal. Splitting up the model into, and having those parts lie flat on the build plate, will also limit the need for multiple supports, resulting in a model with fewer support blemishes. Finally, another reason for splitting a model into smaller pieces is to make large model fit onto a 3D printer with a small build plate. Using the method described next, a large model can be split into smaller pieces that can be then be reoriented and rearranged, ensuring that the large models fit on a smaller 3D printer's build plate.

Figure 6-23. *The dinosaur model has many overhanging features, and if the model is 3D printed on an FDM of SLA 3D printer, supports will be necessary. One way to limit the supports needed is to divide the dinosaur into separate parts, which may help eliminate the number of overhangs on the model. The dinosaur can then be reassembled and glued back together after it is 3D printed*

SPLITTING A MODEL INTO PARTS IN MESHMIXER

1. In the side toolbar, select the Plane Cut tool in the Edit menu. The model will then appear to be sliced into separate parts. One part (the upper half) with be solid, and the lower half will be translucent (Figure 6-24). If you were to hit Accept in the Plane Cut window in the upper-left corner, then the translucent lower half would be deleted, leaving the remaining upper portion.

Figure 6-24. *You can use the Plane Cut tool in the Edit section of Meshmixer's toolbar to divide a model into smaller parts*

2. Use the manipulator at the center of the Plane Cut tool to move the location of the cutting plane to the base of the neck (Figure 6-25). Next, to create two separate halves, in the Plane Cut window, change the type from Cut to Slice. Hit Accept, and the model appears to remain whole.

Figure 6-25. *Use the Plane Cut tool's manipulator (the three colored arrows and curves used to adjust the cutting plane) in the location to create the first division in the model. Use the Slice function, which can be accessed in the Plane Cut window's Type drop-down menu to divide the model into two separate pieces. Using Slice versus Cut will ensure both pieces remain after the Plane Cut operation. (Using Cut will delete the translucent part of the model.)*

3. To finalize the separation process, use the Separate Shells function also found in the Edit menu in the side toolbar. An object browser will appear with two separated objects listed. In parentheses "shell 1" and "shell 2" are listed. Clicking the eye icon next to one of the objects will cause the separate part to appear translucent (Figure 6-26). This indicates that there are now two separate pieces for the dinosaur.

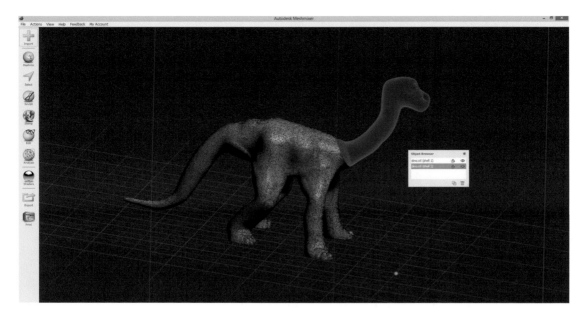

Figure 6-26. *To separate the model into two separate parts that can be adjusted independently, use the Separate Shells function in the Edit section of the Meshmixer toolbar*

5.   Once the dinosaur has been sliced, you can select each section by using the Transform tool. Using the Transform tool, place each selected part of the dinosaur strategically on the build plate, with the length lying flush and parallel on the build plate as a means to minimize supports (Figure 6-27).

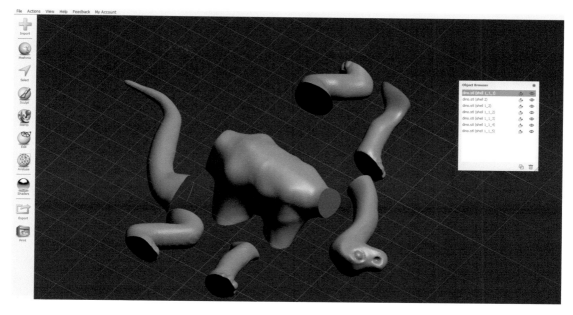

Figure 6-27. *The each separate piece (in other words, shell) is arranged on the build plate. The parts are arranged with the lengthwise parts lying flat to help minimize supports*

Smooth vs. Hard-Edge Parts

Smoothing out parts is another way to help reduce supports. Using a smooth function in a program such as Meshmixer can reduce the number of overhangs by softening the corners of geometry created in Tinkercad and other solid-modeling applications. If accuracy isn't a concern, then smoothing out the geometry can add some aesthetic appeal to the designs you are creating.

In Figure 6-28, the dog model on the left has been softened using both the Make Solid (in the Edit section of the main toolbar) and the Smooth function (in the Deform section of the Select menu in the main toolbar) in Meshmixer. The dog model to the right appears at it originally did in Tinkercad. When supports are added in Meshmixer, the smooth dog has fewer supports under the legs and back. Therefore, with fewer supports, support removal will be an easier, less damaging process for the smooth version.

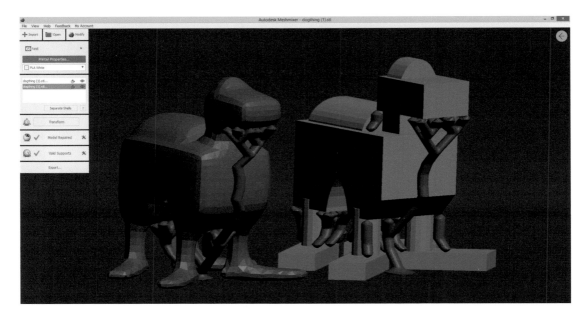

Figure 6-28. *The Tinkercad model was imported into Meshmixer and modified using Meshmixer's Make Solid and Smooth functions. The smooth version now has fewer overhangs than the original Tinkercad model. Respectively, the smoothed version requires fewer supports than the original, making support removal for the smoothed version a far easier, and less damaging, task*

Hollow Parts

With 3D printing, hollow parts are entirely possible. There may be several reasons to make a model hollow. One reason to hollow out a model is to help reduce the amount of material (and therefore significantly lessen amount of time it would take to print the model) during 3D printing. Another reason is to make hollow boxes and vases out of organic and complex forms.

Meshmixer also has the functionality to quickly create hollow parts. The Meshmixer Hollow function is straightforward to use and can be found in the Edit menu of Meshmixer's main toolbar. The Hollow function will allow users to adjust the thickness of the part and designate the amount of hollow space within the object. When the Hollow function is used on a 3D model with Meshmixer, the original surface of the model appears translucent, allowing users to more effectively judge the amount of hollow space that can be created on the model (Figure 6-29). Once hollowed, the object can be split half, if desired, using Meshmixer's Plane Cut tool. Hollowing and then dividing objects within Meshmixer can be an easy way to turn any 3D model into an interesting lidded container or unique vase (Figure 6-30).

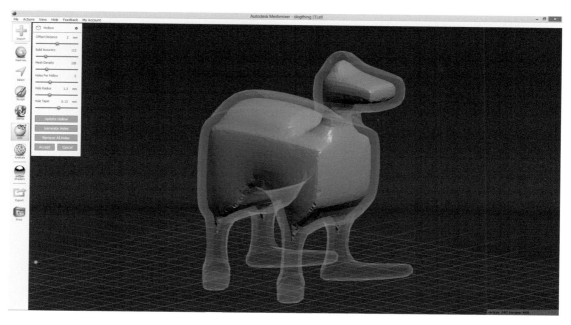

Figure 6-29. *Meshmixer's Hollow function allows designers to turn any 3D model into a hollow object. By hollowing out models, designers can help conserve material and speed up print times*

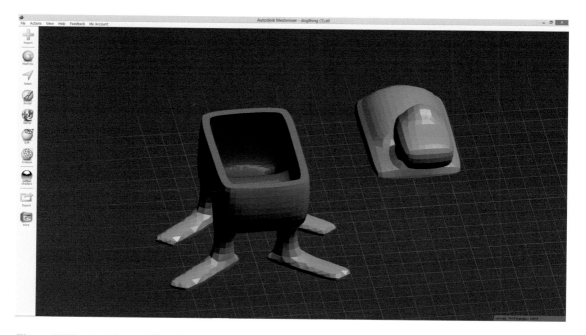

Figure 6-30. *Any 3D model can be hollowed in Meshmixer and then turned into a vase or container using the Plane Cut tool*

Summary

The design strategies provided in this chapter will ideally enable 3D print designers to avoid common design mistakes that may impact the success of a 3D-printed part. To use these techniques effectively, designers should know the 3D-printing processes being used to output their designs. This knowledge will help 3D-print designers print parts more efficiently and eventually, through trial and error, allow for the design of more complex and intricate objects.

CHAPTER 7

■ ■ ■

Basic Solid Modeling Techniques

For those new to 3D modeling, Tinkercad is a great software tool to use to begin exploring 3D design, but it lacks a number of functions found in other solid-modeling applications. With Tinkercad, complex shapes can be made possible by grouping geometric primitives together (along with using Hole objects for Boolean operations), but eventually the need will arise to make intricate objects quickly and with precision. To make the 3D design of elaborate and highly complex geometries more efficient, there are a number of modeling methods (which are unfortunately not found in Tinkercad) that can used to pull and extend geometry in a variety of ways. These methods include using a 2D drawing (or profile curve) as the basis for a 3D design. With a base curve profile, a design can be drawn precisely in 2D and then transformed into the 3D part using techniques such as extruding, lofting, and revolving. Many of these functions can be found in Autodesk's 123D Design, another free software tool in the Autodesk 123D family. Chapter 7 will therefore focus on the wider range of possibilities offered by solid modeling by giving a breakdown of the various solid modeling functions found in 123D Design. This chapter will discuss the benefits of solid modeling used in 123D Design such as drawing curve profiles in order to create more sophisticated parts. Also featured will be a number of techniques such as pattern alignments and more Boolean intersections.

A number of new projects will be presented in this chapter: a desktop organizer, a funnel, a picture frame, a bookmark, and a mini-shelf. Each of these projects utilizes a number of common solid-modeling techniques such as drafting shapes using curves, extruding surfaces, and performing Boolean operations.

The Benefits of Solid Modeling

Like Tinkercad and OpenScad, 123D Design is a solid-modeling application falling into the category of "precision-based modeling" applications. What this essentially means is that designers can use modeling functions to manipulate 3D shapes and 2D profile curves using precise measurements in order to create and construct new geometric forms. Many of the functions found in 123D Design, such as extruding, lofting, and revolving, are common tools found in almost all professional modeling tools used by engineers, such as Autodesk Inventor and Autodesk Fusion 360. Having free access to 123D Design gives first-time designers the opportunity to explore modeling functions found in other more advanced (and more expensive) software tools.

There tends to be some confusion as to what constitutes a solid in a solid-modeling application. Like other modeling tools, a solid-modeling application lets users manipulate 3D solids as well as solids defined by 2D curves. Models are derived by combining solid geometries or by drawing profile curves, which can then be extruded, lofted, or revolved to create the solid forms. Some solid-modeling programs will refer to the curves as sketches, and those sketches can be defined by Beziers, polylines, and/or splines. Since the focus of a solid-modeling application is precision, the users of such tools often input the dimensions of the parts and profiles being built numerically.

■ **Note** *Beziers, polylines, splines,* and *sketches* are common names used to describe the curves that are used to create 2D line drawings in 3D-modeling software. These terms will differ among software packages.

Solid-modeling applications usually excel at generating watertight meshes and error-free geometry because of the simplicity of the curves used in the construction of the geometry. In a solid-modeling program, only the necessary curves are used to define the 3D geometry. Once the solid geometry is exported as an .stl file, the solid geometry becomes a tessellated mesh, and additional edges are added to the model. Comparing gear designed in a solid-modeling program with the .stl tessellated mesh shows the increased faceting in the .stl file (Figure 7-1).

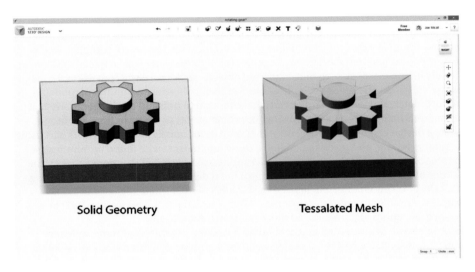

Figure 7-1. *The solid model on the left is clean and lacks the extraneous edges found in the tessellated mesh on the right*

As mentioned in Chapter 2, meshes are often associated with organic sculpting or animation design software since the multiple individual faces of such a mesh can be adjusted to create highly organic forms. Because of the increased number of faces found in a mesh, highly complex meshes can be memory intensive. Most solid programs lack the capability to adjust a mesh directly because of the mesh's complexity. Once the geometry becomes a mesh, it is no longer considered a solid and will be difficult to adjust in modeling programs such as 123D Design.

Discovering 123D Design for Solid Modeling Techniques

Tinkercad provided a basic glimpse into what is possible in a solid-modeling program. 123D Design expands upon what is possible; using it is covered in more detail throughout this chapter.

As part of the Autodesk's 123D series of apps, 123D Design is available for download at www.123dapp.com/design for PCs, Mac OSX, and iPad. Since 123D Design is not a web-based app, it is, in contrast to Tinkercad, ideal for larger files. But 123D Design still takes advantage of the 123D cloud to store and transfer files between 123D applications. Files created in 123D Design can be uploaded to the user's 123D cloud and accessed by both Tinkercad and Meshmixer.

After installing 123D Design and upon opening the application, users will be greeted with a "Welcome to 123D Design" slideshow that showcases new workflow tips for using the 123D Design application (Figure 7-2). New users of 123D Design should take the time to review these slides. The slides go through new and important aspects of the 123D application, such as how to use the Ruler tool, exportable formats (such as .stl files), and the Text tool.

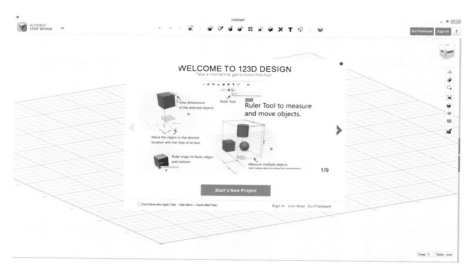

Figure 7-2. *The welcome window for 123D Design introduces users to new features and workflows*

To begin using 123D Design, click the Start a New Project button on the bottom of the welcome window (note, if you don't want to be greeted by the welcome screen every time you open 123D Design, then click Don't Show This Again in the lower-left corner of the screen).

Visually, the workspace of 123D Design looks similar to Tinkercad with a few differences. The main distinction between the two programs is that 123Design is a downloadable application that must be installed on a PC, while Tinkercad is run directly off the Web. Visually, the two applications look quite similar, but 123Design has many more features. The main viewport of 123D Design contains a blue grid that is almost identical to the blue workplane grid in Tinkercad. The 123D Design workplane grid has one additional function: the unit grids are marked on the edge to help with the measurement and placement of geometry on the grid. In the upper-right corner is the ViewCube, which is a common feature found in other Autodesk applications such as 3D Studio Max and Maya. The ViewCube acts as a compass indicator that can help determine the direction in 3D space. The cube is marked top, front, right, left, back, and so on, and follows the navigation of the user.

To create, modify, navigate, and save geometry, users have access to three main menus in the 123D Design interface. In the upper-left corner is the File menu used to save, import, and export designs. On the right side is an icon-list menu with a number of functions for viewing and navigating geometry. The main menu for generating and modifying geometry is represented by a series of icons horizontally on the top of the interface. In addition, a fourth menu appears on the bottom of the screen every time a piece of geometry is selected.

Using 123D Design

On its most basic level, 123D Design creates geometry in the same way as Tinkercad. In the top menu, the fourth icon from the left opens a submenu that allows users to drag primitives (in other words, basic geometric shapes) onto the workplane grid (Figure 7-3).

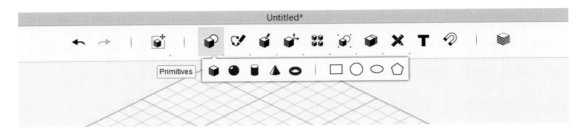

Figure 7-3. *The fourth icon from the right in 123D Design's uppermost menu gives access to a number of primitive shapes and sketch shapes that can be used as base shapes for more complex objects*

But unlike Tinkercad, 123D Design users have many more options to create and modify geometry. In 123D Design's horizontal menu are a number of useful tools that are commonly found in higher-end (and costly) CAD-modeling packages. These tools include the ability to create fillets (the creation of rounded edges), chamfers (the creation of followed beveled edges), and shells (hollowed objects); see Figure 7-4. There are duplication functions that allow designers to create circular and pattern arrays (Figure 7-5); there is also a Boolean function that can create intersections, along with the traditional Boolean functions of add and subtract (Figure 7-6).

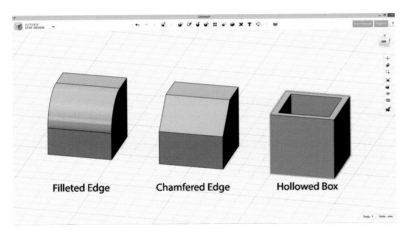

Figure 7-4. *123D Design can modify geometry with a variety of operations. Shown here are examples of a fillet, a chamfer, and a hollowed box*

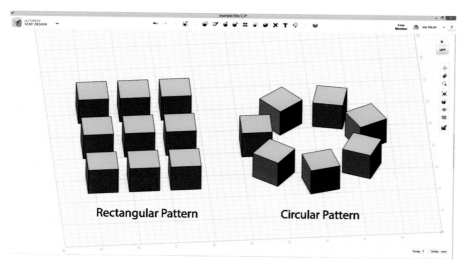

Figure 7-5. *123D Design has can create duplicates of a single object in specific formations. Pictured here are the patterns achieved using the Rectangular Pattern and the Circular Pattern tools*

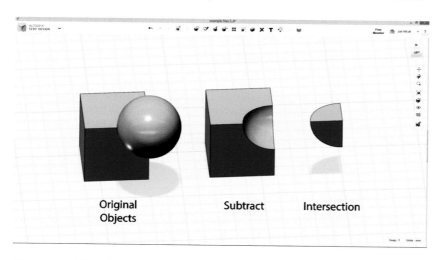

Figure 7-6. *Three "combine" Boolean operations are available in 123D Design. Shown here is the original combination of two geometric objects, and the results from using the Subtract and Intersection functions in the Combine submenu of the horizontal toolbar*

Navigation

In 123D Design, the middle mouse button will drag around the object, the right mouse button will orbit (or rotate) around the object, and the scroll wheel will zoom in and out.

Users of 123D Design can also navigate using the ViewCube in the upper-right corner of the interface (Figure 7-7). Clicking the home icon will return the view to the original home position. Clicking the side or corner of the cube will send the view to the corresponding position as represented on the cube (such as the front, top, left, right, back, and bottom positions). There is also a pop-up menu that can switch between orthographic and perspective views.

205

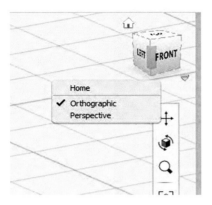

Figure 7-7. The ViewCube in 123D Design offers additional navigation capabilities

Creating Geometry in 123D Design

The following modeling examples will introduce new users to the various geometry creation tools in 123D Design.

■ **Note**   To get a better understanding of how Autodesk 123D Design operates, there are a number of great videos featuring 123 Design workflows at `www.123dapp.com/howto/design`.

There are basically two ways to create geometry in 123D Design. Like Tinkercad, users can drag primitive objects to the grid, and those objects can be combined using Booleans (found in 123D Design's Combine submenu). Designers using 123D Design can also use 2D profile sketch curves, which serve as the basis for more complex 3D objects. These base sketch profiles can be constructed with curve tools such as Polylines, Splines, and Arcs.

Sketch Profiles in 123D Design

The use of sketch profile shapes gives designers a bit more flexibility when developing their models. The ability to create profile curves in any shape allows users to create a broader range of geometric forms, such as the complex shape shown in Figure 7-8. Sketch profiles can be modified using a number of functions such as Extrude, Sweep, Revolve, and Loft.

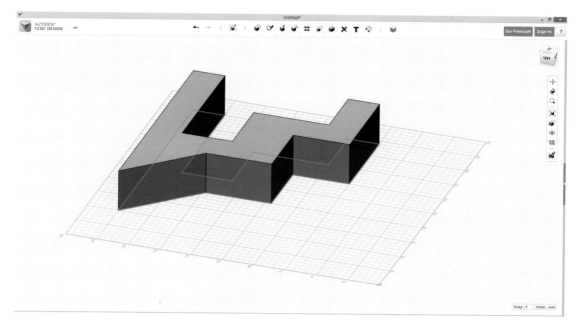

Figure 7-8. *The Polyline sketch tool was used to create the profile for this abstract geometric form. The original sketch was then turned into a 3D object with the Extrude tool*

123D Design's Sketch Submenu

In 123D Design the tools to generate profile sketches are found in 123D Design's Sketch submenu (Figure 7-9).

Figure 7-9. *The Sketch submenu in 123D Design*

In the Sketch submenu, the first four icons represent predefined 2D sketch shape profiles (Rectangle, Circle, Ellipse, and Polygon), the next four icons are drawing tools for creating sketches (Polyline, Spline, 2 Point Arc, and 3 Point Arc), and the last five icons are a special set of sketching tools that will let users modify and adjust preexisting sketches. This last set of five enables additional functions that allow users to trim, extend, and offset sketch profiles.

Polylines, Splines, and Arcs

The most common means to create unique geometric shapes begins with laying down 2D sketches using the drawing tools (the second of icons) in the Sketch submenu. The Polylines sketch tool is used to generate straight lines with sharp corners, as in example A of Figure 7-10. The Spline sketch tool is use to generate curve-linear curves, as in example B of Figure 7-10. There are a couple of arc-drawing tools that can create arcs of various degrees, as shown in example C of Figure 7-10.

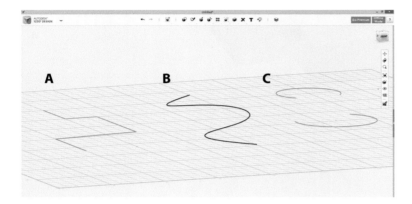

Figure 7-10. *Example A is a polyline (used for generating straight edges). Example B is a spline (use to generate curved edges). The two arc tools (2 Point Arc and 3 Point Arc) can generate the arcs shown in example C*

Snapping Sketch Profiles to the Grid

The Snap functionality, which is accessed in the lower-right corner of the interface, works in conjunction with the sketch tools. The sketch tools respect the spacing of the grid squares. When drawing with the sketch tools on the grid, the small square icon that appears indicates that the point being laid down is being snapped to the grid using the tolerances specified (Figure 7-11).

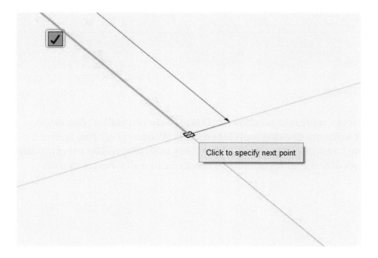

Figure 7-11. *Polylines, splines, and arcs can snap to the grid. A small square indicates that endpoint of any polyline, spline, and arc is snapped to the grid*

A user can set the snap tolerance in the Snap menu found in the lower-right corner of the 123D Design interface (Figure 7-12).

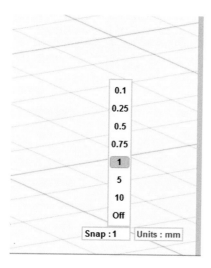

Figure 7-12. *Shown is the snapping menu in the lower-right corner of the Tinkercad interface. Snapping can be set in specified increments for increased precision*

Revealing Angles and Measurements

Clicking a polyline, spline, or arc can reveal useful information. Clicking on a polyline segment will reveal the length of that segment. When clicking on a segment a gear symbol will appear. Clicking on the gear symbol will activate a pop-up menu. Clicking on the Edit Dimension icon that appears in that pop-up menu will reveal additional measuring functions. With Edit Dimensions selected, clicking on any two segments that connect and meet at an angle will reveal the degree of that angle (Figure 7-13).

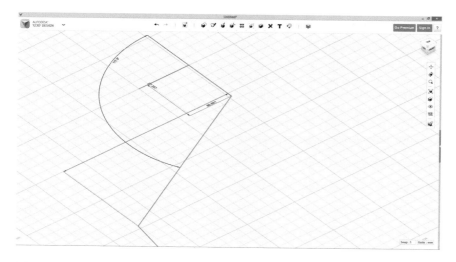

Figure 7-13. *Measurements for polylines, splines, and arcs created in 123D Design can be accessed by clicking on segments*

Enclosed Shapes

When drawing complex shapes, you can use the various sketch tools in combination. Polylines and splines will snap to previously drawn polylines and splines on the grid. Users can snap to the endpoint or edge of a previously drawn line to create fully enclosed shapes (called *closed shapes* in 123D Design). Hitting Enter or clicking the check mark in the green box that appears finalizes the line-drawing process. When determining whether an enclosed shape was successfully made, the inner fill color for the shape should be light blue (Figure 7-14).

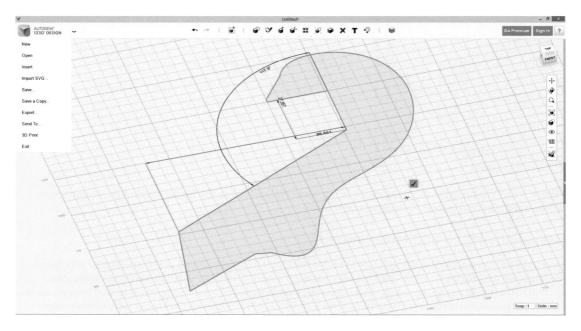

Figure 7-14. *Enclosed shapes can be created by connecting the endpoints and edges of segments. Any combination of polylines, splines, and segments can be combined to create enclosed shapes*

The Fillet Tool

In Tinkercad, creating a fillet was a multistep process. In 123D Design, the creation of fillets are simplified with the Fillet sketch tool. The Fillet tool is the first icon in the third set of tools found in the Sketch submenu. Use the Fillet tool to convert sharp-angled polyline corners to rounded curves (in other words, fillets are basically rounded curves). With the sketch Fillet tool activated, selecting any two lines that connect to form a corner will smooth out that corner into a rounded curve. A red spline indicates the curvature of the fillet, which can also be adjusted in the Fillet Radius pop-up menu, which appears at the bottom of the 123D Design interface (Figure 7-15).

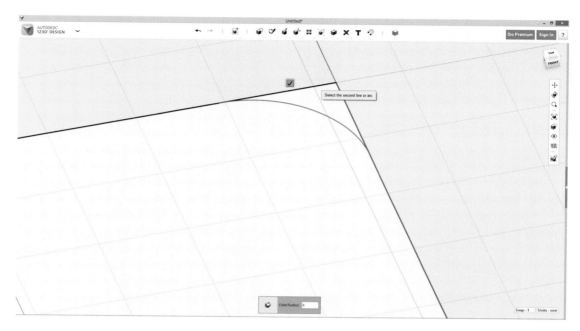

Figure 7-15. *A fillet generated with the Fillet sketch tool*

Trimming and Extending Sketches

Polylines, splines, and arcs can also be edited using the Trim and Extend tools. The Trim tool will delete segments (Figure 7-16). With a Trim tool activated, click any segment to delete it. The segment selected will first turn red; then hit Enter to delete the segment.

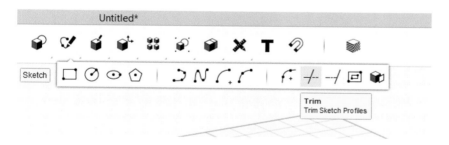

Figure 7-16. *The Trim tool is highlighted in the Sketch submenu*

■ **Note**   Segments can also be deleted by selecting them and simply hitting Delete.

The Extend tool (Figure 7-17) will help enclose gaps to create enclosed shapes. The Extend tool works best when segments used to close the gap are near one another (Figure 7-18).

211

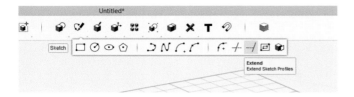

Figure 7-17. *The Extend tool is highlighted in the Sketch submenu*

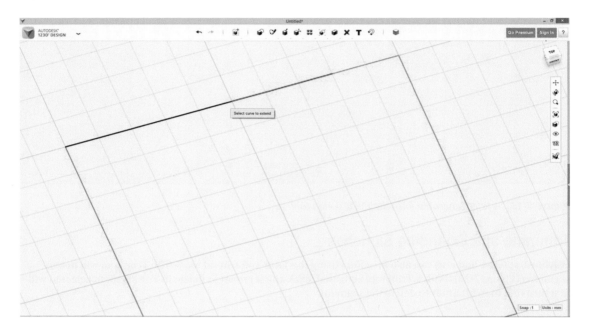

Figure 7-18. *Shown here is the Extend tool in action. The red line indicates the gap that is being extended to create the closed shape*

Offsetting Sketches

The Offset tool (Figure 7-19) will make copies of splines, polylines, and arcs, allowing designers to create shapes with interesting borders and walls.

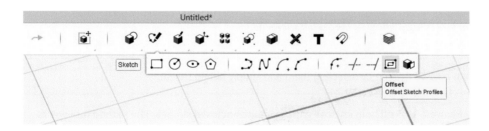

Figure 7-19. *The Offset tool is highlighted in the Sketch submenu*

With the Offset tool activated, click and drag a curve to create a duplicate of that curve (Figure 7-20). The gaps can then be filled using either polylines or the Extend tool.

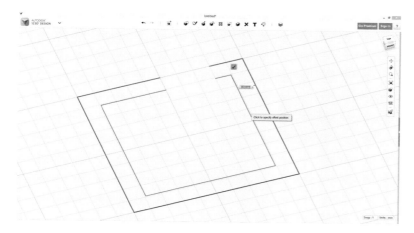

Figure 7-20. *A duplicate curve is created using the Offset tool*

The Construct Menu: Extrude, Loft, Sweep, and Revolve

As mentioned, you can use profile curves to create more complex 3D forms by applying the modeling functions in the Construct menu (Figure 7-21). The additional modeling operations in the Construct menu are, from left to right, Extrude, Sweep, Revolve, and Loft. To use one of the tools in the Construct menu, first select the tool of preference (Extrude, Sweep, Revolve or Loft) and then apply it to a closed 2D shape to create a three-dimensional object. Each construct tool will provide pop-up instructions detailing the exact procedure to follow. These additional modeling operations are explained in the following sections.

Figure 7-21. *In the Construct menu, from left to right: Extrude, Sweep, Revolve, and Loft*

Extrude

The Extrude operation is a simple procedure. When the Extrude tool is selected, clicking any 2D enclosed shape (which will be light blue in color) will allow users to extend that shape into space (Figure 7-22). A small arrow will appear when the Extrude tool is activated, allowing users to extend the form in the direction of the arrow. For precise distances, users can input the desired length in the small window that appears at the bottom of the 123D Design interface.

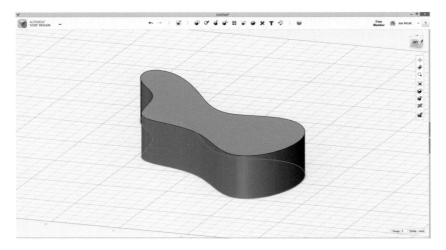

Figure 7-22. *The Extrude tool has been applied to a 2D, closed shape*

The Extrude tool can also extrude the face of a preexisting 3D object. When the Extrude tool is activated, hovering over a face of a 3D object will produce a green highlight around the edges of the face to be extruded.

Furthermore, the Extrude tool can perform Boolean operations. In the small window that appears when the Extrude tool is activated, users have the option of merging, subtracting, intersecting, or creating a new solid. Creating a new solid will turn the extrusion into a separate object that can be adjusted independently.

Loft

Lofting will connect two faces of a 3D object or two closed shapes, creating 3D geometry to bridge the selected faces or shapes (Figure 7-23). The objects used in the Loft operation can be different in shape, but the results will not always be predictable or may produce unexpected 3D objects (for instance, lofting a square to a hexagon generates a pyramid). You can also loft a closed shape to the face of 3D solid. To loft more than two closed shapes/faces together, Shift+select each object to be lofted, then click the gear icon that opens a pop-up menu, and finally select the Loft icon.

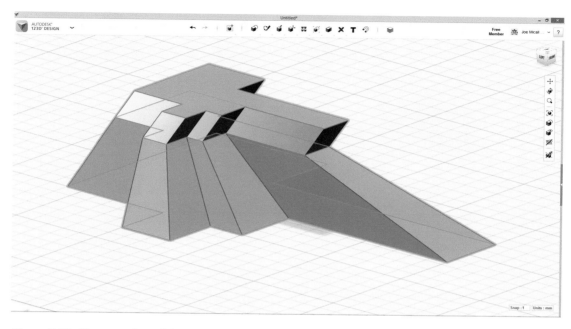

Figure 7-23. *Two complex polylines have been used to create a 3D form using the Loft tool*

Sweep

The Sweep function in the Construct menu uses a polyline/spline to extend a face or a closed shape. The newly generated 3D form follows the path of the polyline/spline (Figure 7-24). When enabled, a small window will appear, giving the option to start the sweep using a profile or a path. By default the option is set to Profile. A profile is the face of geometry (or the closed shape) that will be extended. The path is the polyline/spline that the sweeping geometry will follow. Once the profile and path are selected, an arrow will appear letting you control the length of the sweep. Note that if the polyline/spline is overly complicated, the operation may fail.

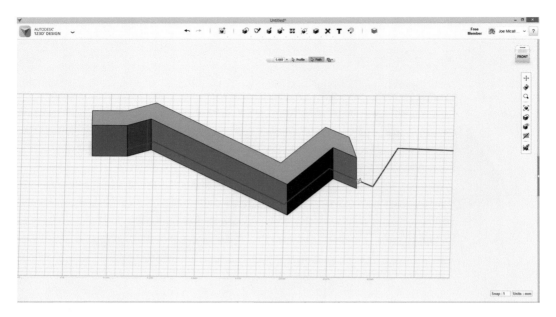

Figure 7-24. *New 3D geometry is generated using the Sweep tool. The polyline determines the flow of the new geometry*

Revolve

Revolve will rotate a closed shape or face around a selected axis (Figure 7-25). When the Revolve tool is selected, a small window will appear asking for a profile and axis. The axis can be the edge of the geometry being revolved or a separate profile polyline.

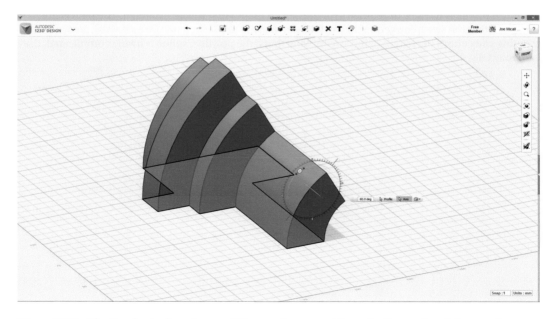

Figure 7-25. *The Revolve tool creates new 3D geometry around the axis of an enclosed shape or face*

The Shell Tool

Beyond the construction tools mentioned, there are many more features in 123D Design that will come in handy. Indeed, with all the functions available, 123D Design deserves its own book to go through all the details. Some of the tools in 123D Design will be easy to grasp (such as text generation), but unfortunately not all the tools can be mentioned here. But there is one more tool worth explaining: the Shell tool. (Also note some additional 123D Design tools not featured previously are featured in the projects discussed at the end of this chapter.)

The Shell tool (Figure 7-26) is a similar to the Hollow tool in Meshmixer, with one exception: the initial face selected by the Shell tool will create an "opening" for the object selected, making the Shell tool a quick way to create open vases and boxes (Figure 7-27).

Figure 7-26. *The Shell tool is found in the Modify submenu*

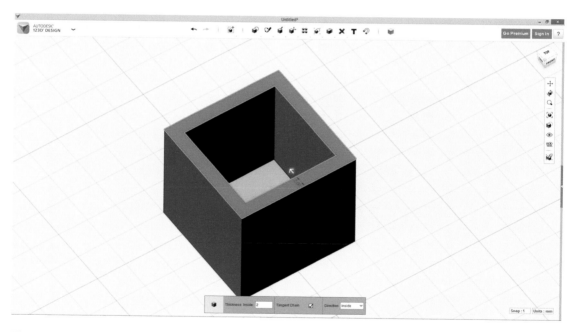

Figure 7-27. *The Shell tool can be used to create a hollow object with an opening on one end*

Projects Using 123D Design

The following sections will delve a bit deeper into 123D Design with several projects that take advantage of 123D Design's solid modeling workflows. The step-by-step examples below will use 123D Design's Polyline, Spline, Loft, Boolean and Extrusion tools to make a desktop organizer, bookshelf, picture frame, funnel, and paper click bookmark.

Creating a Desktop Organizer

In this exercise, you will take advantage of the 123D Design's Shell tool and a number of other common solid-modeling techniques to create a desktop organizer. The process of designing the desktop organizer featured here uses solid modeling techniques that every 3D-print designer should become familiar with. In addition to using the Shell tool, other solid-modeling methods featured in this exercise include using Polylines, the Extrude tool and Booleans to combine and divide objects. Pictured in Figure 7-28 is a 3D printed example of the desktop organizer featured in this step-by-step tutorial.

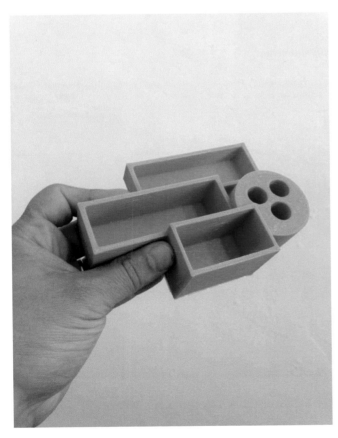

Figure 7-28. Here is a 3D printed example of the desktop organizer featured in the lesson below

BUILDING THE DESKTOP ORGANZIER IN 123D DESIGN, STEP BY STEP

1. Begin by inserting a box primitive into the scene.

2. Use the Pull tool in the Modify menu to grab a side of the box and stretch it out. The keyboard shortcut to access the Pull tool is P. Hover over the right side (in other words, the face) of the box and select that face while it is highlighted in green (a small tooltip will also pop up asking you to "select the face of a solid to pull/press"). Select and drag the arrow icon that appears (which will turn yellow when selected). Drag the face away from the box to turn the box into an elongated rectangle. Click outside of the box or hit Enter to complete the operation.

3. If you want to pull the face of the box a precise distance, you can input the measurements into the small menu next to the Pull tool's arrow icon. For my particular desktop organizer, I want the boxes to serve as business card holders; therefore, in my circumstance, the width of box should be 3.5" wide (or 88.9 mm). Since the initial width of the box is 20 mm, I will pull the side out an additional 75 mm, giving myself plenty of space to create the walls for the box (which will probably be 3 mm wide).

4. Repeat this operation for the back of the box.

5. Duplicate the box three or four times by copying and pasting. The keyboard shortcuts for Copy and Paste are Ctrl/Cmd+C and Ctrl/Cmd+P, respectively. Each time the box is duplicated with Copy and Paste, the Move manipulator will appear allowing you to move and rotate the box. Move each new box away from the initial box. The number and size of each box are totally up to you (you can use Figure 7-29 a guide) but should be influenced by the build volume of the 3D printer being used. In other words, as you build out the base for the desktop organizer, be mindful of the 3D printer you will be outputting to. It's easy to get carried away creating something that exceeds the 3D printer's build size.

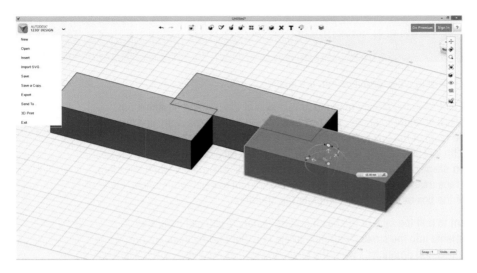

Figure 7-29. *The boxes are duplicated using Copy and Paste (Ctrl/Cmd+C and Ctrl/Cmd+V). Each box will eventually become a compartment for the desktop organizer*

6. Each box in this desktop organizer will act as a compartment to hold business cards, paper clips, and anything else you want to organize. (Ultimately what you want to use the boxes for is up to you.) Again, precise measurements will be required if you want to use these box compartments for something specific (like a business card). Otherwise, duplicate the boxes as you see fit. The key here is to ensure that the boxes overlap slightly since this desktop organizer being created will be printed as a single, complete object.

7. To add some variety to the configuration of rectangles, use the Pull tool to adjust the height of boxes in order to add variation in the design. Pull upward or downward to make the boxes taller or shorter (Figure 7-30).

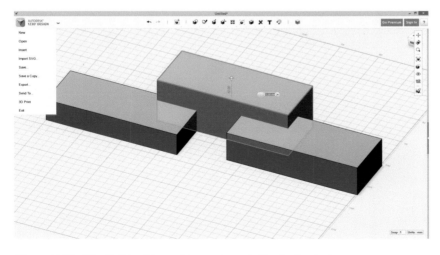

Figure 7-30. *The Pull tool is used to create variation in the design*

8. Use the Shell tool to hollow out the individual boxes (the Shell tool is in the Modify menu), as shown in Figure 7-31. The Shell tool will remove the upper face of the box and extrude the inner sides. Use the J keyboard shortcut to quickly access the Shell tool. Hover over the object you would like to use the Shell tool on (again, a green highlight will surround the box you hover over). A white arrow will appear to allow you to extrude the inner surface inward. For more precision, use the window bar that appears in the lower half of the interface to input an exact measurement. In this example, let's make the shell wall 3 mm. Clicking outside the box or anywhere in the interface completes the operation.

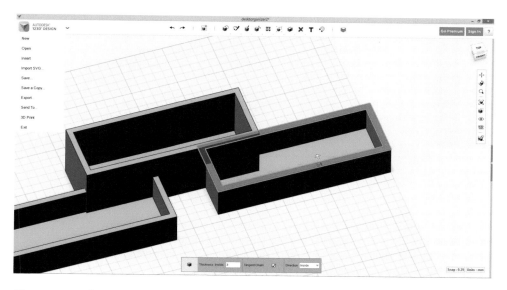

Figure 7-31. *The Shell tool is used to turn the boxes into hollow compartments*

■ **Note** If the Shell tool appears not to be working, it is possible that you forgot to pull inward with the arrow icon selected. If this happens, the Shell tool creates the extrusion inside the box. Since the top of the box appears to be unchanged using the Shell tool a second time will cause an error to occur. If this happens, use the Extrude tool to correct the error. After the Shell tool error appears use the Extrude tool to push the top face of the box downward. Extruding downward will reveal the inner shell and automatically delete the upper face. After you fix the box with the Extrude tool, you can also use the Pull tool (keyboard shortcut P) to pull the inner faces inward to create wider walls for the fixed box.

9. Your series of overlapping boxes may have a couple of overlapping spaces (Figure 7-32) that you may want to get rid of. This will be a good opportunity to use the Subtract tool in the Combine menu to remove the unwanted overlaps.

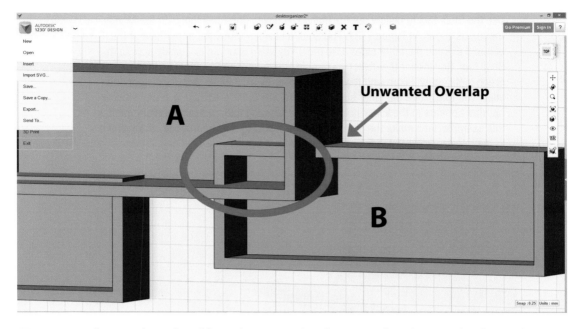

Figure 7-32. *There may be undesirable overlaps in your box design. Use the Subtract tool in the Combine menu to remove any overlaps*

First press Ctrl/Cmd+C to copy the box that will be used to subtract the geometry. Second, press Ctrl/Cmd+V to paste the geometry, effectively creating two duplicates of the box, one on top of each other. You are now ready to use the Subtract tool to remove the unwanted, overlapping geometry.

10. Use the Subtract tool (the keyboard shortcut for the Subtract tool is]) to begin the process of removing the unwanted intersection. When the Subtract tool is selected, a small window will appear with two buttons. The highlighted button on the left will prompt for a target selection, and the button on the right will prompt for a source solid/mesh. The target selection is the part of your box you want to keep, and the source is the part that will be removed. In this instance, you are using the Subtract tool to isolate the intersection; therefore, first click box A in Figure 7-32. That box will now be highlighted blue. Then select box B in Figure 7-32 and hit Return. Box B will have now been used to remove a slice of geometry from Box A, leaving the overlapping geometry as a separate part.

11. Select the overlapping part and hit Delete. The overlapping geometry is now removed, as in Figure 7-33.

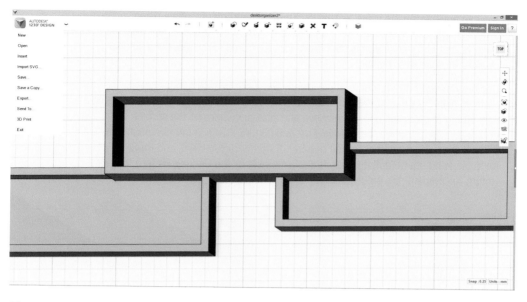

Figure 7-33. *The overlapping part was isolated with the Subtract operation and has been deleted*

12. To add more functionality to this desktop organizer, let's include a pen/pencil holder and incorporate that into the design. You will use a cylinder for the base of the pencil holder and then subtract three smaller cylinders from that base to hold the writing instruments. Therefore, from the Primitive Shape submenu, drag a cylinder to the grid. Give this main cylinder a radius of 25 mm by entering that measurement in the menu bar that appears in the lower portion of the 123D Design interface. Then move the cylinder into position using the Move tool (Figure 7-34).

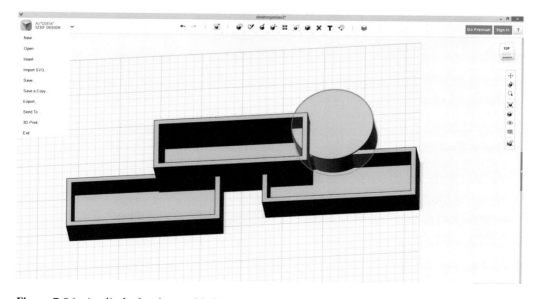

Figure 7-34. *A cylinder has been added to the desktop organizer to serve as a pen/pencil holder*

13. You can now create the holes to hold your writing instruments, again using cylinders. The average diameter of a pencil is 7 mm; therefore, create a new cylinder that is 7 mm wide. Use the Move tool (Ctrl/Cmd+T) to move the smaller cylinder in place over the larger cylinder.

14. Use the Circular Pattern tool to make create two more cylinders in a circular pattern. With the Circular Pattern tool, first select the solid to duplicate, select the axis button in the small pop-up window, and click anywhere on the surface to create an axis to revolve the cylinders around (Figure 7-35). In our circumstance, three is the perfect number for the number of cylinders you want, and three happens to be the default number of duplicates set by the Circular Pattern tool. Hit Return to complete the process.

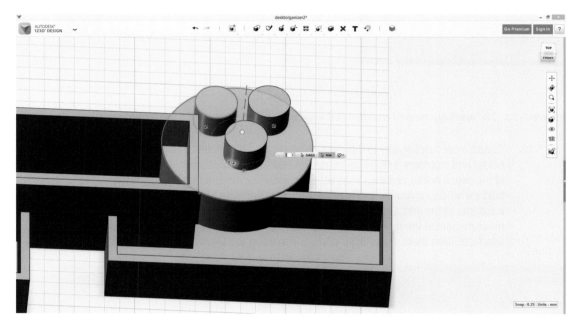

Figure 7-35. *Smaller cylinders have been added to the larger cylinder and arranged using the Circular Pattern tool. The small cylinders will be used to subtract geometry from the larger cylinders*

15. Group the cylinders together. Create a group selection of the smaller cylinders by holding down the Shift key while right-clicking each cylinder. When all three small cylinders are highlighted in green, group them together using the Group function in the Grouping toolbar (or use the keyboard shortcut Ctrl/Cmd+G).

16. Use the Transform tool to roughly center the smaller three cylinders in the larger cylinder. Use the upward-pointing arrow in the Transform tool to raise the three cylinders upward from the main cylinder.

17. To complete the pencil/pen holder for this desktop accessory, use the Subtract function in the Combine menu to create the holes in the larger cylinder. With the Subtract tool activated, first click the main cylinder (the object you will be subtracting from), then click the three smaller cylinders (Shift+click each cylinder), and finally hit Return/Enter to create the holes (Figure 7-36).

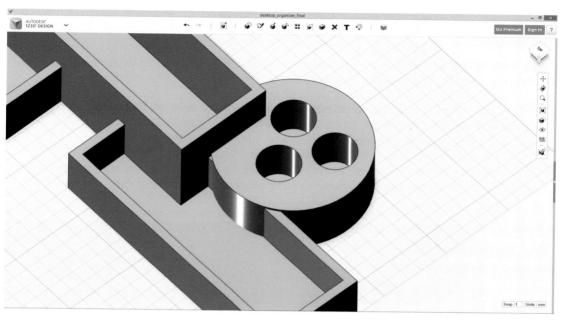

Figure 7-36. *The Subtract tool was used to subtract the geometry of the smaller cylinders from the larger cylinder*

18. To finally clean up the model, look for any more overlapping surfaces that you may want to remove. If it's necessary to remove more overlapping geometry, repeat the process in step 9.

19. Once the model is complete, save the file. You have the option to save the file locally to your hard drive or to your projects folder on the cloud if you are a premium member of Autodesk 123D Design.

20. Finally, to prepare the model for 3D printing, you have the option to send the completed desktop organization directly to Meshmixer. If you create a selection around the model, a small menu bar will appear at the button of the screen. The third from the last button on the menu bar will send the model to Meshmixer (Figure 7-37). (You also can export an .stl file directly from 123D Design's main menu.)

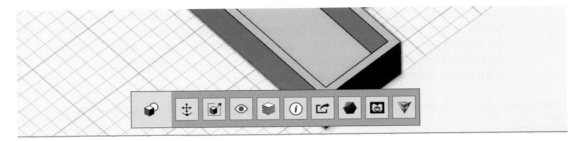

Figure 7-37. *When the whole desktop organizer is selected, a toolbar will appear at the bottom of the screen. The third icon from the left will send the model to Meshmixer to prepare it for 3D printing*

21. Upon clicking the Meshmixer button (if you have Meshmixer installed), the desktop organizer will automatically be imported into Meshmixer (Figure 7-38). When bringing the desktop organizer into Meshmixer, you may notice that you have several separate objects. While this may be OK for 3D printing purposes, it may be best to combine the parts into one solid. If you click the Print button in Meshmixer's Tool menu, you will see that Meshmixer automatically corrects the file as well.

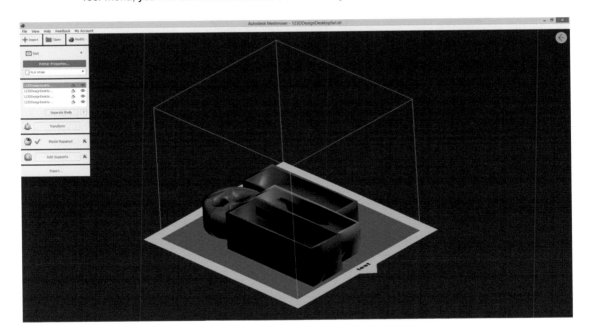

Figure 7-38. *The desktop organizer has been brought into Meshmixer via 123D Design*

22. Since the model has no errors, it is ready to be printed. If you have a 3D printer compatible with Meshmixer, you can send the desktop organizer to that printer via Meshmixer. Otherwise, click Export to create the .stl and then import it into the 3D-printing software of your choice to create the final g-code. In the example in Figure 7-39, the desktop organizer .stl has been brought into Cura to generate the g-code necessary for 3D printing.

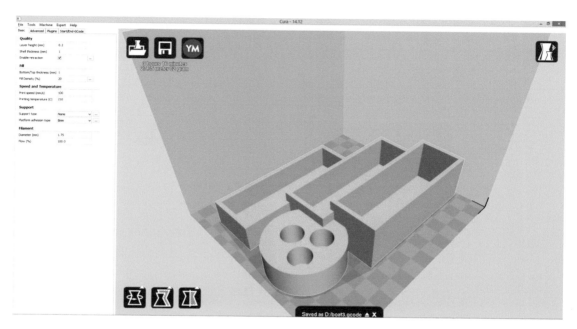

Figure 7-39. *The desktop organizer* .stl *has been brought into Cura to generate the g-code for 3D printing*

Creating a Picture Frame

The following exercise goes through the process of creating a simple picture frame. Figure 7-40 shows an example of completed, 3D-printed frame.

Figure 7-40. *An example of a 3D-printed picture frame designed using solid-modeling techniques*

PICTURE FRAME

1. Start with a box. Drag a box from the Primitive submenu onto the grid (Figure 7-41).

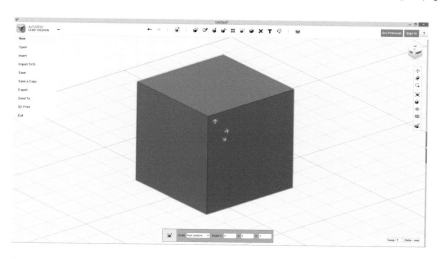

Figure 7-41. *To design the picture frame, begin by dragging a box onto the grid*

2. Scale the box (use the S keyboard shortcut). In the Scale window that appears at the bottom of the screen, change the scale from Uniform to Non-uniform. When the scale is set to Non-uniform, you will notice three arrows appearing around the box. Click and drag the arrows to scale down and flatten them into a flat rectangle, as shown in Figure 7-42.

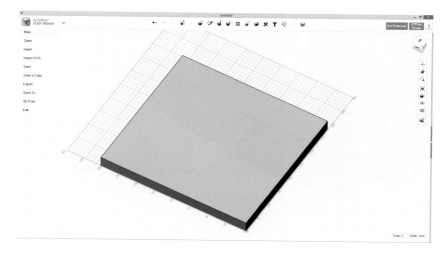

Figure 7-42. *The box should be scaled down into a flat rectangle to create the main structure for the frame*

229

3. To precisely scale the box, use the grid as a guide. Drag to the origin of the grid, with the corner of the box aligned to the corner of the grid (it should snap into place). Make the box 100 mm by 100 mm (Figure 7-43).

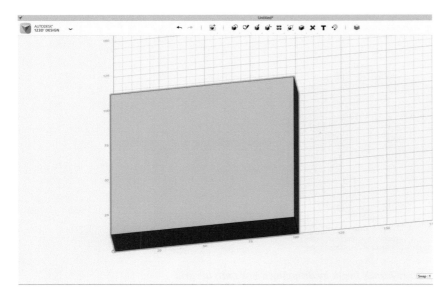

Figure 7-43. *The box should be scaled to 100 mm by 100 mm using the grid as a guide*

4. Cut and paste the initial box to create a duplicate. Scale the duplicate down with the Scale tool (Figure 7-44).

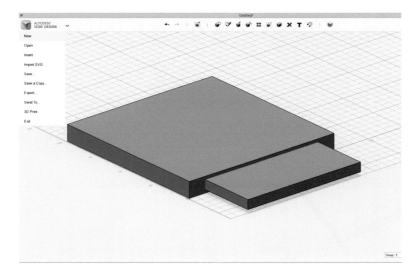

Figure 7-44. *A duplicate of the main box is made and will serve as the frame backing*

5. The dimensions of the smaller box should be half the height of the large box and roughly 20 mm smaller in length and width. Position the duplicated smaller box so one edge aligns flush with the edge of the larger box. The smaller box will be the back panel of the frame (Figure 7-45).

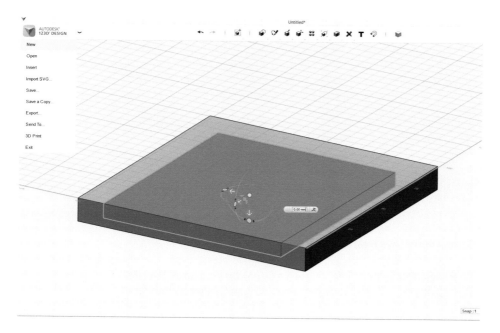

Figure 7-45. *Align the back panel of the frame*

6. Copy and paste the smaller box and then use Combine and Subtract operations to delete the smaller box from the larger box (Figure 7-46). The smaller box that remains will be the backing for the frame. Pull in the side edges slightly using the Pull tool. Pull .1 mm in on the right and left sides of the frame back. Setting the snap tolerances to .1 can help with this operation.

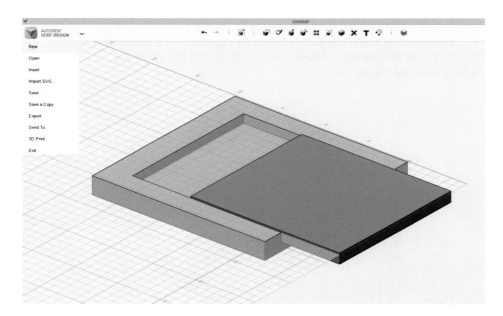

Figure 7-46. *Subtract the frame back from the main frame*

7. To create the opening for the frame, create a new box that is smaller than the small back. Center the box on the larger frame and have it intersect the frame (Figure 7-47).

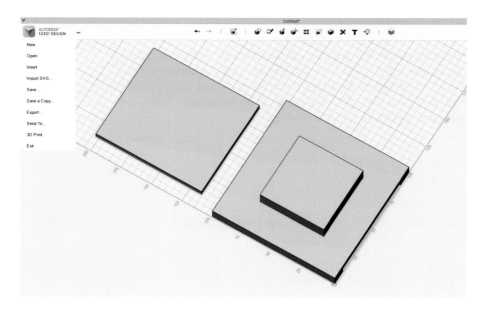

Figure 7-47. *Intersect a box with the main frame*

8. Use another Combine/Subtract operation (Figure 7-48) to create the opening by first selecting the large frame and then select the smaller box with the Subtract tool selected. Hit Enter to complete the operation.

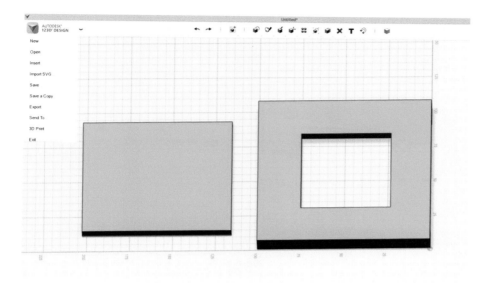

Figure 7-48. *Use a Subtract operation to finalize the frame*

Creating a Funnel

A funnel is incredibly easy to make and is one of the items you may never have to buy again once you master the construction in 123D Design. This exercise demonstrates how to use the 123D Design's Revolve tool, which is a common tool found in most other solid-modeling applications.

FUNNEL

1. Start with a profile curve that will represent the outer edge of the funnel (Figure 7-49). For this, use a polyline a draw the profile of the funnel on the grid.

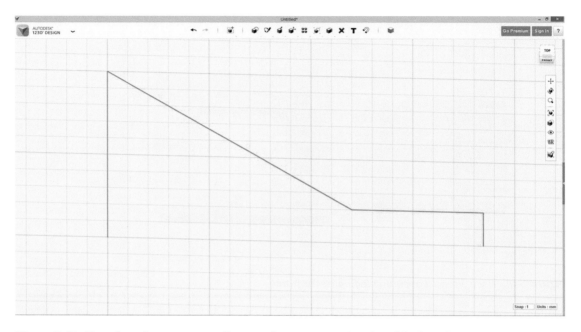

Figure 7-49. *Use a funnel to create a profile curve that represents the edge of the funnel*

2. The funnel profile will have to be an enclosed shape for the revolve to work; therefore, complete the funnel by placing the last point onto the first point where you began drawing the funnel with the Polyline tool (the enclosed shape will be highlighted light blue), as shown in Figure 7-50.

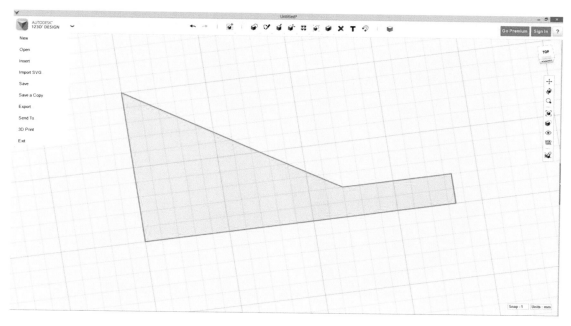

Figure 7-50. *Make sure the funnel profile is fully enclosed*

3. Then use the Revolve tool in the Construct menu bar to create the funnel geometry; in the small pop-up window that appears, you will be asked to select a profile, which can be a 2D shape or face of a solid. After the profile is selected, select the axis you want to revolve around, which in this case will be the longest straight polyline of the profile shape. After the axis is selected, a circular gizmo will appear over the previously selected axis. Grabbing the two arrows on the circular gizmo will allow the Revolve tool to be adjusted manually. For more precision, enter **360** in the small pop-up window that appears next to the Revolve tool to create a full revolve. Hit Enter to complete the revolve operation (Figure 7-51).

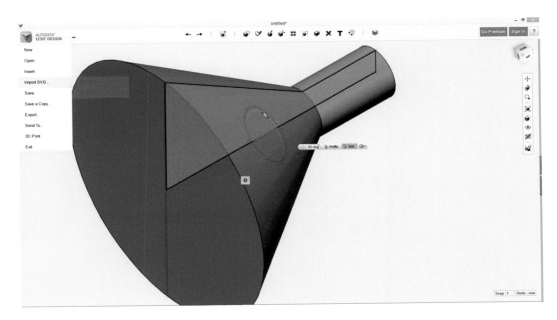

Figure 7-51. *Use Revolve to create the funnel's 3D geometry*

4. Once the funnel is fully revolved, it's time to make it hollow. The easiest way to do this is to use the Shell tool in the Modify menu (keyboard shortcut J). Click the funnel, select the small arrow icon, and pull inward about 4 mm (you can keep track of the distance being pulled inward by noting the number found in the "thickness inside" window that appears at the bottom of the screen when using the Shell tool (see Figure 7-52).

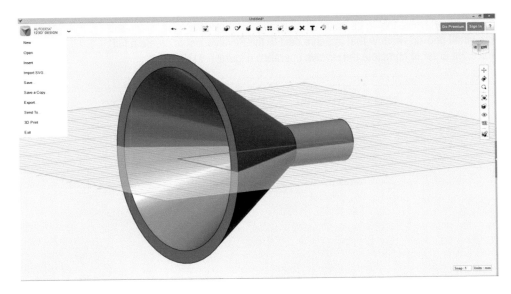

Figure 7-52. *Use the Shell tool to hollow the inside of the solid funnel form*

5. The Shell tool works great, but the end cap of the funnel will still be enclosed. To finalize the funnel use the Pull tool to pull the end of the funnel inward. Pull in far enough until you see the interior circle of the funnel end appear. Hit Enter, and the funnel will be completely hollow on both sides (see Figure 7-53).

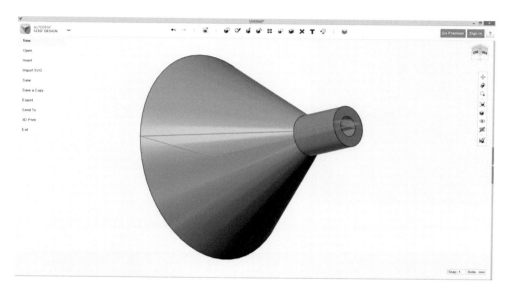

Figure 7-53. *Use the Pull tool on the narrow end of the funnel to ensure that the funnel is hollow at both ends*

Make a Paper Clip Bookmark

This particular bookmark will look somewhat like a giant paper clip. Instead of drawing the curves of the paper clip, you will create hard-edged angles instead and then use the Fillet tool to create the actual curves. Figure 7-54 shows an example of the final bookmark design.

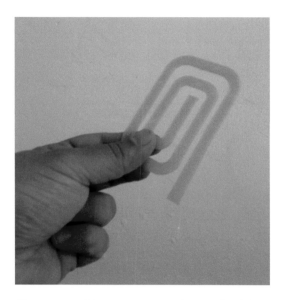

Figure 7-54. *Here is a 3D printed example of the paperclip bookmark that is featured in the lesson below*

BOOKMARK

1. Again start with a profile curve. Use the Polyline tool and Grid Snapping function of the grid to draw a paper clip design that spirals inward (Figure 7-55).

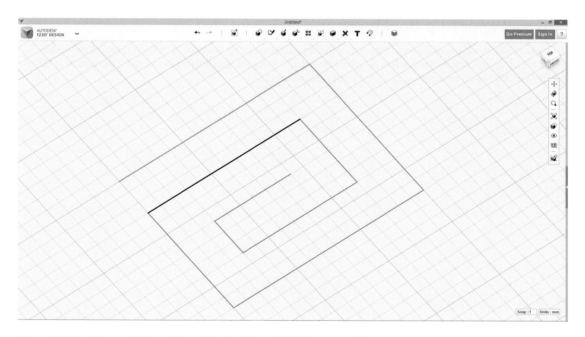

Figure 7-55. *Use a polyline to draw the initial profile of the paper clip*

2. Use the Fillet sketch tool to round the corners of the paper clip bookmark design. With the Fillet sketch tool selected, click the edges of the corner that should be rounded. After clicking the second edge, an approximation of the round corner will appear in red (Figure 7-56).

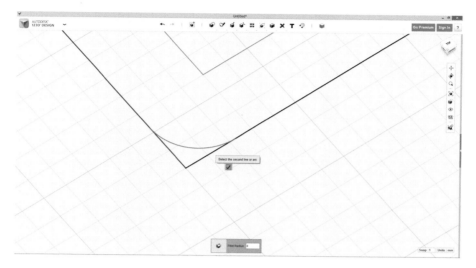

Figure 7-56. Fillet the corners of the paper clip polyline

3. To finalize the shape, use the Offset tool to duplicate the curve. Use the Polyline tool to enclose the ends of the paper clip design to create the final enclosed shape (Figure 7-57).

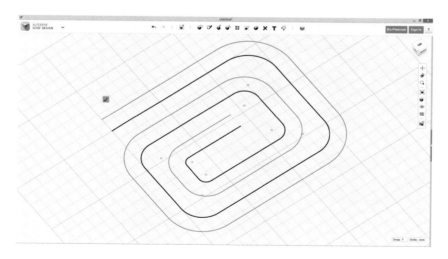

Figure 7-57. Offset the original polyline

4. Close the ends of the paper clip using a polyline, which should result in a closed shape, as shown in Figure 7-58.

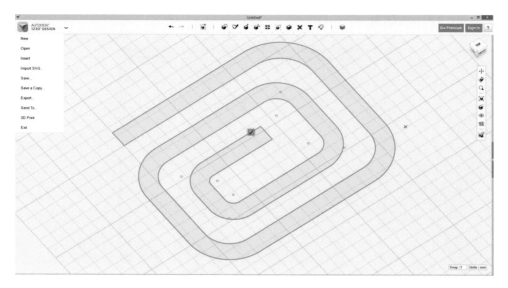

Figure 7-58. *Make sure the paper clip design is a fully enclosed shape*

5. Finalize the design by extruding the paper clip (see Figure 7-59).

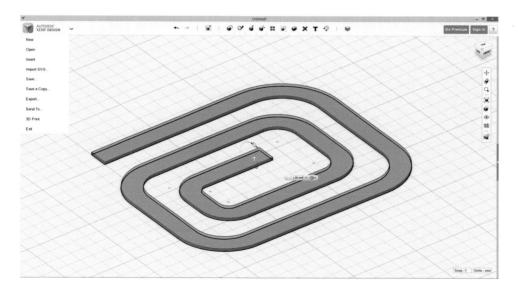

Figure 7-59. *Use the Extrude tool to complete the paper clip bookmark*

Create a Mini-Shelf

Here is quick recipe to create a mini-shelf for displaying your other 3D-printed designs (see Figure 7-60). The exercise shows how extruded objects can be combined to create a complex assembly.

Figure 7-60. *Several 3D-printed mini-shelves on display*

ORNATE MINI SHELF

1. Start by making profile curves for the shelf support and the main shelf. You will need three profiles.

2. The shelf support will consist of two profiles. Draw the first part of shelf profile using a polyline and match the profile, as shown in Figure 7-61.

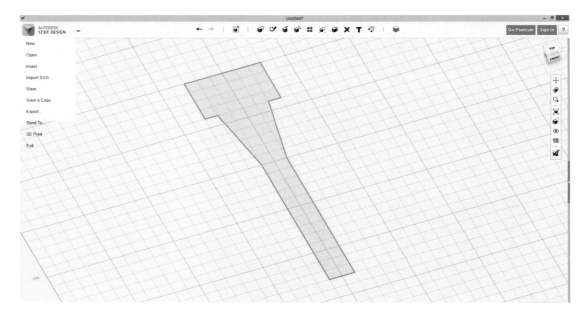

Figure 7-61. *Use a polyline to draw the initial profile for the back of the shelf*

3. The second part of the base will extend from the wall and be the main support for the shelf. Use a polyline to draw that part, as shown in Figure 7-62.

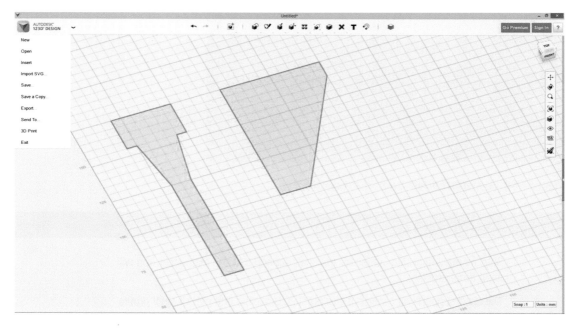

Figure 7-62. *Create another profile of the back support*

4. To draw the shelf, use a spline to create a curvy profile for a more interesting shelf. Create a curvy shape similar to the curve, as shown in Figure 7-63.

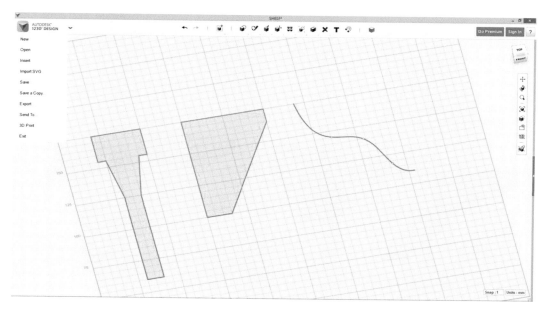

Figure 7-63. *A spline tool is used to draw the main shelf profile*

5. Use the Polyline tool as in Figure 7-64 to make the final enclosed shape.

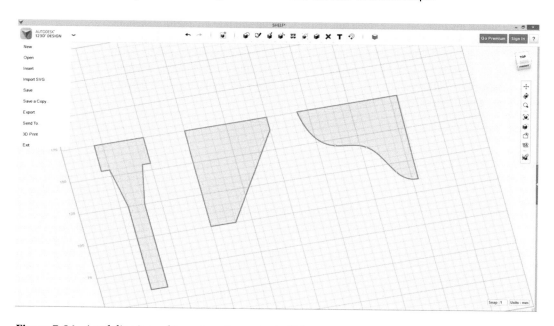

Figure 7-64. *A polyline is used to enclose the main shelf shape*

6. Use the Extrude tool on the three shapes that were made in the previous steps. With the Extrude tool activated, you can extrude all three enclosed shapes at once. Extrude the shapes 5 mm and .hit Return (Figure 7-65).

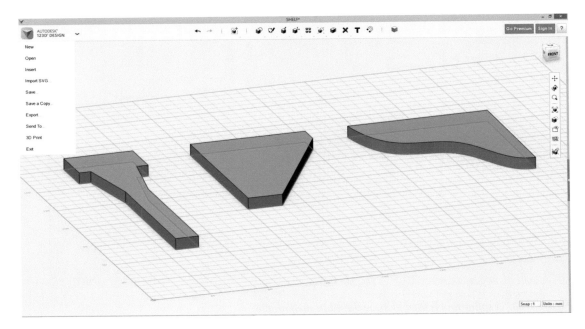

Figure 7-65. *All three parts are extruded*

7. Finalize the main shelf by using the Mirror tool. You can find the Mirror tool in the Pattern menu. With the Mirror tool activated, drag and select the main shelf piece. Then click the Mirror Plane button in the small pop-up menu and select the edge of the shelf to be used for the mirror axis. A red rectangle will appear defining the mirror axis. Hit Enter, and the shelf will be fully mirrored, combining both halves into one single piece (Figure 7-66).

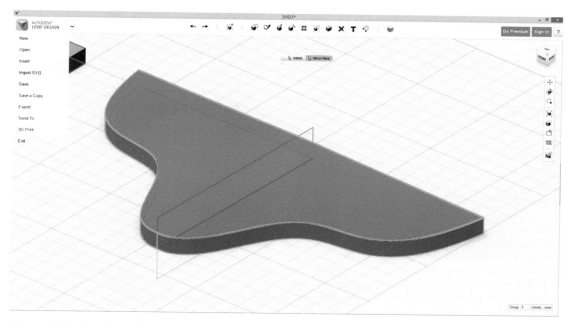

Figure 7-66. *The Mirror function is .used to complete the main shelf*

8. Now you'll finalize the shelf by combining the separate components. To do this, use the Snap tool, which is represented by the magnet icon at the end of the main horizontal toolbar.

9. Start by snapping together the two support pieces. Select the Snap tool (Figure 7-67) and then first click the back edge. of the triangular support. Then click the surface you will be snapping to, which will be the back of the T-shaped support. Hit Enter and then both pieces should combine nicely. Once the two pieces are snapped together, use the Merge function to combine both sections into the final shelf support.

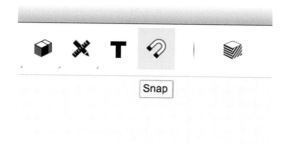

Figure 7-67. *The Snap tool will align and connect. the shelf components*

10. Finally, snap the main shelf to the base support. With the Snap tool selected, click the top face of the base first (the part of the shelf that will mount to the wall), and then click the bottom of the shelf second (Figure 7-68). Hit Enter, and the sections will come together.

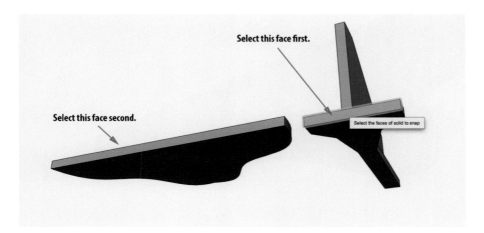

Figure 7-68. *Use the Snap tool to align and fit the base to the shelf. With the Snap tool active, first select the top face of the base then select the bottom face of the shelf*

11. Some minor translations and scaling may be required to align the pieces properly. To adjust the pieces individually they must first be ungrouped using the Ungroup tool (Figure 7-69).

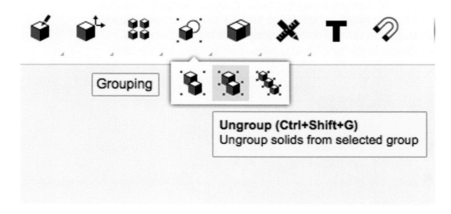

Figure 7-69. *To adjust the pieces individually, the must be ungrouped using the Ungroup tool*

12. Try to look at the shelf from various angles to ensure the pieces are properly assembled. If the shelf looks good, use the Merge function to combine the support with the main shelf, which will finalize the design (Figure 7-70).

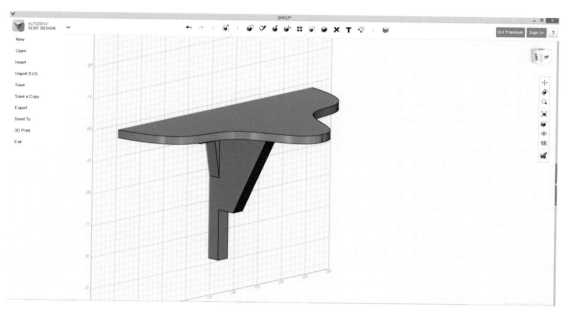

Figure 7-70. *The Merge function .is used to finalize the shelf design*

Summary

In this chapter, you were introduced to 123D Design to gain a broader knowledge of solid-modeling workflows. Provided was a basic understanding of how polylines and splines can be used for profile shapes, allowing for the exploration of a wider range of complex structures. Also presented were methods for turning 2D profiles into 3D designs. The various projects in this chapter demonstrated a number of common solid techniques that will be commonly found in more advanced solid-modeling applications. Being familiar with the methods discussed, which included the Extrude, Revolve, and Loft modeling tools, will allow aspiring 3D-print artists to tackle more complicated solid-modeling projects as they progress in their 3D-printing careers.

CHAPTER 8

■ ■ ■

Organic Modeling Techniques

The previous chapter introduced a variety of solid-modeling techniques that use polylines, extrusions, and predefined primitives in 123D Design. These basic modeling methods allow 3D-print designers to input precise measurements for developing well-engineered 3D models, providing the assurance that the parts being created work exactly as expected. But 3D printing isn't strictly intended for engineered parts. For many artists, the freedom of creation enabled by 3D printing offers the opportunity to manifest visually compelling sculptures, abstract shapes, and free-flowing forms. Using solid-modeling techniques to construct such highly organic forms presents a challenge. When using solid-modeling methods to create complex, flowing, and organic designs (such as an abstract sculpture), every curve has to be strategically placed, point-by-point, and the adherence to such precision can be extremely time-consuming. For many designers and artists, 3D printing offers an opportunity for visual experimentation and the constant use of exact measurements and precisely placed curves are not always necessary.

While artists still use measuring in some capacity, many times organic designs, abstract sculptures, statues, busts, toys, and maquettes are created intuitively with artists "eyeballing" a structure to discover and explore spatial relationships. Artists and designers also rely on a number of tips and tricks, such as using templates and reference imagery, to ensure accuracy in their 3D models, without having to constantly measure every aspect of a design. For artists, constantly having to input measurements can be time-consuming and disruptive to the creative flow.

Artists with sculpting backgrounds, who already have an innate skill in developing multidimensional objects, may prefer to use tools that let them work uninhibited. The software modeling tools of choice for such artists would fall into the category of organic modeling tools (also known as *digital sculpting tools*). Organic modeling tools present users with a digital "ball of clay" that can be stretched, molded and carved into, allowing artists to sculpt and build in a traditional manner that is familiar and intuitive. Organic modeling tools can be useful for engineers to learn as well. An interesting way to use organic sculpting is in combination with more precision-based solid-modeling tools. For example, organic tools can add ornamentation to otherwise normal-looking parts, bringing the Arts and Craft movement into the digital age. But before delving deeper into combining software tools, a brief introduction into organic modeling techniques is required.

Pixologic's ZBrush is popular modeling software that falls into the category of organic 3D-modeling tools. Sculptors, jewelry artists, and entertainment designers venerate ZBrush as a quick and efficient means to create highly detailed geometry. The premise behind ZBrush is similar to other organic, digital sculpting tools. In ZBrush users can sculpt and modify high-resolution geometry using familiar functions such a rake, clay build-up, pinch, and flatten.

Similar digital sculpting software that falls into this category includes Sculptris (which is also owned by Pixologic), SculptGl (which is a web-based app that is similar to Sculptris), Autodesk Meshmixer (which was already covered in previous chapters and will be again touched upon in this chapter but in more detail), Autodesk123D Sculpt, Autodesk Mudbox, and 3D Coat. Blender, Modo, and Maya also provide some sculpting capabilities.

Since the software is free to everyone reading this book, this chapter will first focus on Sculptris and then provide some details on the sculpting tools in Meshmixer. Also discussed will be methods on how to combine software tools, by importing and exporting geometry, primarily from Sculptris to Meshmixer. Importing/exporting geometry is an important skill that every 3D-print designer should become familiar with and will also be touched upon in later chapters.

Organic Modeling with Sculptris

Sculptris is a good place to begin the journey into digital sculpting. Sculptris' bare-bones interface ensures new users won't be overwhelmed with too many tools. Once users feel comfortable with Sculptris, it will be easy to switch to more elaborate sculpting tools such as ZBrush.

Since the main focus of Sculptris is digital sculpting, a "ball of clay" will appear center stage in the Sculptris interface (Figure 8-1) when you open the software. The interface may seem foreign to some users since there is no horizontal menu at the top of the screen and the long vertical toolbar that most designers are familiar with is missing. Instead, users are greeted with a dashboard of icons on the far-left side of the interface. While this may appear strange at first, the intention is to have the designer focus on the sculpting and not get lost in too many menus and interface options.

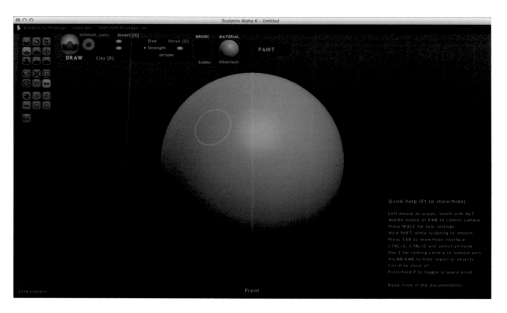

Figure 8-1. *Upon launching, Sculptris designers are greeted with a ball of digital clay. This is where the digital sculpting process begins*

Sculptris: Getting Started

Sculptris is a free application for both Windows and Mac OS that can be downloaded at http://pixologic.com/sculptris/. Sculptris is easy to download and install. There is no need to sign up for an account, and, unlike Tinkercad, Sculptris is not a web-based application (it is not connected to the cloud in any way).

Freeform Design in Sculptris

The challenge with most CAD, precision-based modeling tools is that the solid-modeling design process can be time-consuming. Organic modeling tools such as Sculptris offer immediate satisfaction by allowing designers to pull, stretch, and contort a digital "ball of clay." While initially the process is less precise, the digital ball of clay can be refined to create highly detailed objects. A model being developed using Sculptris' freeform techniques is similar to sculpture created by an artist using clay in the real world. With Sculptris, highly intricate and organic forms can be developed quickly, giving the designer instant satisfaction as the digital model is being developed.

Levels of Detail

Models created in freeform, organic tools such as Sculptris are no different from models found in most other 3D-modeling applications since a 3D model in Sculptris is nothing more than a polygonal object composed of tessellated faces. The main difference is that the faces on a model using a digital sculpting application such as Sculptris can number into the thousands, or even millions. The polygon faces found on a Sculptris model are extremely small, sometimes the size of pixel. Since the polygons are so small, they are imperceptible as the designer manipulates and stretches the Sculptris model to create new forms. Because of the many polygonal faces involved, models in organic sculpting packages such as Sculptris are referred to as *high-resolution* geometry. This high-resolution geometry can be more clearly seen by observing a Sculptris model in wireframe mode.

■ **Note**   Hitting the W key in Sculptris allows users to see the wireframe of the model, which reveals the many triangle faces with greater clarity. This is called *wireframe* mode.

One of the key features that Sculptris, and other organic modeling tools offer, is the ability to change the resolution of a model at any time by increasing or decreasing the number of small polygons that make up the model. The ability to increase or decrease the number of polygons allows an artist to work at different "levels of details" (Figure 8-2). Increasing the number of polygonal faces on the model will allow the designer to sculpt more detail into those areas, provided that they have an increased resolution.

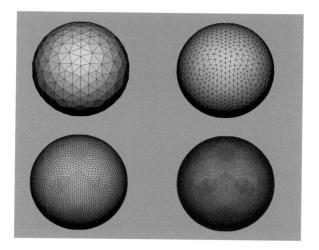

Figure 8-2. *Increasing levels of detail (in other words, resolution) of the digital model in Sculptris. As the number of faceted polygon triangles increases, a greater level of detail can be sculpted into the model*

■ **Note**   The method of increasing the resolution of model is also known as *subdividing* the model.

Most organic modeling applications have the ability to create subdivisions in some capacity and oftentimes will let users subdivide a model repeatedly. Each time a model is subdivided, the number of polygons increases, allowing more detail to be sculpted onto the subdivided surface. Very high-resolution models (in other words, models that have been subdivided multiple times) will be smooth without any noticeable faceting. Models at lower subdivision levels will have less detail and require less computing power, whereas high-resolution models that are composed of millions of tiny polygons may require more computing power and may be more difficult to work with.

Navigation in Sculptris

Clicking and dragging freely allows users to rotate the model they are working on. Pressing Alt/Option while clicking and dragging will pan the view. Pressing Ctrl/Cmd while right-clicking and dragging will allow you to zoom in and out of the scene. The scroll wheel on a three-button mouse will allow zooming in and out as well.

How to Use Sculptris

The workflow for Sculptris is pretty simple. When the application is first opened, centered in the screen will be a spherical, digital ball of clay. In the upper-left corner are the sculpting tools that will let you push, pull, and distort the clay sphere (Figure 8-3).

Figure 8-3. *Here are the icons in the main Sculptris toolbar that, when selected, will allow the designer to sculpt and distort the digital ball of clay*

Try testing some of the various sculpting tools to see how the digital sphere reacts. If this is your first time using digital sculpting, it may take a little time to become comfortable.

EXPERIMENT AND EXPLORE

1. Begin by manipulating the spherical ball with the Draw tool. The Draw tool, if not already selected (selected tools are highlighted in orange), can be accessed by pressing the D keyboard shortcut.

2. Play with several of the sliders in horizontal menu as you draw.

3. Increase or decrease the Size slider to change the area being sculpted (Figure 8-4).

Figure 8-4. *The modifiers in Sculptris' upper horizontal menu allow users to change the settings on the sculpting tool being used. Circled is the setting that will increase or decrease the size of the sculpting tool selected*

4. Increasing or decreasing the Strength slider changes the intensity of the brush (Figure 8-5). Increasing the value affects the amount of surface detail affected and applies a higher level of distortion (depending on the sculpting tool selected) to the digital clay.

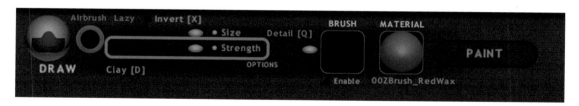

Figure 8-5. *Circled is the Strength slider that increases or decreases the intensity of the tool being used*

5. As you draw, you will first notice that your actions are duplicated on the other side of the sphere. This is because, by default, Symmetry is enabled. If you want to disable Symmetry, turn off the Symmetry button circled in Figure 8-6. When Symmetry is turned on, the button is highlighted in orange.

Figure 8-6. *Circled in the vertical toolbar is the Symmetry button. When Symmetry is turned on (indicated by the button's orange highlight), sculpting on the left side of the model (or vice versa) will create the same results on the opposite side*

6. Another option to pay attention to is the Detail slider in the horizontal toolbar (Figure 8-7). The Detail slider will allow you to add greater levels of subdivision to the areas that are being sculpted. Raising the value increases the level of subdivisions and the amount of detail that can be sculpted onto the surface of the model (Figure 8-8). The Q keyboard shortcut will toggle between low detail (the lowest value in the slider) and high detail (the highest value in the slider).

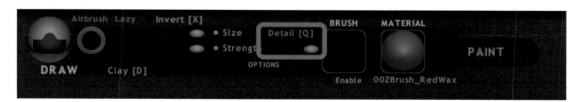

Figure 8-7. *The Detail slider (circled) will increase the number of subdivisions in the model as the model is being sculpted*

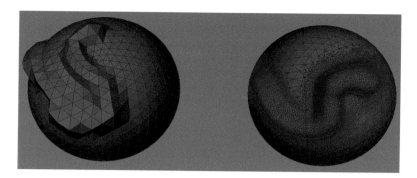

Figure 8-8. *Shown here are the effects of the Detail slider being applied. To the left, the Detail slider is set at its lowest value; therefore, no subdivisions have been applied. At the lowest level, the sculpted surface will appear rough and faceted. To the right, the Detail value has been raised, increasing the subdivisions and the quality of the sculpted form*

7. Experiment with various brushes as you get used to the sculpting process. Adjust the size, strength, and quality as you sculpt. If things get messy, try using the Smooth tool and reduce the complexity of the model (Figure 8-9). You can also activate the functionality of the Smooth tool by using the Shift key as you sculpt (to learn more about the Smooth tool and other sculpting tools, please consult the following section).

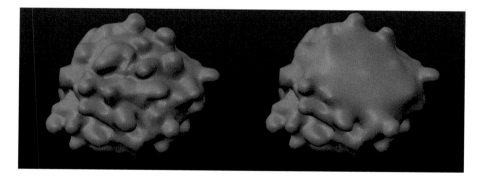

Figure 8-9. *The bumpy model on the left has been smoothed using Sculptris' Smooth tool to create a flattened, less-complete form, as shown in the model to the right*

A Breakdown of the Sculpting Tools in Sculptris

A commonality among digital sculpting software packages is that they have tools that are analogous to real-world sculpting techniques. Here is a breakdown of the common modeling methods in Sculptris. Since Sculptris isn't trying to overwhelm new users with too many tools (there are nine basic sculpting tools in the Sculptris toolbar), new users should have an easy time grasping each tool and its capabilities. Once you have mastered the Scupltris toolkit, you will be better prepared to tackle similar tools in other sculpting packages.

The Crease Tool

The Crease tool makes a sharp indentation into the sculpted surface. The effect is similar to using a sharp stick to draw gouges into clay (Figure 8-10). Inverting the brush (hit the X key or hold down Option/Alt while you sculpt) will create sharp ridges (Figure 8-11).

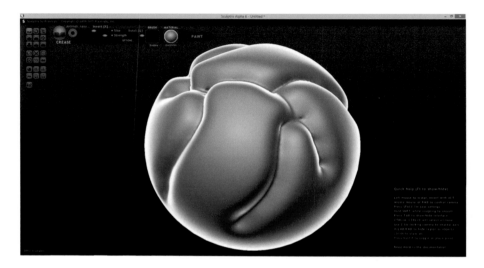

Figure 8-10. *The results of using the Crease tool on the digital ball of clay in Sculptris*

Figure 8-11. *Inverting the Crease brush by hitting the X keyboard shortcut or by sculpting while holding down the Option/Alt key produces sharp ridges*

The Draw Tool

The Draw tool creates a rounded, hill-like extrusion on the surface on the model (Figure 8-12). Selecting Inverse creates a trough-like recess in the surface (Figure 8-13). Using the Clay option creates a flatter plateau on the surface (Figure 8-14). The Soft option helps give the stroke smoother edges.

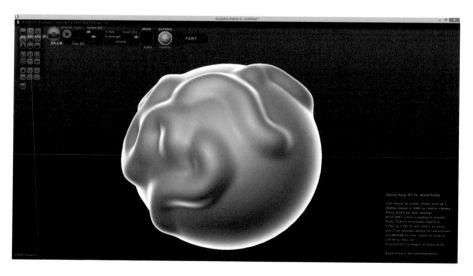

Figure 8-12. *The Draw tool creates hill-like protrusions on the surface of the model*

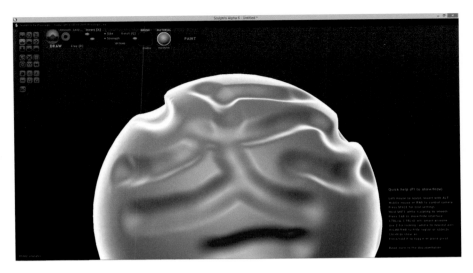

Figure 8-13. *Inverting the Draw tool creates trough-like gouges in the model's surface*

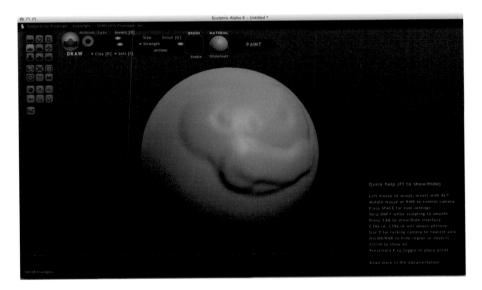

Figure 8-14. *The Draw tool produces flatter surface details with the Clay option activated*

The Flatten Tool

The Flatten tool levels the surface off to a flat plane (Figure 8-15).

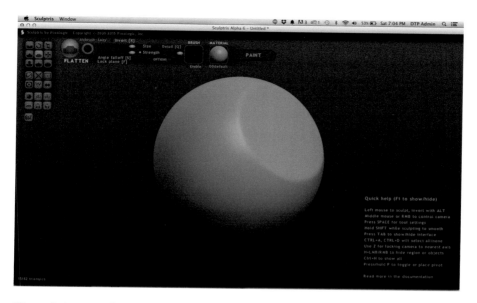

Figure 8-15. *Use Flatten to create flat surfaces on the sculpted model*

The Inflate Tool

Inflate will make an area balloon outward. If the detail is set to the highest setting and Inflate is used multiple times, it's possible to create long tentacles that extend out from the surface (Figure 8-16). Using the Alt/Option keyboard shortcut has the opposite effect, creating hollows and holes in the surface (Figure 8-17).

Figure 8-16. *Inflate causes the surface to balloon outward. Apply it multiple times to create tentacles*

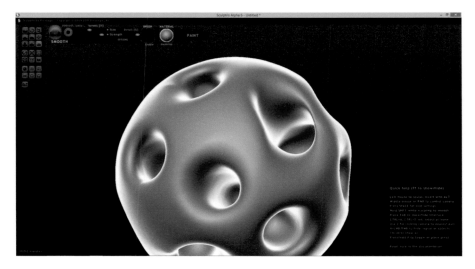

Figure 8-17. *Inverting (hit Alt/Option to invert the Inflate tool as you sculpt) the Inflate tool will create deep holes in the model*

The Pinch Tool

Pinch draws the polygons on the surface to create creases and ridges. Using Pinch is a good way to get hard edges on the surface of the sculpted object (Figure 8-18).

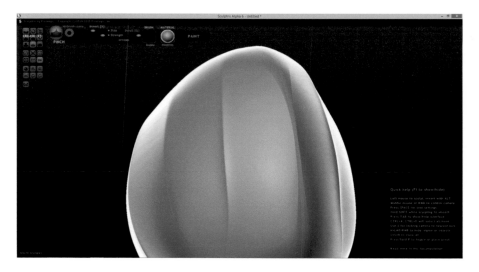

Figure 8-18. *The Pinch tool is used to create hard edges on the model*

The Grab Tool

The Grab tool will push and pull large sections of the model. This is a great way to develop the initial form of a model before more detailed sculpting occurs

The Smooth Tool

The Smooth tool will diminish areas of high detail and bring back the original surfaces.

■ **Note**   Holding the Shift key while sculpting will provide the equivalent functionality of using the Smooth tool.

MAKE A BABY BRONTOSAURUS

Let's put to use more of the tools mentioned earlier by sculpting a baby brontosaurus in this exercise. The steps described here will be useful for developing all sorts of quadruped creature sculpts.

1. For this tutorial, start with the default digital clay ball in Sculptris.

2. You'll begin the sculpting process for the brontosaurus by stretching out the digital ball of clay with the Grab tool. The digital ball of clay will be used to make the brontosaurus body.

3. Use the Grab tool to elongate the sphere to form the body. With the Grab tool selected, turn off the Global option and turn on the Limit option in the Grab tool's parameters. This will let you grab and stretch portions of the sphere, rather than moving the whole sphere. Also, use a large brush size. (Drag the Size slider almost all the way to right. You can also use the] key to increase the brush size.) Pull the front and back of the sphere to elongate it. To give the sphere a beanlike shape (which will be the body of the brontosaurus), push the bottom of the sphere up slightly (Figure 8-19).

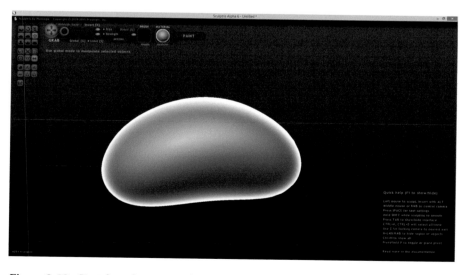

Figure 8-19. *Stretch and compress the digital ball of clay with the Grab tool to make the dinosaur's body. The final form should have a beanlike shape*

4. The next step is to drag out the legs. Again, use the Grab tool, but this time use a smaller-sized brush. Make sure Symmetry is enabled as you sculpt. Having the Symmetry option enabled will apply any sculpting on one side of the mesh to the opposite side of the mesh. Use the Grab tool to stretch out legs for the bronto (Figure 8-20) on the left side of the mesh; you will notice that with Symmetry enabled, the same results will be produced on the right side of the mesh. As you drag down with the Grab tool, you may also notice that the legs get a little pointy, which may be undesirable. To avoid this, instead of dragging down once (which would create the leg in one fell swoop), drag down multiple times in shorter increments. When you drag down the legs, you may also notice some stretching and distortion (Figure 8-21). To remedy this, smooth out the distorted by pressing the Shift key as you sculpt (Figure 8-22). Smoothing as you sculpt is generally a good practice when using digital sculpting tools.

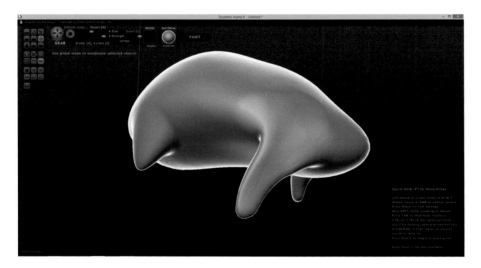

Figure 8-20. *Use the Grab tool to drag out the legs*

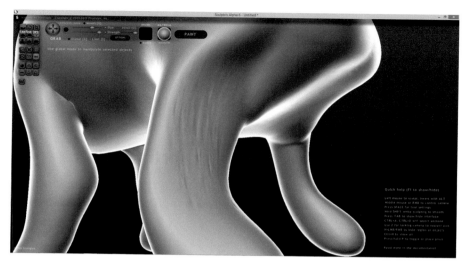

Figure 8-21. *As the legs are pulled, some stretching may occur*

Figure 8-22. *Use Smooth to clean up any stretching*

5. Continue to define the legs by using a combination of tools. Use the Flatten brush to level areas that are too rounded. Use the Grab tool (global turned off) to pull in areas that protrude too far out. If any area feels too pinched, use the Inflate tool to bring back some roundness to the form.

6. Now begin the process of creating feet by using the Inflate brush. Use the Inflate brush to fatten up the ends of the legs (Figure 8-23) and then flatten the bottom of the legs with the Flatten brush (Figure 8-24). When flattening the ends of the legs, work on the model facing down (orbit the scene until the word *bottom* appears in the interface) to ensure the Flatten brush creates a level surface.

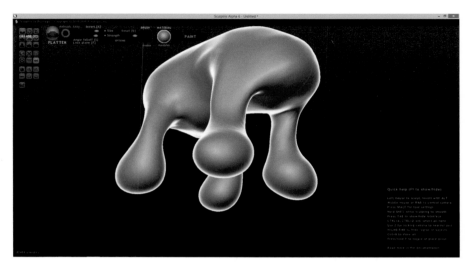

Figure 8-23. *The Inflate tool is used to create the feet*

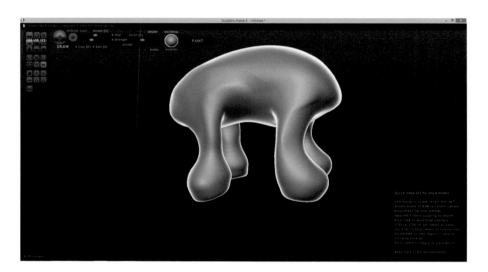

Figure 8-24. *Use the Flatten tool to refine the bottom of the feet*

7. Continue to refine the feet and legs by using some of the other brushes. Use the Grab tool to pull in bulbous areas. Reduce protrusions by using the Flatten and Smooth tools. Also use the Draw tool to add definition.

8. Add creases where the legs meet the body with the Crease tool (Figure 8-25). Also, add creases where the limbs naturally bend. This will add an extra bit of realism to the models.

Figure 8-25. *Refine the legs further with the Crease tool*

9. Pull out the neck and tail with the Grab tool. As you did with the feet, work in smaller increments as you pull the sculpture outward with the Grab tool (Figure 8-26). Each time you grab the surface and pull outward, use the Smooth shortcut (by pressing Shift while sculpting) to smooth out any distortions that may appear on the stretched surface. Since Symmetry is still turned on, be careful not pull in two separate directions. If you pull the neck in two separate directions, you may accidently turn the neck into a "Y" shape. (Figure 8-27). To eliminate any accidental deformation of the neck, work at an angle and observe the neck and tail as you pull and grab the surface.

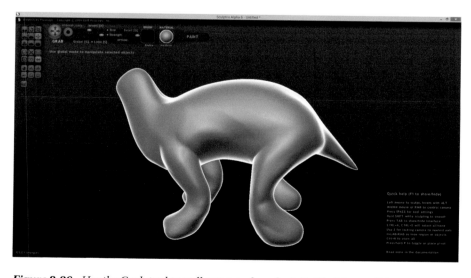

Figure 8-26. *Use the Grab tool to pull out a neck and a tail. Work in small increments*

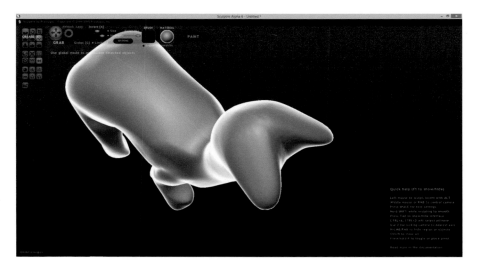

Figure 8-27. *Be careful not to separate the neck into a "Y" shape when pulling out the neck with the Grab tool*

10. To help refine the neck as you pull it outward, try using the Inflate tool as well (Figure 8-28).

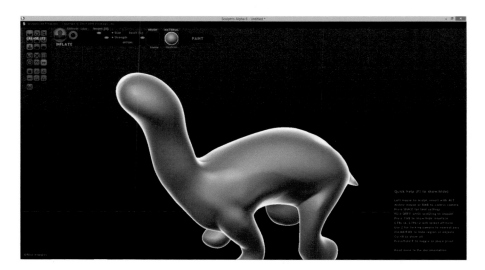

Figure 8-28. *The neck emerges with the help of the Inflate tool*

11. The Inflate tool will also come in handy when creating the dino's head (Figure 8-29). Use it in small increments to build out the head from the neck.

Figure 8-29. *Use the Inflate tool at the end of the neck to create the dino's head*

12. Add more details and begin refining with the Crease tool. Smooth out or flatten areas that appear to be too bulky. Using the Draw tool can help add even more detail (Figure 8-30). Try sculpting details such as the eyes and the folds of skin. Use the X keyboard shortcut with Draw to invert the Draw tool, which will allow for quick indentations such as nostrils.

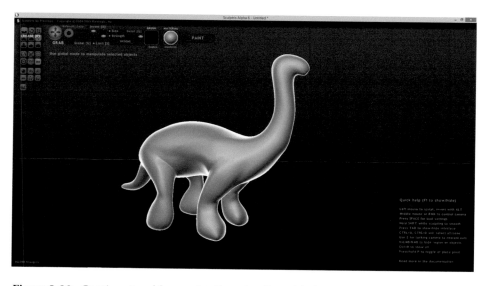

Figure 8-30. *Continue to add more details to the dino with the Crease brush*

13. Continuing sculpting until you feel comfortable with the final product (Figure 8-31). Once you reach a point where you are satisfied, export the dinosaur as an .obj file, and then you can prepare the file for 3D printing using Meshmixer.

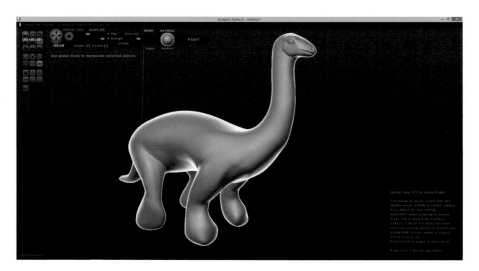

Figure 8-31. *Once the dinosaur is complete, export it as an .obj file*

14. Bring the dinosaur .obj file into Meshmixer. Launch Meshmixer and import the dinosaur .obj file (Figure 8-32).

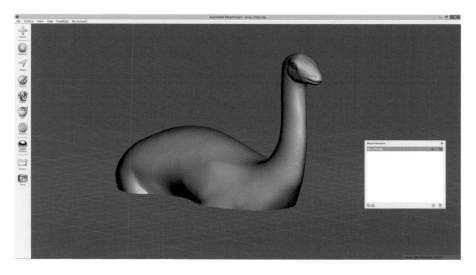

Figure 8-32. *The dinosaur is imported into Meshmixer. Note that the scale of the model will be off and located partially below the ground plane. The Transform tool in Meshmixer's Edit menu will help rectify this*

15. Initially the dino will be tiny (Figure 8-33). Zoom out using Meshmixer's navigation tools to see the size of the dinosaur in proportion to the size of the print bed.

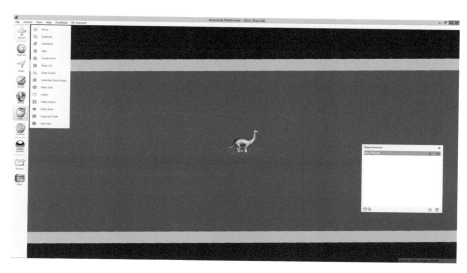

Figure 8-33. *Zoom out using Meshmixer's navigation tools to see the size of the dinosaur in proportion to Meshmixer's print bed*

16. Use Transform (in Meshmixer's Edit menu located in the left-side toolbar) to the move the dinosaur to the surface of the Meshmixer grid. Use the Transform tool to scale up the dinosaur as well (Figure 8-34). Scale the dinosaur up to a reasonable size, but do not go beyond the boundaries of the grid. The scale you determine here will be the final size output to the 3D printer.

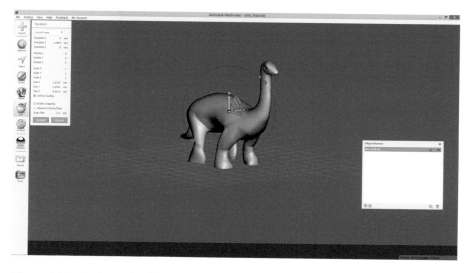

Figure 8-34. *Scale up the dinosaur and move upward in the Y direction (the feet should now be level with the print bed) using the Transform tool in the Edit menu*

17. To ensure that the feet are completely flat and level, use the Plane Cut tool (Figure 8-35) (also in the Edit menu). Lower the Plane Cut plane so it is level with the print bed (it should slightly cut off the bottom of the dino's feet). In the Plane Cut pop-up window that appears, hit Accept.

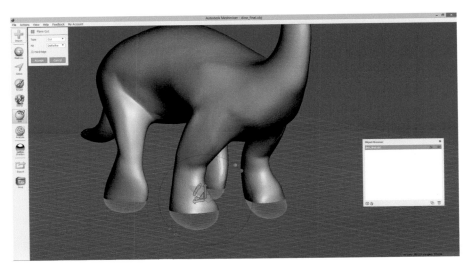

Figure 8-35. Use Meshmixer's Plane Cut tool in the Edit menu to make the dino's feet flush with the print bed

18. In preparation for 3D printing, generate supports for the model. In the Analysis menu, click the Overhangs option. In the Overhangs pop-up window that appears, click Generate Supports and then click Done (Figure 8-36).

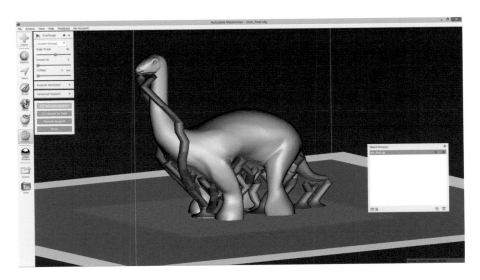

Figure 8-36. Overhangs are generated for the dinosaur using the Overhangs option in the Analysis menu in the side toolbar

19. Export the model as an `.stl` file by hitting Export in the left-side toolbar menu. Then import the `Brontosaur.stl` file into Cura or MatterControl to generate the g-code for 3D printing. Figure 8-37 shows an example of the final 3D-printed brontosaur.

Figure 8-37. *Here is the 3D-printed result from the brontosaurus lesson*

SCULPT A 3D FACE

The simplicity of moving and stretching the digital ball of clay to create arms and legs makes it easy to see the advantages of using digital sculpting for organic forms. To achieve the same results using polylines, extrusions and other solid-modeling techniques would be a quite a challenge. Another type of project that organic sculpting lends itself to is the design of realistic busts, masks, and grotesque faces. Like the dinosaur project, the process used to sculpt a face with Sculptris is fairly simple and opens up opportunities for all sorts of artistic experimentation.

1. Begin with the digital ball of clay and start by making impressions for the eyes. Make sure Symmetry is turned on. Use the Draw brush and sculpt an indentation into the surface with the Alt/Option key pressed down (Figure 8-38).

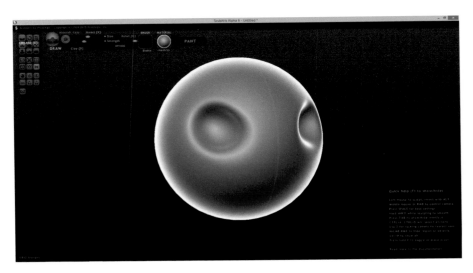

Figure 8-38. *Sculpt an eye into one side of the face with the Draw tool and with Symmetry turned on. Keep Alt/Option pressed down in order to carve into the model*

2. Add a nose with the Draw tool. Use the Shift modifier to smooth out and refine the nose as it is being drawn on the face (Figure 8-39).

Figure 8-39. *Add a nose to the face with the Draw tool*

3. Now add a mouth. Again use the Draw tool in combination with the Alt/Option key pressed to create an indentation. With the eyes and nose already laid out, you will begin to see the face come to life (Figure 8-40).

Figure 8-40. *Add a mouth by using the Draw tool with the Alt/Option keyboard combination*

4. Begin to add more "secondary details" to the face such as lips, nostrils, a chin, cheeks, eye ridges, and a forehead. Continue to use the Draw tool to make slight adjustments. Throughout this stage of adding secondary details, the Draw tool's options can be set to Clay and Soft. This will allow you to build up the details gradually. Details can be gradually developed by lowering the Strength setting as well. For larger areas such as the chin and cheeks, use a larger brush to gradually increase the details on the surface. For smaller areas, such as the forehead and eye ridges, use a smaller brush. For nostrils, use the Alt/Option keyboard shortcut to dig into the surface. As you sculpt, refine the surface by using the Smooth function (hold Shift as you draw to smooth areas). Also, don't be afraid to carve into the surface in some areas to adjust the mass of the face (Figure 8-41).

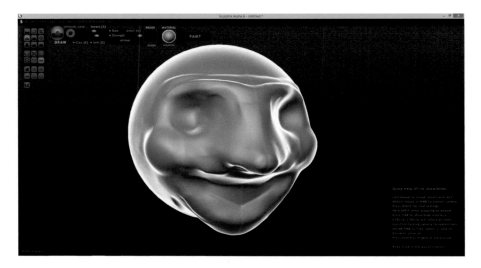

Figure 8-41. *Use the Draw tool to add more details such as lips, nostrils, cheeks, eye ridges, and a forehead*

5. Use the Grab tool with Global turned off to adjust the surface. Keep Strength set low to make gradual adjustments. Push out the forehead and the chin. Push in the sides of the jaw, the back of the head, and the bridge of the nose. Try not to get too extreme since it may heavily distort the face (Figure 8-42).

Figure 8-42. *Use the Grab tool with Global turned off to change the proportions of the face*

6. To push and pull the face with a bit more finesse, trying using both Flatten and Inflate. Smooth out areas that become too pronounced. When using Inflate, keep the settings low; otherwise, you may distort the model when Strength is set too high (Figure 8-43).

Figure 8-43. *When shaping the face, use both the Flatten and Inflate tools to add definition*

7. After adjusting the model with the Grab, Flatten, and Inflate tools, return to the Draw tool to do a final detail pass. Correct any areas that feel off. Also, try to use the Crease brush to add details such as ridges and wrinkles. When using the Crease brush, keep the settings low; a high setting may produce unwanted and overly dramatic results (Figure 8-44).

Figure 8-44. *Add some final definition to the face with the Draw and Crease tools*

8. Once you are satisfied with the face, save it as an .obj file. You will create the other parts of the character in the next lessons and then bring all the parts together into Meshmixer for final 3D printing.

CREATE A BODY

What is a head without a body? Don't worry, the next exercise will give the head a body to rest on. After completing the body, there will be lessons on sculpting the hands and shoes as well. The final lesson in this chapter will bring all the pieces together using Meshmixer to combine the parts and prepare the model for 3D printing.

1. Start with the Sculptris sphere and create a mask for the area on the body where the neck will protrude. Creating a mask allows you to pull out the neck without interfering with body. Use the Ctrl/Cmd key and paint the area on the sphere to define the area where the neck will grow (Figure 8-45).

Figure 8-45. *Using the Ctrl/Cmd keyboard modifier, paint a mask onto the sphere defining the area where the neck will protrude from*

2. The mask protects the model from being modified during sculpting. In this circumstance, to create the neck without affecting the rest of the sphere, the mask needs to be inverted. Invert the selection by clicking anywhere outside the model with Ctrl/Cmd pressed (Figure 8-46).

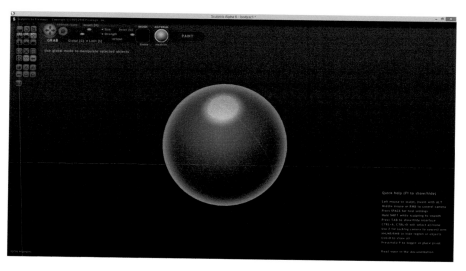

Figure 8-46. *The mask in inverted by clicking outside of the sphere (click anywhere in the Sculptris interface, just not on the sphere) while the Ctrl/Cmd key is pressed down*

■ **Note**   The process called *masking* is a common technique found in most digital sculpting software applications. Throughout this chapter masking will be used to isolate and protect parts of the model being worked on. A mask is usually indicated by a darker color on the surface of the model. A mask protects a digital model. Tools and brushes won't affect the masked portion of a model or functions that change the surface detail on that the model. Masking is a great way to focus only on parts of model that you want to sculpt while protecting the areas that should remain intact. In Sculptris, create a mask by keeping Ctrl/Cmd pressed while painting on the surface of the model.

3.   Once the mask is inverted, the neck can then be pulled up with the Grab tool (Figure 8-47).

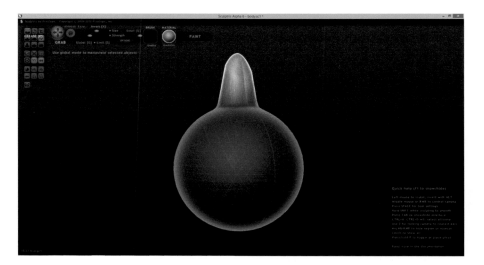

Figure 8-47.   *The neck is pulled up with the Grab tool. Only the unmasked area is affected*

4.   Once the neck has been pulled up with the Grab tool, follow the same procedures as in steps 1 through 3 for the arms. Paint a mask for the arm using the Ctrl/Cmd keyboard modifier (Figure 8-48). Then invert the mask and then pull out the arms with the Grab tool (Figure 8-49). After the arms have been pulled out, delete the mask by Ctrl/Cmd+clicking and dragging outside of the sculpted torso.

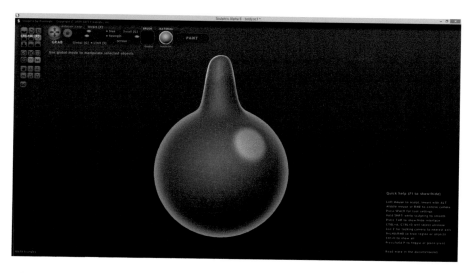

Figure 8-48. *A mask is created for the area where the arm will protrude from*

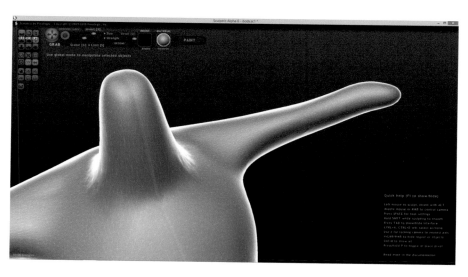

Figure 8-49. *The Grab tool is used to pull out the arm from the main sphere*

5. Use the Draw brush to create musculature for the arms. When using the Draw tool, the strokes applied to the model should be subtle. To get a more subtle effect, turn on the Clay and Soft options. Also keep Strength set to a lower value. This will allow you to build up the detail gradually. Don't be afraid to carve into the model by inverting (use the Alt/Option modifier) the brush to cut away details. Also, add definition to the arms using a combination of Grab, Smooth, and Inflate (Figure 8-50).

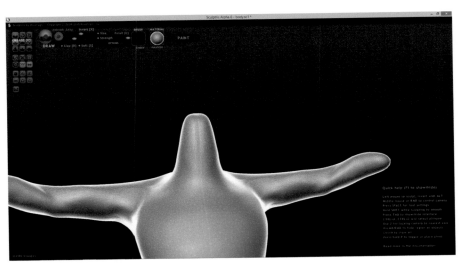

Figure 8-50. *Musculature is sculptured into the arms using the Draw brush with the Clay and Soft options turned on. Inflate, Grab, and Smooth are used to add detail as well*

6. Elongate the torso with the Grab tool. Also, use the Grab tool to push in the back and the chest (Figure 8-51).

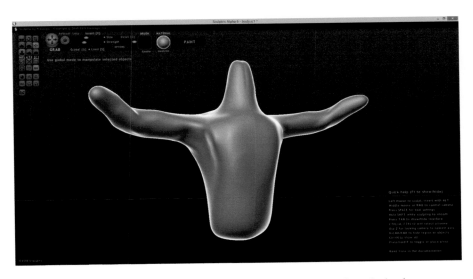

Figure 8-51. *The Grab tool is used to pull down the torso and push in the back*

7. Make the legs with the same process as you did with the arms and neck. First mask out the areas where the legs will protrude from using the Ctrl/Cmd keyboard modifier. Then invert the mask by using Ctrl/Cmd and clicking outside the model (Figure 8-52).

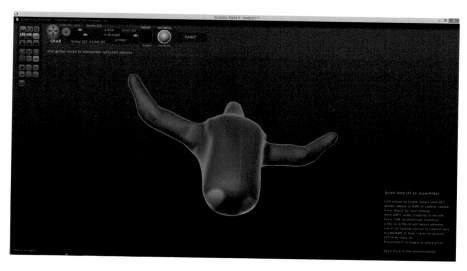

Figure 8-52. *A mask is drawn on the model using the Ctrl/Cmd keyboard shortcut modifier to indicate the placement of the legs. The mask is then inverted using Ctrl/Cmd and clicking outside the model*

8. Once the mask is inverted, pull out the legs with the Grab tool (Figure 8-53).

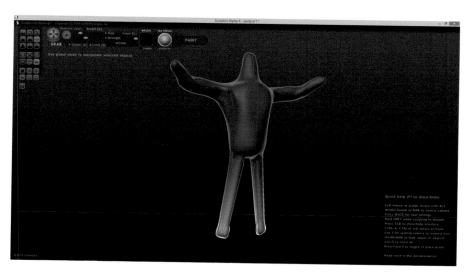

Figure 8-53. *The legs are pulled out with the Grab tool*

9. Define the musculature of the legs by using a combination of Draw, Inflate, Smooth, and Grab. Remember to build up detail slowly be keeping Strength set at a low value (Figure 8-54).

Figure 8-54. *Add definition to the legs using a combination of Grab, Draw, Inflate, and Smooth*

10. When you are happy with the final sculpt of the body, export it as an `.obj` file. You should now have two `.obj` files: a body and a head. Next you will work on the hands and the shoes for this character. In the final steps of this process, you'll be importing the various individual parts (the body, head, hands and shoes) into Meshmixer to combine them into the final body.

MAKE A HAND

1. Begin with a sphere. Use the Flatten brush to flatten the top and bottom of the sphere. Set Size and Strength to the highest level (Figure 8-55).

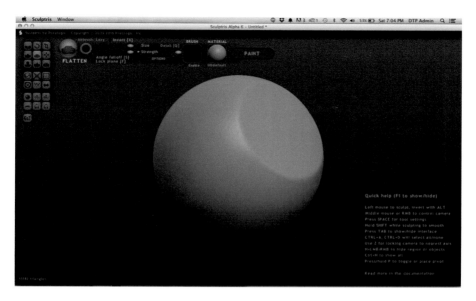

Figure 8-55. *Flatten the top of the Sculptris sphere with the Flatten tool*

2. Scale the hand to flatten it even further using the Scale tool. To effectively flatten the hand using Scale, you must turn off the XYZ modifier (Figure 8-56).

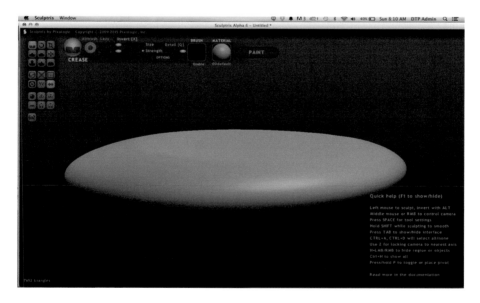

Figure 8-56. *Use the Scale tool to flatten the sphere into the initial hand shape*

3. Use Inflate to create the beginning points of where the fingers will grow from the base of the hand (Figure 8-57).

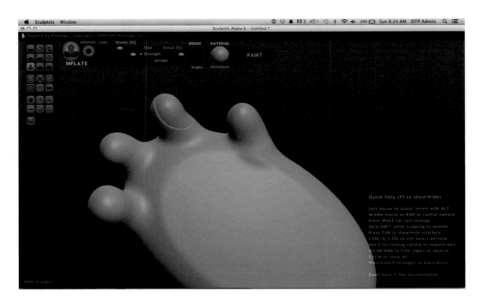

Figure 8-57. *Use the Inflate tool to extend the fingers and thumb from the hand*

4. To create the fingers, you will extend each finger individually using the Grab brush. Since you want to focus only on the thumb, begin by painting a mask over the thumb protrusion, which will be the area you want extend with the Grab tool. After the thumb area is painted in black, inverse the mask by Ctrl/Cmd+clicking outside the hand surface. The thumb area will now appear white with the rest of the surface appearing dark gray (Figure 8-58).

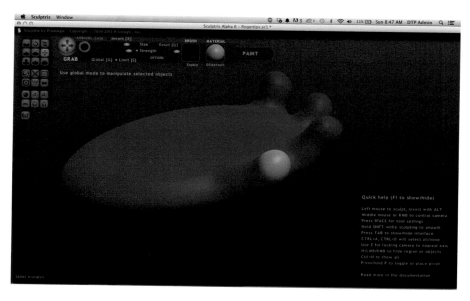

Figure 8-58. *Mask out the tip of the thumb and then inverse the mask*

5. Now you can use the Grab tool to extrude the thumb away from the hand, elongating the thumb without disturbing the rest of the model. When isolating part of the hand using a mask, the Grab tool can remain set to Global, and only the fingertip will move (Figure 8-59) when the Grab tool is used.

Figure 8-59. *Extend the thumb with the Grab tool*

6. Once the thumb is extended, the mask can be deleted, and you can focus on the remaining fingers. To delete the mask, click and drag with the mouse while keeping the Ctrl/Cmd key selected. The model will now be free of the original mask, and you can continue to mask the fingers. Proceed to mask off the fingertips, just as you did in the previous section. This time around, let's mask off all three fingertips simultaneously, as in Figure 8-60.

Figure 8-60. *Further extend the thumb with the Grab tool*

7. Invert the mask (Ctrl/Cmd+click), grab downward with the Grab tool, and set it to Global. When you pull the fingers down with the Grab tool, it may be easier to have the hand facing you, which will allow you to keep the fingers straight as you grab downward (Figure 8-61).

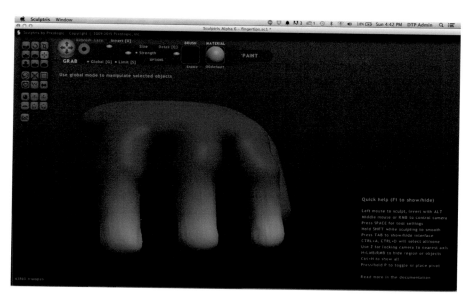

Figure 8-61. *Extend all three fingers simultaneously with the Grab tool*

8. Once the fingers and thumb have been established, begin to refine the hand with the other brush tools. Begin by smoothing out the fingers and thumb by brushing over the model with the Shift key pressed. Then use the Grab tool (with Global turned off) to give the round hand a more handlike shape. Also use the Grab tool to shorten the two outer fingers and the thumb (Figure 8-62).

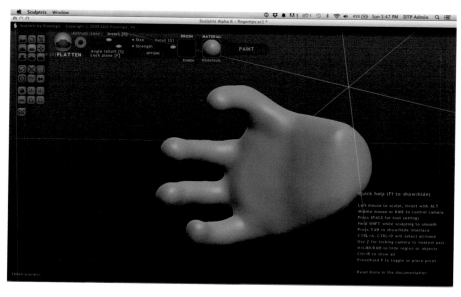

Figure 8-62. *Use the Grab tool to refine the hand and shorten the fingers*

9. Add more definition by using the Inflate tool on the knuckles. Use a low value and gradually apply Inflate to reach a look you feel comfortable with. Also, use the Draw tool to give some indication of bones, again with a low value. Add any definition that you think is necessary. Here you are not striving for a perfect-looking hand; something cartoony will suffice. Once the hand is brought to completion, go ahead an export an `.obj` file.

MAKE A SHOE

This lesson will create a shoe for the cartoony character. Note that this lesson is not meant to create a wearable shoe, but there are a few designers who are creating 3D-printable shoes that you can actually wear.

1. Create a new scene and start with a sphere (Ctrl/Cmd+N).

2. Use the Grab tool to push in the sides of the sphere. Also use the Grab tool to pull out the toe and the heel. The size of the Grab tool should be at its highest setting (Figure 8-63).

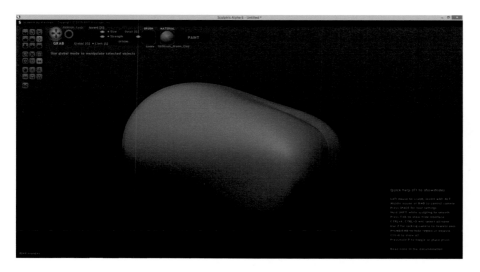

Figure 8-63. *Use the Grab tool to push in the sides of sphere*

3. Smooth the oblong shape by using the Shift key modifier and adjust the proportions of the sphere. The final shape should start to slightly resemble a shoe (Figure 8-64).

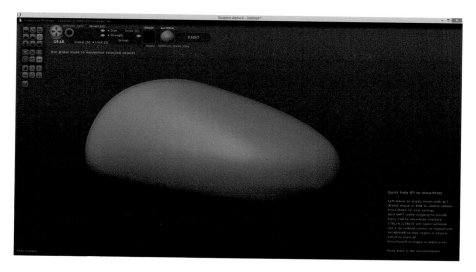

Figure 8-64. *Smooth out the distorted sphere. The shape should start to resemble a shoe*

4. Flatten the bottom of the foot. Again, set the Size setting to a high value (Figure 8-65).

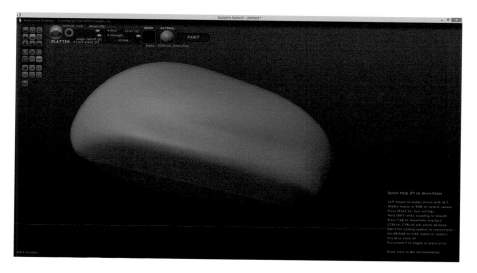

Figure 8-65. *Flatten the bottom of the shoe to create a heel with the Flatten tool*

5. Again use the Smooth modifier to smooth out any distortions caused by the Flatten tool.

6. Use the Grab tool again to develop a more shoelike shape (Figure 8-66).

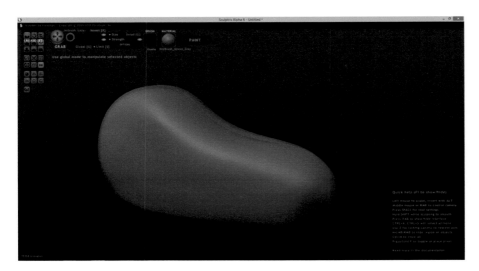

Figure 8-66. *Use the Grab tool to bring more definition to the shoe form*

7. To give a better indication of a heel, use the Draw tool around the lower perimeter of the shoe. Also, you can use the Crease brush to give more definition to the heel (Figure 8-67).

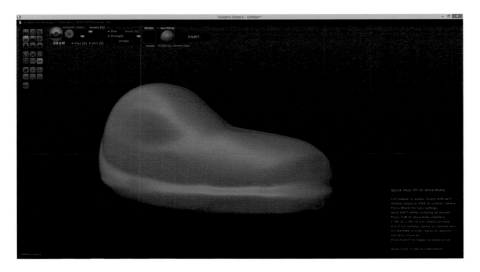

Figure 8-67. *Use the Draw tool to indicate the part of the heel that transitions into the shoe. Use the Crease tool as well to give the heel a bit more definition*

8. Finally, level out the top of the shoe with the Flatten tool (Figure 8-68).

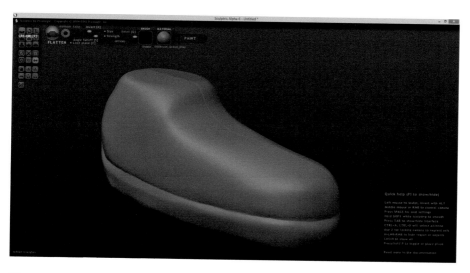

Figure 8-68. *Level off the top of the shoe with the Flatten tool*

9. To finalize the shoe, clean up the geometry a bit with the Smooth tool. Don't worry if it's not perfect at this stage. The final step will be to export it as an `.obj` file.

Combining Parts in Meshmixer

The following exercise will take you through the process of combining the parts you previously developed in Sculptris by taking advantage of the geometry-merging capabilities in Meshmixer. You will go through the process of importing each part into Meshmixer to fuse the various pieces (the body, head, hands, and shoes) together in order to create one complete mesh. You will also utilize some sculpting tools in Meshmixer to clean up the model. Finally, you will take advantage of Meshmixer's 3D-printing capabilities to create supports for the model.

COMBINING OBJECTS IN MESHMIXER

1. First import the body `.obj` file into Meshmixer. Click the large plus sign in the main Meshmixer toolbar to import the model.

2. Scale up the body if necessary using the Transform tool in the Edit section of the main toolbar. The body should fit within Meshmixer's build plate representation (Figure 8-69).

Figure 8-69. *Import and scale up the body.obj file in Meshmixer*

3. Next import `head.obj`. Again, click the plus sign in the main toolbar to import the head. A window may appear asking you to append or replace the imported mesh. Click Append since you are adding the head to the body (Figure 8-70).

Figure 8-70. *When importing another object into a current Meshmixer scene, a window will appear asking you to append or replace. Click the Append button and proceed*

4. The head may be tiny in relationship to the body. If that is the case, another window may appear asking you to scale up the head. Click Yes to scale up the head automatically (Figure 8-71).

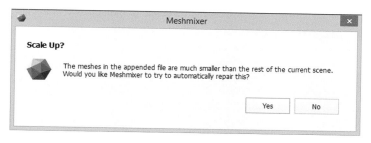

Figure 8-71. *If the model to be imported into the scene is tiny in relationship to the current scene size, a window will appear asking you to scale up the model*

5. When you import the head.obj geometry into Meshmixer, notice it will appear on its own layer in the Object Browser window (Figure 8-72).

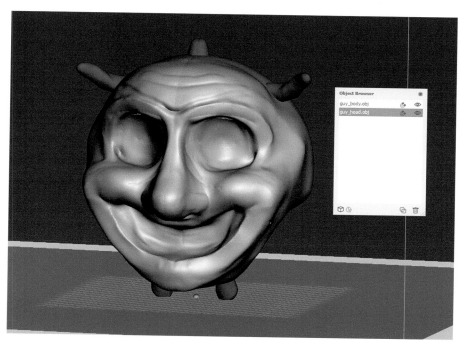

Figure 8-72. *When there are multiple pieces of geometry in a Meshmixer scene, each object will appear on its layer in the Object Browser*

■ **Note**   The Object Browser is Meshmixer's way of keeping track of multiple appended objects in a scene. Users of Meshmixer have the option of merging objects together into one layer or keeping objects on a separate layer to keep projects organized. When geometry is kept on separate layers in the Object Browser, one layer can be accessed at a time (inaccessible objects will be "grayed out" and cannot be edited or manipulated until they are selected in the Object Browser or in the Meshmixer scene).

6. Select the head either directly in the interface or in the Object Browser panel to adjust its size and positive. To scale and move the head, use the Transform function, which is found in the Edit section of Meshmixer's main side toolbar (Figure 8-73).

Figure 8-73. *The head is moved to the top of the body and scaled down using the Transform function in the Edit menu in Meshmixer's main toolbar*

7. Next, import the hand geometry and append it to the scene (Figure 8-74). Follow the same sequence of steps used for the head geometry.

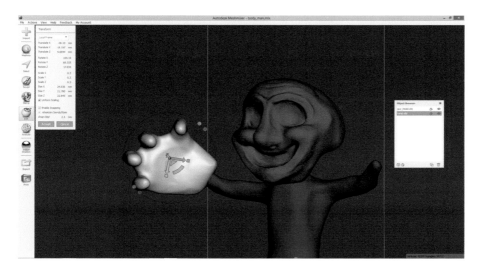

Figure 8-74. *Append the hand geometry into the scene*

8. Adjust the hand geometry, again using the Transform function in the Edit menu. Make sure that hand.obj is selected in the Object Browser (Figure 8-75).

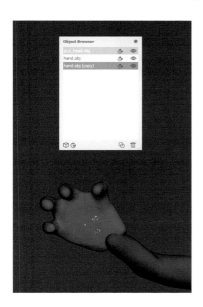

Figure 8-75. *The hand.obj geometry is selected in the Object Browser*

9. Rotate and scale the hand into position with the Transform control manipulator.

10. Input directly into the Transform dialog pop-up if necessary.

11. Hit Accept when you are satisfied with the scale and position of the hand.

12. Now mirror the hand in order to duplicate it to the opposite side of the character's body. If you have trouble seeing the mirrored hand, click the purple arrow that is displayed as part of the Mirror tool's control manipulator. Hit Accept once the hand has been mirrored (Figure 8-76).

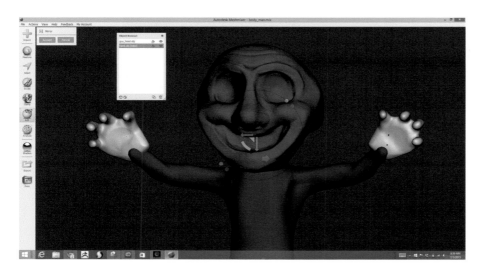

Figure 8-76. *The Mirror function is used to mirror the hand*

13. Import the shoe and follow the same mirroring procedure as you did for the hand.

14. Scale the shoe and put it in position with the Transform tool. If you have challenges using the Transform control manipulator, you can numerically input values into the Transform dialog box.

15. When positioning the shoes, Meshmixer's print bed representation may block out the view, making it difficult to properly place the shoe. To make things easier, turn off Show Print Bed in the View menu.

16. Once the shoe is in position again, use the Mirror tool to reflect a duplicate to the opposite side of the body (Figure 8-77).

Figure 8-77. *The shoe is duplicated to the opposite of the body using the Mirror function*

17. Let's make a base for the character using primitive shapes found in Meshmixer's
     Meshmix menu. A base will ensure the character stands upright without falling over.
     Drag the cylinder from the Meshmix menu onto the grid.

18. Scale the cylinder down in the Y direction by grabbing the green square located on
     the Transform manipulator and dragging downward (Figure 8-78).

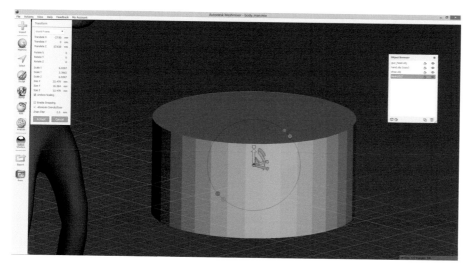

Figure 8-78. *A cylinder is dragged from the Meshmix menu and scaled down in the Y direction*

19. Use the Transform control manipulator to drag the cylinder into position beneath the shoes (Figure 8-79). The placement doesn't have to be perfect at this stage, but do make sure that the cylinder and shoes slightly intersect. In a later step, you will use Meshmixer's Align function to ensure that the base is properly aligned.

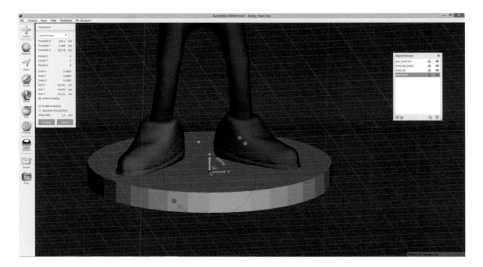

Figure 8-79. *The flattened cylinder is placed beneath the shoes of the character*

20. Merge the remaining body parts by using Combine (the Combine option becomes available in the pop-up in the upper-left corner of the interface when multiple parts are selected in the Object Browser). In Meshmixer's Object Browser window Ctrl/Cmd+select the head, hand, and shoe and then select the Combine option in the pop-pop window. After the parts are combined, there should be two objects left in the Object Browser, the main body and the base, as shown in Figure 8-80.

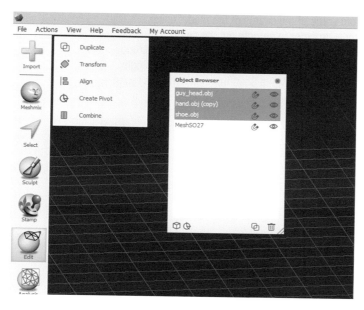

Figure 8-80. *The separate elements (head, hand, and shoe) are selected in the Object Browser and then merged using the Combine function*

21. Although the parts are combined, they are still separate pieces and can be selected individually if necessary. You will notice that when the combined geometry is selected in the Object Browser, each individual piece is represented in a different color when selected. The colored geometry is used to help group the pieces, making each piece easier to select with the Select tool (Figure 8-81). This is a great way to isolate parts of a model, but having separate pieces can be problematic in areas where pieces touch since the seams will be noticeable.

Figure 8-81. *When merged, the pieces that make up the model are still considered to be separate objects and are color coded for easy selecting*

22. At this stage you can smooth out some of the seams of the model using Meshmixer's set of sculpting tools. In order to smooth out the seams correctly you will need to ensure that the model is one single piece rather than a group of combined parts like it is now. To merge the separate pieces into one single, seamless model, you can use Meshmixer's Make Solid function, which is found in the Edit menu (Figure 8-82).

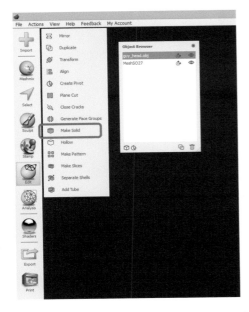

Figure 8-82. *To make one completely merged object, use the Make Solid function*

23. With the model selected in the Object Browser, use Make Solid to merge the parts. The Make Solid procedure will run, and the individual parts will be fused together. Initially the fused model will appear to be faceted and of poor quality (Figure 8-83). Raising Solid Accuracy and Mesh Density in the Make Solid pop-up window will help deliver smoother results.

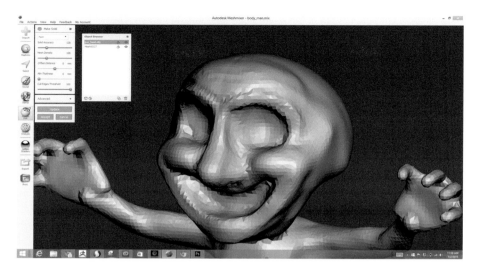

Figure 8-83. *Increase the Solid Accuracy and Mesh Density values in the Make Solid pop-up window if the character appears overly faceted*

24. Raise the value of Solid Accuracy to 430 and the value of Mesh Density to 320 and then click Update (Figure 8-84). The Make Solid procedure will run again and deliver much better results.

Figure 8-84. *Increasing the Solid Accuracy and Mesh Density values improves the resolution of the character*

25. Once you are pleased with the results of the Make Solid function, hit Accept. The model will now be merged as one seamless object. You will notice that in the Object Browser the original model is retained (Figure 8-85).

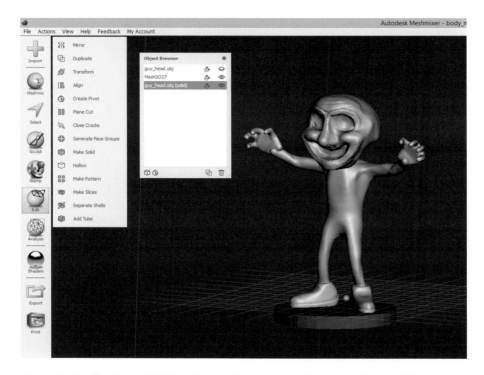

Figure 8-85. *The Make Solid function retains the original version of the model*

26. Next align the base with the main character. Select both the character and the base in the Object Browser. In the resulting pop-up window, select Align (Figure 8-86).

Figure 8-86. *Use the Align function to line up the base and the character mesh*

27. In the resulting Align pop-up window, select Base Point for the Source and World Origin/Y-up for the destination (Figure 8-87). The character and base will now be flush and aligned to the ground plane grid Meshmixer.

Figure 8-87. *The Align function will ensure that the character is flush with the ground plane*

28. With the base and character aligned, let's combine the two using Combine. Follow the same procedure as mentioned in step 23. Select the character and the base parts in the Object Browser and then select Combine.

29. Again, use Make Solid to turn the whole sculpture into one single mesh. Use the process as outlined in step 26. Make sure the model is selected in the Object Browser and then select Make Solid in the Edit menu located in the vertical toolbar. Keep Solid Accuracy at 320, set Mesh Density to 400, and click Accept.

30. Let's add some eyeballs to add a finishing touch. In the Meshmix menu in the vertical toolbar, select a sphere (Figure 8-88) and drag it to the eye cavity. Adjust the size and location by selecting icons that appear on the sphere. These small icons will appear on any Meshmix object that is dragged from the Meshmix menu and into the scene. The small white globe will allow you to adjust the position, and the triangle arrow (it looks like a house) adjusts the scale (Figure 8-89). The icons will be highlighted in blue when selected. First scale the eyeball down using the arrow icon and then use the globe icon to move it into position. You can also adjust the Scale value in the Drop Solid menu that appears when a Meshmix object is dragged into the scene.

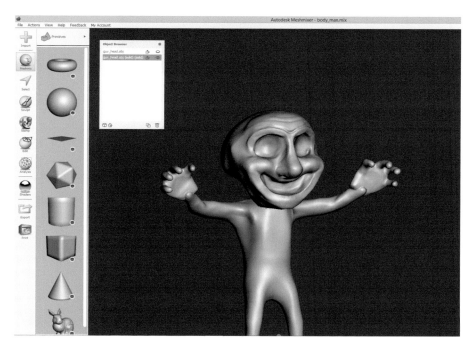

Figure 8-88. *Drag a sphere from the Meshmix menu into the scene to create eyeballs for the character*

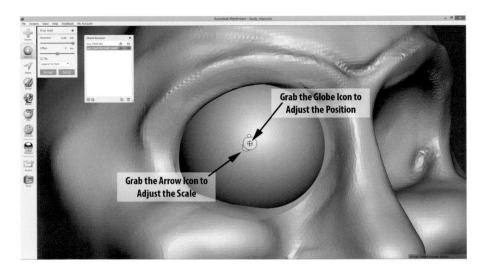

Figure 8-89. *A transform controller appears in the center of the placed sphere. The central globe controls the sphere's position. The house-shaped arrow icon controls the scale*

31. In the Drop Solid pop-up window, hit Accept to finalize the placement of the sphere, but before you do, select Create New Object (Figure 8-90) in the Drop Solid drop-down menu. This will ensure that the sphere remains a separate object from the main character model. You want to keep the sphere separate in order to mirror it and create the second eyeball on the right side of the face.

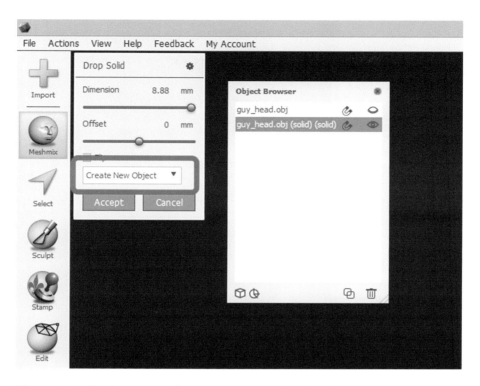

Figure 8-90. *The Create New Object option ensures that the sphere will be a separate object and placed on a separate layer in the Object Browser*

32. Now mirror the eyeball. Select Dropped Part in the Object Browser. Then, in the Edit menu in the vertical toolbar, select Mirror. Remember, if you don't see the mirrored copy, click the blue arrow. Once the eyeball is mirrored, hit Accept.

33. Once again use Combine and Make Solid on the individual parts. Select the eyes and main body in the Object Browser and then select Combine in the pop-up menu. Then select Make Solid in the Edit menu. Again, use a value of 320 in Solid Accuracy and 400 in Mesh Density. In the Make Solid pop-up window, hit Update and then hit Accept.

34. To finalize the model, let's use some of the sculpting tools in Meshmixer to fix some areas that may feel a little off. The sculpting brushes in Meshmixer are similar to the brushes in Sculptris (Figure 8-91). In Meshmixer you have Drag (which is similar to the Sculptris Grab tool), Inflate, Pinch, Flatten, and Smooth. You will also notice a toggle that will allow you to alternate between volume and surface brushes. Both volume and surface brushes operate the same way. Volume brushes build up more detail, and surface brushes tend to be subtler. For now, use the Bubble Smooth brush in the volume category and paint over seams in the hands, eyes, and neck. Make sure Symmetry is turned on as you do this. If you want to scale the Smooth brush up or down, you can use the square bracket keys. [will scale the brush down, and] will scale the brush up.

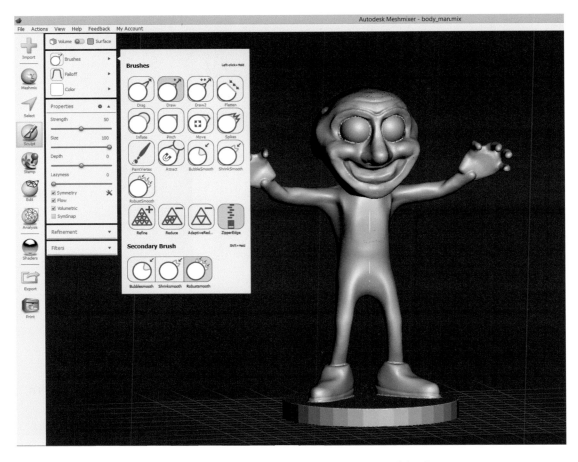

Figure 8-91. *Using the sculpting tools in Meshmixer to clean up the seams of the character*

35. To finalize the character and get it ready for 3D printing, turn the Show Printer Bed option back on in the View menu and then run the Overhang function in the Analysis menu to create supports. In the Overhangs pop-up window that appears, click Generate Supports (Figure 8-92). Note that the support generation process may take a few minutes.

Figure 8-92. *Click Generate Support in the Overhangs menu to generate supports for the character*

36.   Once supports are generated, the character will be ready for 3D printing. Either print directly from Meshmixer (if you have a 3D printer set up to work with Meshmixer) or export an `.stl` file for Cura or MatterControl to generate g-code. Figure 8-93 shows two 3D-printed versions of the character. Some modifications were made on the smaller character, such as thickening the arms and legs, to ensure printability.

Figure 8-93. *Here the character printed at two separate sizes. The smaller character was modified slightly (the arms and legs were thickened) to make the character more durable*

Summary

The various exercises presented here, using Sculptris and Meshmixer, represent a small sampling of what is possible using digital sculpting tools. Based on the lessons provided, designers should have no problem exploring Sculptris, Meshmixer, and other digital sculpting tools in greater detail. Having some digital sculpting experience will allow artists, designers, and engineers to take their 3D-printing projects to a whole new level, allowing for the development of any form imagined. Once designers have mastered Sculptris, they should be comfortable using other sculpting tools such ZBrush. Regardless of the sculpting tool used, having some familiarity with digital sculpting will also allow for the customization of both artistic and engineered 3D-printable designs. Quick customization on a project-to-project basis using digital sculpting techniques is what separates 3D printing from other manufacturing workflows and will be explored in more detail in the next chapter.

∎∎∎

CHAPTER 9

Customization Techniques

Mass customization is one of the big advantages that 3D printing provides over other types of manufacturing technologies. Because the 3D-printing production pipeline is tightly integrated with 3D-modeling software, each file that is sent to a 3D printer can be modified or customized by using a variety of software-based customization tools. This chapter will explore a few of those techniques that will allow for unique variations in every 3D-printed product that you design.

Customization can be enabled in the 3D-printing process in a number of ways. One way to add customized details is with digital sculpting. The freedom to sculpt and craft unique features into otherwise ordinary objects can result in an interesting array of 3D-printed products. By providing added appeal to 3D designs, digital sculpting increases the value of common engineered objects, and clients will appreciate the personal touch and additional attention given.

Adding digital sculpting details to a design is just one of the many forms of customization being integrated into the 3D-printing process. Other types of customization include algorithmic tools and randomization methods that can make changes to a 3D model using a custom-designed interface. Kit bashing is another technique being used, allowing for objects to be combined in unique ways, where two completely different objects are merged seamlessly using a tool such as Meshmixer. In addition, logos and text can be used to customize 3D prints to allow for personal marketing experiences.

This chapter will explore some of these many methods of customization, building upon your knowledge of Tinkercad, 123D Design, Sculptris, and Meshmixer. In this chapter, you will let Meshmixer combine elements for you so you can create a range of customized solutions.

Adding Variation

To begin the customization process, let's return to the head sculpture project in the previous chapter to explore variations that can be quickly developed using Sculptris. With the knowledge gained of the digital sculpting process, try to explore variations by stretching, distorting, smoothing, and adding new details to the initial sculpture. If desired, start from scratch and use your sculpting knowledge to create an entirely new design. Explore different emotional states, add animalistic features, or make something completely alien (Figure 9-1).

Figure 9-1. *With the sculpting knowledge you gained in the previous chapter, come up with several new sculpted heads*

As you explore adding variation in a design using digital sculpting, here are some additional sculpting tips to help you in the creative process:

- If you are developing a new design, use the Grab brush to create a rough form for your shape.

- Sometimes it helps to draw directly on the model and map out the areas to sculpt. Use the Crease tool to draw the areas you want to sculpt.

- Don't distort the model too extremely in the beginning stages. Draw at the lowest settings and build up detail gradually.

- Smooth it out if things get messy. Reduce the resolution as well if necessary.

Each new sculpted head should be seen as a part or asset that can be combined with the preexisting model from Chapter 8. It's easy to see how the sculpting tools in Sculptris help quickly modify and make new designs and how those new designs can add variety to a preexisting model (Figure 9-2).

Figure 9-2. *The sculpted heads add variety to a preexisting model*

When creating sculpted parts to add variation to a model, it's a good idea to keep polygon counts as low as possible, which can be especially challenging when creating parts that are highly detailed. Small impressions on a scuplted surface such as wrinkles, pores, fine embossings, thin lines and intricate textures are possible due to the millions of polygons being used, but such high-level details can increase the model's file size. The millions of tiny polygons on a digitally sculpted object are similar to pixels used in Photoshop document. Similar to adding pixels to a Photoshop document, adding more polygons to a digital scupture can increase the detail but it will increase the file size of the model as well. Keeping the polygon counts at a manageable level is important, especially if the sculpted parts are going to added and combined with another model. For example, the sculpted head in Figure 9-3 has more than 20,000,000 polygons, making the size of the file around 75MB. Alone, as a single model, this would be fine but if the head was added onto another object (let say the head is added to a body of some sort) then adding 20 million polygons would result in an extremely large file.

As you sculpt it is good to be aware of the total polygon count of a model. If the polygon count becomes unreasonably high, the software application being used will become very slow, or even potentially crash. In Sculptris the polygon count is listed in the lower-left corner of the screen (Figure 9-3). In Meshmixer, you can find the polygon count of an imported file in the lower-right corner of the screen (Figure 9-4). If the file size of a model or part to be used in model becomes unreasonably high it can be optimized in Meshmixer using the steps in the section that follows.

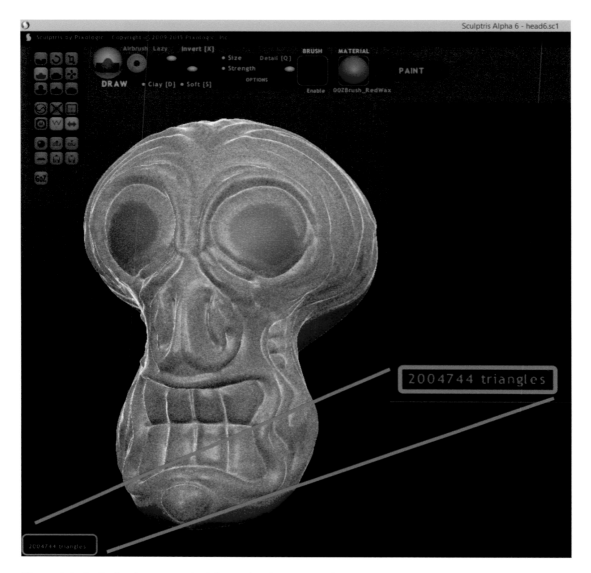

Figure 9-3. *In Sculptris, you can find the total polygon count (in other words, the number of triangles that make up the model) in the lower-left corner of the interface*

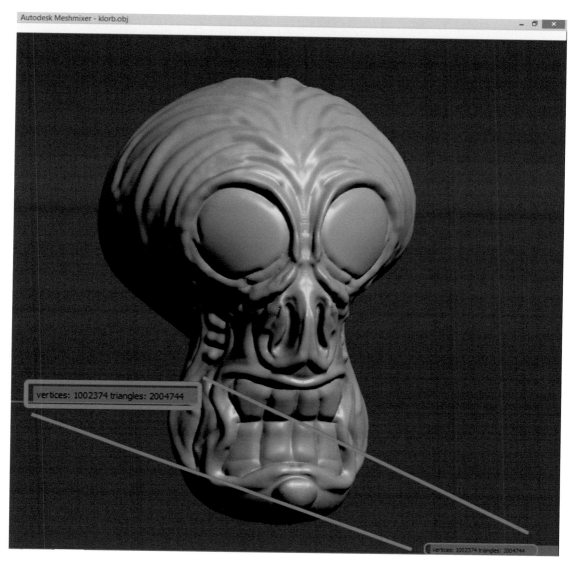

Figure 9-4. *In Meshmixer, you find the polygon count in the lower-right corner of the interface*

Optimizing High-Resolution Files in Meshmixer

While the high number of polygons is what makes the act of digital sculpting possible, there may be areas of the model where the dense number of polygons is not necessary. Meshmixer can be useful in optimizing these high-resolution files, which is helpful for keeping file sizes at a manageable level; this is important as you build up models using customized parts (and is something that service bureaus will appreciate).

USE THE REDUCE OPTION IN MESHMIXER

1. Import the file into Meshmixer.

2. Click the Select tool (it's the third icon from the top) in the toolbar and double-click the model to select it. When selected, the model will be highlighted in brown.

3. Then, in the Edit pop-up window, select Reduce (Figure 9-5).

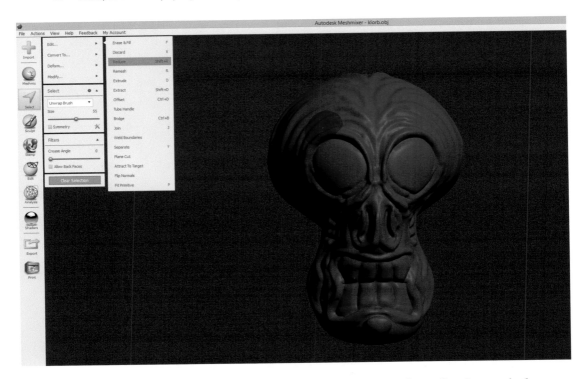

Figure 9-5. *In Meshmixer, use the Reduce function to globally reduce the resolution (in other words, the number of polygons) of a model. Reduce is found in the Edit menu, which is located in the pop-up window when the Select icon is activated in Meshmixer's main toolbar*

4. Using the Reduce option, use a value in the range of 50 to 80 percent to reduce the polygon count accordingly (Figure 9-6).

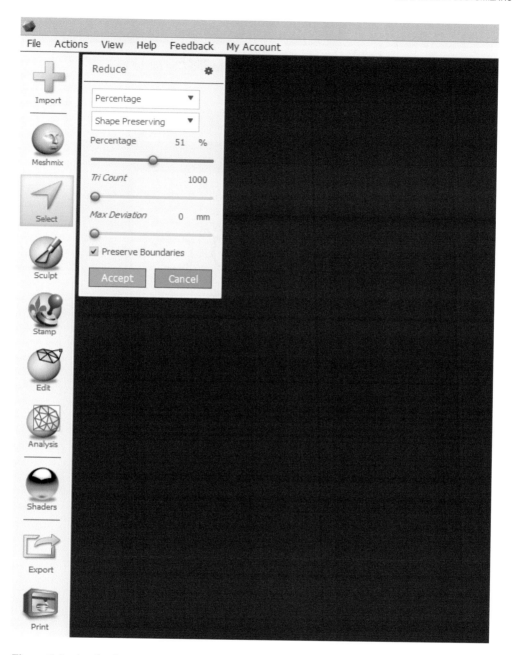

Figure 9-6. *A value between 50 and 80 percent will reduce the triangle count (in other words, the model's resolution) without significantly impacting the detail of the model*

USE THE REDUCE BRUSH IN MESHMIXER TO OPTIMIZE SELECTIVELY

1. Another option is to use the Reduce brush and selectively paint on the model the areas to be reduced (Figure 9-7).

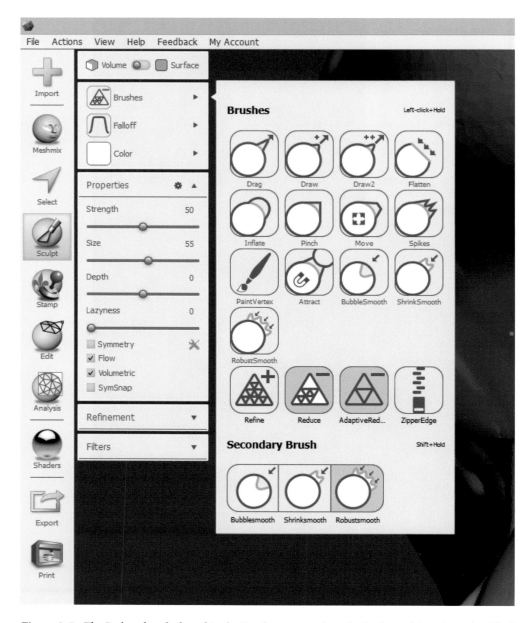

Figure 9-7. *The Reduce brush, found in the Brushes menu when the Sculpt tool is activated, will allow you to selectively reduce areas of model*

2. It's best to reduce in areas of low detail and in areas that are not easily noticeable, such as the base or back of an object.

USE MAKE SOLID TO ADJUST THE POLYGON COUNT IN MESHMIXER

The Make Solid function will also globally reduce the resolution of the model. If set too low, the Make Solid function will reduce the resolution significantly, which will produce faceting that will degrade the quality of the model. Set the value to around 400 for best results.

Combining Hard-Edge and Organic Modeling Techniques

VASEHEADS AND BOXHEADS

With a library of sculpted heads at your disposal, think of all the fun things you can create. This exercise pays homage to ornamental architecture and the work of Antoni Gaudi by integrating organic sculpted forms with the hard-edge shapes developed using the solid-modeling techniques of 123D Design.

For this project you can use the head created in Chapter 8, or you can use another head sculpt that you've created on your own. This lesson won't go through the process of sculpting the head since you should be familiar with that process by now. The main point of this lesson is to emphasize the process of combining different workflows from distinct applications. Here you are combining solid modeling with organic modeling techniques.

1. The assumption is you have already sculpted a head of some sort. If not, quickly create something or use the model from the previous chapter. Save that for now because you will input it into Meshmixer after you create the main vase in 123D Design. The sculpted face is one asset for this project, which will be combined with other assets (such as a cylinder that will be used for a Boolean Subtract operation and the vase itself) to create the final project.

2. In 123D select a cylinder and drag it onto the canvas. Don't adjust it in any way. Leave it at its default settings (Figure 9-8).

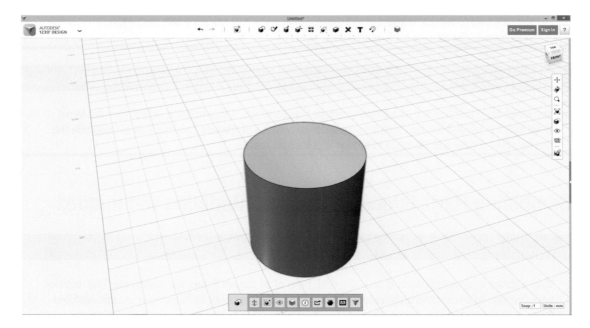

Figure 9-8. In 123D Design, create the vase using a cylinder. Drag a cylinder from the top menu bar in 123D Design onto the grid

3. In the menu bar at the bottom of the 123D Design interface, click the Meshmixer icon and send the cylinder directly to Meshmixer (Figure 9-9).

Figure 9-9. Click the Meshmixer icon in the bottom menu bar to immediately send the cylinder to Meshmixer. You will use the cylinder to "cut out" the back of the sculpted head to ensure it fits nicely around the vase

4. This initial cylinder shape that you sent to Meshmixer will be used for a Boolean Subtract operation that will ensure that the head sculpt can be fitted to the vase properly. From this point forward, you will import the remaining pieces using export in 123D Design and import in Meshmixer (if you click the Meshmixer icon again, it will open another version of Meshmixer, which can make things confusing).

5. Back in 123D Design use the Shell tool to create the vase. Select the cylinder and drag inward to create a hollowed vase (Figure 9-10).

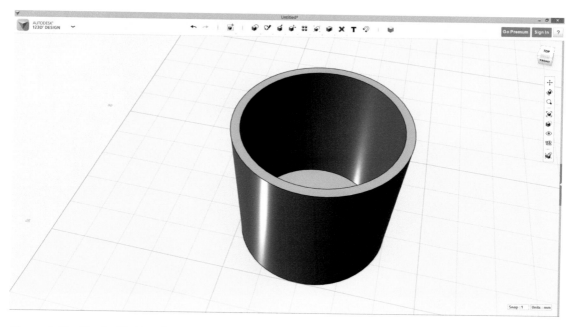

Figure 9-10. *Use the Shell tool in 123D Design to create a quick vase*

6. Export the vase as an .stl file.

7. Return to Meshmixer and begin to import your other assets for the assembly: the sculpted head and the hollow vase.

8. If you are asked to scale up your models, hit Yes (Figure 9-11).

Figure 9-11. *When a new model asset is imported into Meshmixer, it may be too small in relationship to other objects already in the scene. If so, Meshmixer may ask you to scale up your model. Hit Yes and then all the models will be scaled in proportion to one another*

9. If you imported an asset but it isn't appearing in the scene, it may be hidden by another object. To make sure everything has properly imported, review the list of objects that appear in the Object Browser. There should be three objects in the Object Browser (Figure 9-12).

■ **Note**   *Assets*, *objects*, and *subassemblies* are common terms for "parts" that make up a digital model. Each modeling package will use its own terms, and each term is synonymous. When designing a more intricate project, composed of many parts, the individual parts can be referred to as *assets*, *objects*, or *subassemblies*. When these parts are combined, the model is referred to as an *assembly*.

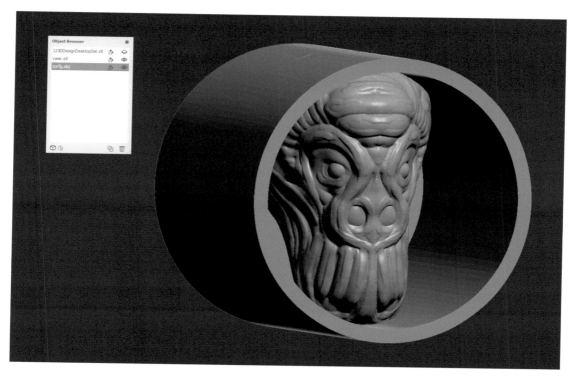

Figure 9-12. *Every model that is imported into Meshmixer will appear as a separate object in the Object Browser. If you cannot find an imported model in a scene, explore the Object Browser to ensure that the model was imported properly. Clicking the eyeball icon will turn off the visibility of objects, which will help you find an imported model that is hidden by a model on top of it*

10. You will notice the positions of the objects in the scene may be off. Use Edit and Transform to rotate the vase and cylinder upright. You will need to rotate the vase and cylinder -90 degrees. Then select the sculpted head in the Object Browser and move it to the outside of the vase/cylinder. You may want to scale it up a bit as well (Figure 9-13).

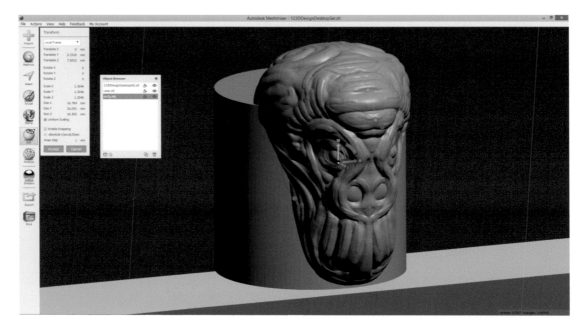

Figure 9-13. *Use the Transform tool to adjust the objects imported into Meshmixer*

Next, use the cylinder that was initially created in a Boolean Subtract operation to cut away the inside of the imported head model. This will ensure that your vase is completely hollow without the head sculpture getting in the way. To effectively cut away the whole backside of the head model, the cylinder will need to be a little bit taller.

11. To lengthen the cylinder's height, use the Extrude tool, which is in the Edit portion of the Select menu. To properly extrude the model, the top of the model needs to be selected. A quick way to do this is to draw a selection around the base (Figure 9-14) and then invert the selection (Figure 9-15).

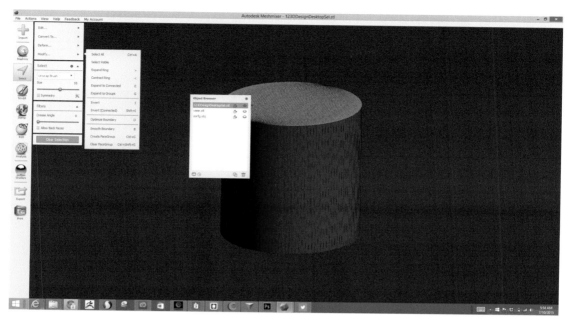

Figure 9-14. *To quickly isolate the top of model for the extrusion operation, first draw a selection around the base of the model with the Select tool. During this process, it will be helpful to turn off the visibility of the vase object in order to clearly select the cylinder*

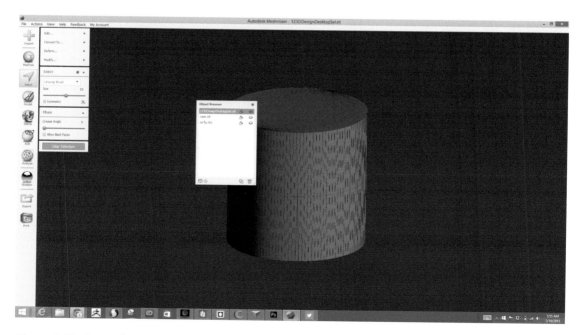

Figure 9-15. *Invert the selection by using Invert in the Modify menu*

12. Once the selection is inverted, an Extrude operation can be performed on the top of the model. Extrude upward and ensure that the cylinder is taller than the model (Figure 9-16).

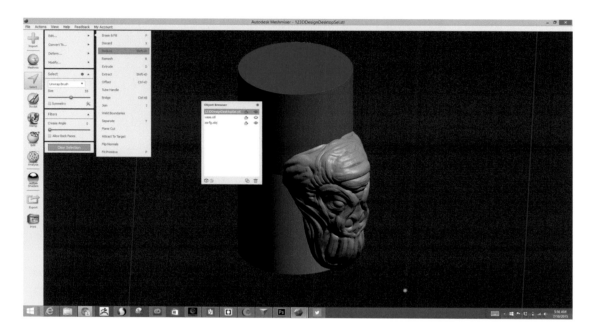

Figure 9-16. *The Extrude function is used to increase the height of the cylinder. Extrude is found under Modify in Meshmixer's Select menu*

13. Use the taller cylinder to cut away from the back of the head model. Select the head object and then select the cylinder object (you can select the objects in the Object Browser). With the two objects selected, select the Boolean Subtract option in the pop-up window that appears. Hit Accept in the next window. The cylinder will now disappear, and the head model will be sliced into two separate objects. Select the back of the model with the Select tool and hit Delete (Figure 9-17).

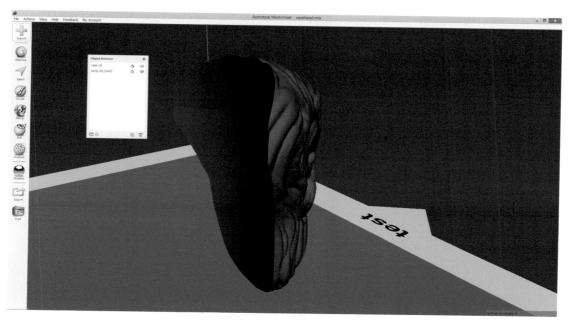

Figure 9-17. *After performing a Boolean Subtract on the head model using the cylinder object, you can delete the back of the head sculpt*

14. Turn the visibility of the vase back on in the Object Browser, and it should align nicely with the head sculpture (Figure 9-18).

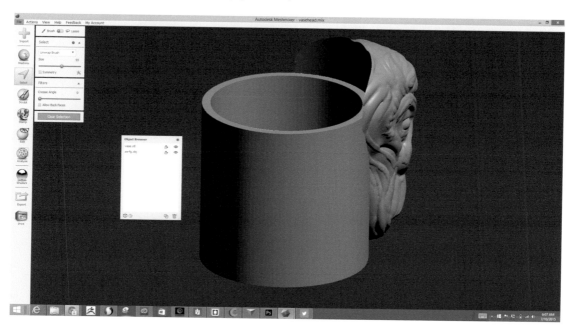

Figure 9-18. *Once the back of the head is removed it should fit nicely around the hollow vase*

15. Use the Transform tool to push the head sculpture into the vase object (Figure 9-19).

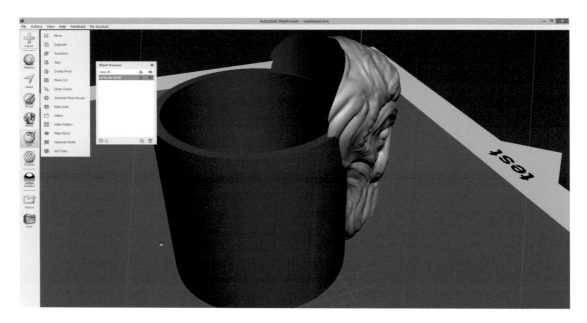

Figure 9-19. *Caption here*

16. Smooth out the model to create nicer transitions in the connected pieces. Also clean up the Object Browser and delete unnecessary objects (there should be only one object left in the scene, the final vase head). Once you are satisfied with the vase head, send it to print in Meshmixer. In the preview, scale up the vase head and add supports if necessary (Figure 9-20).

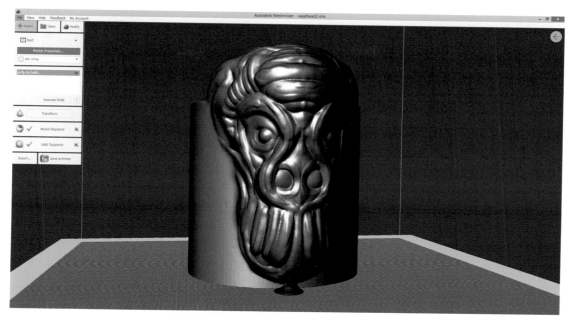

Figure 9-20. *Blend the sculptured details into the main vase with the smooth brush, delete unnecessary objects in the Object Browser, and then hit the Print icon in the main toolbar to prepare the vase head for 3D printing*

17. Finally, export the finished vase head as an `.stl` file by hitting the Export button. Import the final `.stl` file into the 3D-printing validation software of your choice to slice the model and create g-code. In Figure 9-21, the file is being prepared in Cura. Figure 9-22 shows the 3D-printed vase head, along with a version that has been customized with different sculpted details.

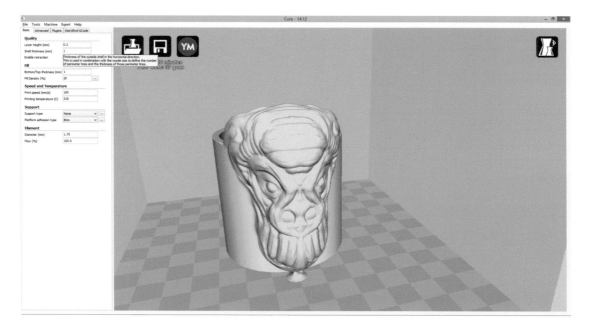

Figure 9-21. *The final vase head .stl file is sent to Cura for slicing and g-code creation*

Figure 9-22. *Here are two 3D-printed versions of the vase head. One is the original vase head from the previous lesson; the other has been customized with unique sculpted details*

ORNAMENTAL CANDLESTICK HOLDER

The vase head idea can evolve into something more ornate, such as a candlestick holder or maybe a trophy with an elaborate base. One possibility involves using the Revolve tool in 123D Design to create a curvy form (Figure 9-23) and then combine that with the sculpture that was created in Sculptris.

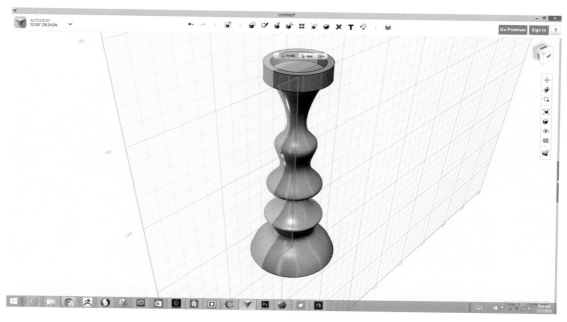

Figure 9-23. *Use 123D Design to create a more elaborate object, such as this candlestick holder*

1. To create the initial candlestick holder, use the Spline tool, found in the upper horizontal toolbar's Sketch menu to draw a curvy polyline on the grid (Figure 9-24). This will represent the outer edge of the candlestick holder.

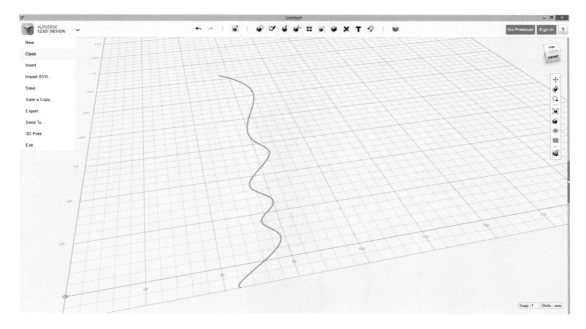

Figure 9-24. *Use the Polyline tool to drive a curvy line to represent the outer edge of the candlestick holder*

2. Use the Polyline tool to draw the internal axis of the candlestick holder. Draw two additional polylines to connect the curvy spline to the first polyline to create a closed shape. The closed shape will be used to make the revolved candlestick holder (Figure 9-25).

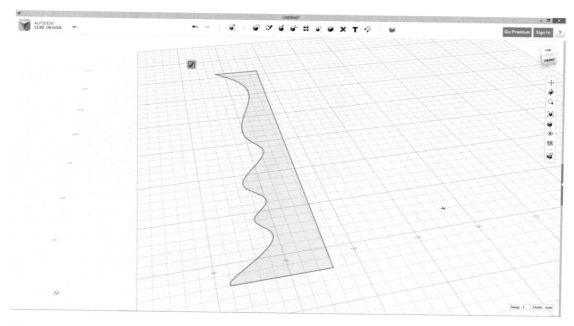

Figure 9-25. *Close the curvy spline by using three polylines to make an enclosed shape. This will serve as the profile for the Revolve tool in step 3*

3. Use the Revolve tool, which is found in the Construct menu, to create the final geometry for the candlestick holder. When you click the Revolve tool, first you will be asked to select a profile, which is the closed shape created in steps 1 and 2. Then select the axis to revolve around. Once the axis is selected, the Revolve manipulator will appear along with a small pop-up menu asking for a measurement. Enter **360** into the pop-up menu and then hit Enter to create the fully revolved candlestick. (Figure 9-26). Once the candlestick is complete, export it as an .stl file.

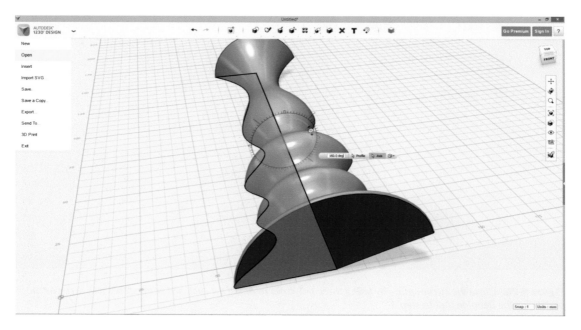

Figure 9-26. *Use the Revolve tool on the enclosed shape profile to create the geometry for the candlestick holder*

4. The candlestick .stl file can now be imported into Meshmixer and combined with the head sculpture (or anything else you have created) from the previous lesson. This time around, use the Boolean Unite operation to merge both objects (Figure 9-27). Follow the same steps as for the vase head procedure. Smooth out any rough edges and then prepare the final file for 3D printing.

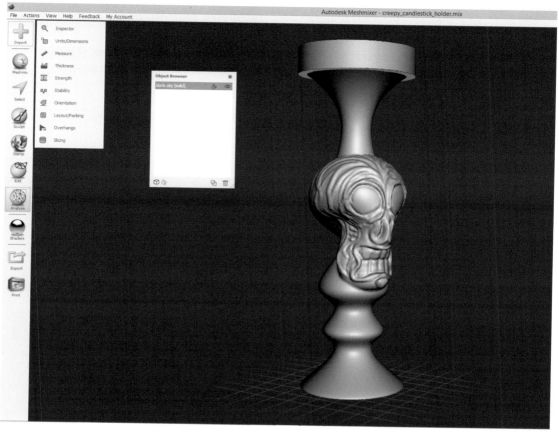

Figure 9-27. *The candlestick holder is imported into Meshmixer and combined with another 3D model to create a custom candlestick holder*

CREATE CUSTOME JEWELRY FROM CUSTOM SCULPTURES

With Meshmixer it's also easy enough turn 3D sculpts into rings, pendants, and other forms of jewelry. Here is a quick lesson on adding a loop to the surface of a model to turn any object into a pendant.

1. Import the sculpture you want to turn into a pendent.

2. In the MeshMix menu, under Miscellaneous, select the last MeshMix object in the list (it's the small loop shown in Figure 9-28).

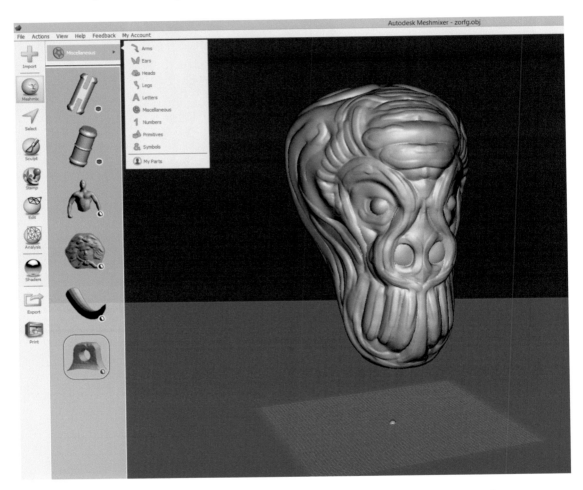

Figure 9-28. *Import the sculpture you want to turn into a pendent. In the MeshMix menu, under Miscellaneous, select the last MeshMix object, which looks like a small loop*

3. Drag the loop onto the head model. It will automatically align itself to the surface of the model. Grabbing the central circle icon will allow you to place the "loop" exactly where you want. Selecting and dragging the triangle icon will increase the size of the loop (Figure 9-29).

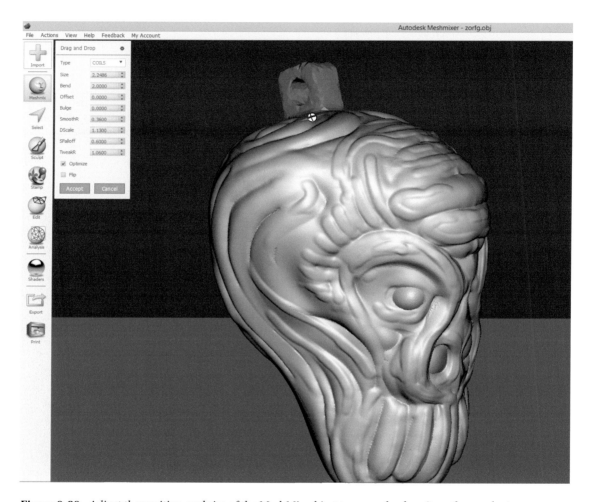

Figure 9-29. *Adjust the position and size of the MeshMix object to properly place it on the pendent*

4. To finalize the pendant, have it lie flat on the workplane grid, with the backside flush to the print bed to avoid adding unnecessary supports. Go through the same procedure as outlined in previous exercises to generate supports using Meshmixer. Use your preferred software to generate the slices and g-code. You may want to consider sending this file to a service bureau such as Shapeways, iMaterialize, or Sculpteo to have the file pendent printed in a metal material, which is a good option to explore when designing jewelry.

Summary

The ideas presented only scratch the surface of what is possible when customizing parts and works of art. As you become more experienced in the various design software methods being taught here, you will find new ways to combine tools and workflows to create unlimited variations in your 3D-printable designs.

■ ■ ■

CHAPTER 10

3D-Scanning Techniques

An invaluable aid to 3D-print designers is a 3D scanner. Having the capability to scan objects around you can be extremely useful. Scanned objects can be reversed engineered, modified for artistic purposes, or used as placeholders for other geometry.

There are many 3D scanners on the market today, and while many of those options are inexpensive, even the most affordable 3D scanner can be out of the price range of the average consumer who is starting to explore 3D printing for the first time. For designers on a budget there is one 3D-scanning method that is completely free, which will allow anyone to transform real-world objects into digital 3D models. This scanning technique uses a process called *photogrammetry* to turn a series of photos of an object into 3D geometry.

Photogrammetry is the process of taking measurements from photographs. The photogrammetry process began in the Renaissance when artists began to study perspective, but really took off with the invention of photography. The digital photogrammetry used today is based of the earlier methods, and uses algorithms to match and triangulate matching points on multiple photographs to generate 3D geometry.

This chapter will detail how designers can use photogrammetry to create 3D geometry using another free application from the Autodesk 123D series of applications: 123D Catch.

Getting Started

As part of the Autodesk 123D family, 123D Catch is a free app and is available at `www.123dapp.com/catch`. Users must sign up to get access to the 123D Catch app. If you are already signed up to use Tinkercad, then you can use that same login and password.

How to Use 123D Catch

To begin your first 3D scan, click the plus sign in the upper-right corner of the app. You will be greeted with a short tutorial with directions for using the app.

SCAN A SMALL OBJECT WITH 123D CATCH

The challenge with any type of 3D scanning is preserving small details. With photogrammetry, retaining detail in intricate objects will be a challenge. Another challenge is avoiding bringing unnecessary objects into the scan. This exercise will demonstrate the various issues related to photogrammetry and how those issues can be resolved using Meshmixer to clean up the data.

1. For this exercise you will need a small object to scan. In this example, I am using a small Buddha statue (Figure 10-1). You will also need to have room to navigate around the statue and will need consistent lighting to ensure that the photos being taken are clear and in focus. Sometimes the best area to scan objects with photogrammetry is a wide-open space outdoors. Also, since you need to take photographs from various angles, it is a good idea to place the scanned object on a small table that is waist level in height or higher.

Figure 10-1. *Find a small object to be scanned. In this exercise, I am using a small Buddha statue*

2. Launch the 123D Catch app. To begin the photogrammetry process, click the plus sign in the upper-right corner of the 123D Catch app's interface.

3. If this is your first time using 123D Catch, you will be greeted with a tutorial going through the photogrammetry process. You will be asked to keep the photographing device being used (which will most likely be an IPhone, iPad, or Android phone) stable and steady as the photos are being taken. You will be instructed on the best ways to take your photo as you navigate around the object to be scanned.

4. Click the check mark to start taking your photos of the object that will be converted to 3D geometry. The process will require you to take about 40 photos total. In the lower-left corner of the interface is an icon representation showing your current position. The icon consists of two layers of circular-arrayed rectangles. A rectangle will turn light blue when you are in the proper position to take a photo. If the image is properly focused and centered, then take a photo. The small rectangle for the position you are in should then turn a darker blue. Orbit around the object and proceed to take photos until every rectangle is blue (Figure 10-2).

Figure 10-2. *In the lower-left corner of the 123D Catch interface is a series of rectangles arrayed in a circle. The photos represent the proper position that the photographer should be in as the photo is being taken. Each rectangle will turn blue once a photo is properly taken*

5. Once all the rectangles turn blue, 123D Catch will let you process the images. Here you will continue to the next step. Click the check mark to continue. The next screen will display all the photos that were taken (Figure 10-3). Here you can delete or retake photos that were poorly taken. Once satisfied, hit the Submit button, and the photos will be uploaded to the cloud to be converted to 3D geometry.

Figure 10-3. *After all the photos are taken, an option is given to remove unwanted ones or to retake unsatisfactory images*

6. The photogrammetry process may take a bit of time, usually about an hour, as the images are sent to cloud to be computed and translated into a 3D image. Once the process is complete, users will be asked to review the image and "keep" (in other words, publish) the 3D scans (Figure 10-4). Once published, the scanned image will be available on the 123D Catch web site.

Figure 10-4. After submitting the photos to the cloud, the conversion process may take up to an hour. Once the conversion is complete, you will asked to keep the final 3D geometry

7. To access the geometry, users will have to visit the 123D Catch web site where the geometry can then be downloaded (Figure 10-5). The geometry can be downloaded as `.obj` or `.3dp` files.

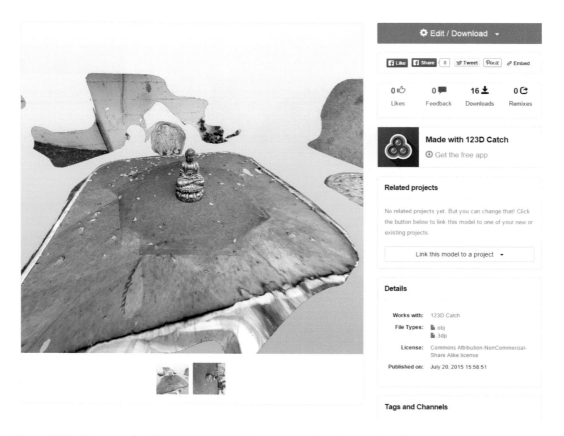

Figure 10-5. *To access the 3D geometry, go to the 123D Catch web site. There the geometry can be downloaded as a .obj or .3dp file*

CLEAN UP THE SCAN IN MESHMIXER

Once this is complete, you will notice that a lot of unwanted geometry is part of the final scan. A lot of this data can be discarded. To do so, some of the scan data will need to be selected and deleted. This exercise will go through the steps of cleaning up the scanned data in Meshmixer.

1. Import the scanned geometry into Meshmixer as an .obj file. The scan will probably consist of several islands of geometry. Unwanted islands need to be selected and deleted. The quickest way to delete the unwanted geometry is to select the object that is to be retained (Figure 10-6) and then invert the selection using the Select menu. Hit Delete to remove the unwanted geometry.

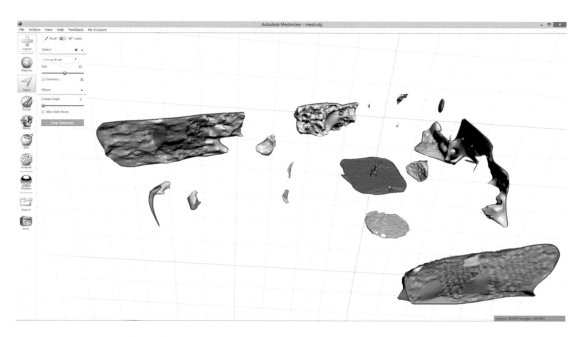

Figure 10-6. *There will be a lot of unwanted geometry left over from the conversion process. You can remove unwanted geometry in Meshmixer*

2. Once the unwanted geometry is deleted, you will notice that the main geometry is not properly centered in the Meshmixer view. Use the Transform tool in the Edit menu to properly center the geometry (Figure 10-7).

Figure 10-7. *It may be necessary to move the geometry into a better position. Use the Transform tool to correct the position of the geometry*

3. You will find that there is still unwanted geometry in the scene, particularly the surface (in other words, table or floor) that object was placed on when it was originally scanned. To remove this unwanted geometry, use the Plane Cut tool in the Edit menu. Once properly removed, only the main geometry that is meant to be 3D printed will remain.

4. You will notice that some details were lost during the photogrammetry conversion process. You may want to return to those areas and rebuild sections using the Sculpt tools. Another option is to modify the sculpt with additional geometry. In Figure 10-8, the face is replaced with a higher-resolution head geometry.

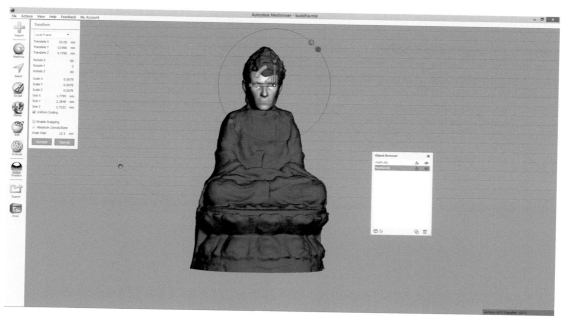

Figure 10-8. *Sculpt in lost details or add geometry to the scan*

5. If geometry is added to the scan, be sure to use the Make Solid function in the Edit menu to fuse all the objects together into one seamless object (Figure 10-9).

Figure 10-9. *Use the Make Solid function in the Edit menu to fuse together added geometry*

Summary

Not every 3D design needs to be built from scratch. Using a 3D scanner, or the photogrammetry process, is a great way to create base geometry that can be modified and refined in greater detail with other 3D-modeling tools. The greatest benefit of photogrammetry is that it's accessible to everyone thanks to applications such as Autodesk 123D Catch. The photogrammetry process detailed in this chapter will allow designers to turn everyday, real-world objects into 3D geometry and provide designers with valuable workflows that can be used to clean up data from any 3D scanner.

■ ■ ■ ■

CHAPTER 11

Intermediate Solid-Modeling Techniques

Up until this point, most of the emphasis has been placed on software tools that are tailored toward beginners. Tinkercad, 123D Design, 123D Catch, and Sculptris are great tools for first-time users, who may have little to no previous CAD or 3D-modeling experience. The motivation for software companies to release free and easy tools such as these is to help develop a user base while providing new users the confidence and skill to build a range of 3D models, from simple to complex. The audience for 3D modeling is growing as tools such as Tinkercad and 123D Design demonstrate how anyone can pick up and learn 3D modeling. Naturally, this increased implementation of easily-accessible 3D modeling tools helps demystify the belief that CAD is too difficult for the average user.

While the tools such as Tinkercad have been simplified for the average user, one shouldn't trivialize the value of introductory 3D-modeling applications since, with skill and imagination, highly complex parts can be developed. As gateway software, introductory tools help pave the way for more advanced applications that can be used to create complex assemblies and elaborate mechanical contraptions.

This chapter will provide a better understanding of how complex projects can be developed using 123D Design and FreeCAD. The tools taught in previous chapters have provided the stepping-stones leading up to this point where articulated assemblies and interactive parts can be developed for 3D printing.

To illustrate how complex, articulated assemblies can be designed specifically for 3D printing, two projects will be explored: a ball and socket joint in 123D Design and two interactive gears in FreeCAD.

Designing Articulated and Mechanical Objects in 123D Design

BUILDING A BALL AND SOCKET JOINT IN 123D DESIGN, STEP BY STEP

1. Start with a primitive sphere. In the top-row menu toolbar, click the Primitives icon to access the Primitives menu and drag a cylinder onto the workspace grid.

2. Duplicate the sphere twice. Press Ctrl/Cmd+C to create a copy and then use Ctrl/Cmd+V to paste it. After the first duplicate is pasted into place, move it upward in the Z direction using the "move controller" that appears. Press Ctrl/Cmd+V again to paste the second duplicate, and move that sphere upward as well.

■ **Note**   You can duplicate objects in 123D Design by using the traditional keyboard shortcuts for copying and pasting, which are Ctrl/Cmd+C to copy and Ctrl/Cmd+V to paste. When the object is pasted, a "move controller" appears, which consists of three arrows pointing in the X, Y, and Z directions, along with a rotate icon, letting users change the position and rotation of the duplicate.

3. Drag a box to the workspace grid and move it onto the first sphere on the grid. Have the box overlap the sphere. Allow one-fourth to peek through the top of the box (Figure 11-1). You will have to use the Scale tool and Move tool to properly overlap the cube with the sphere.

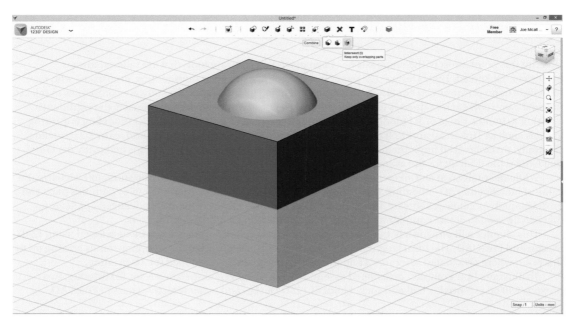

Figure 11-1. *A box is dragged to the grid and scaled up to overlap the first sphere. The box will be used as a Boolean to slice off the top of the sphere*

4. Use the box to cut the box three-quarters of the way from the bottom of the first sphere using Combine Intersect (Figure 11-2).

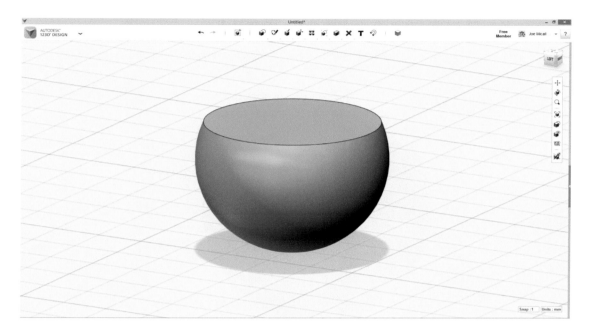

Figure 11-2. *Here are the results of the Combine Intersect operation*

5. Scale down the middle sphere by .8 by entering **.8** in the dialog box that appears after the Scale tool is activated (Figure 11-3).

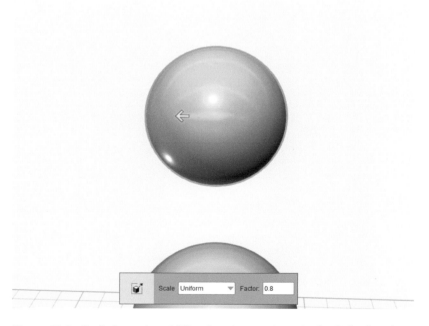

Figure 11-3. *Scale down the middle sphere by entering .8 in the dialog box that appears after the Scale tool is activated*

351

6.   Move the middle sphere into the lower sphere (Figure 11-4).

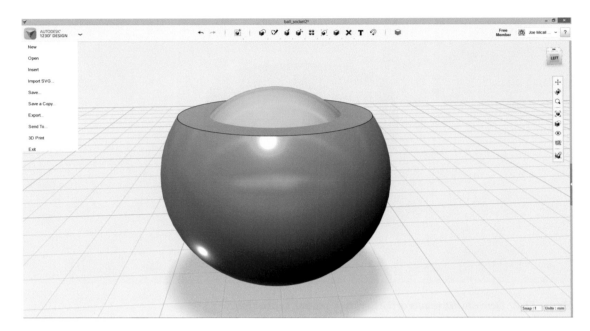

Figure 11-4.   *The middle sphere is moved to the center of the lower sphere in preparation for the Boolean Subtract operation*

7. Use the Subtract Combine Boolean operation on the lower two spheres to create a hollow sphere (Figure 11-5).

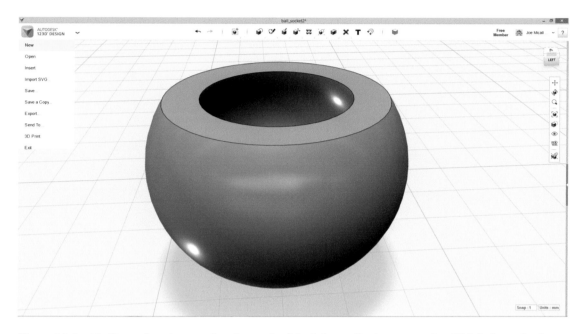

Figure 11-5. *A hollow sphere is created as the result of the Subtract Boolean operation. This is the socket for the ball and socket joint*

8. Scale down the uppermost sphere by 6.5. This will give it enough clearance to move within the lower sphere.

9. Move the upper sphere into the new hollow lower sphere (Figure 11-6).

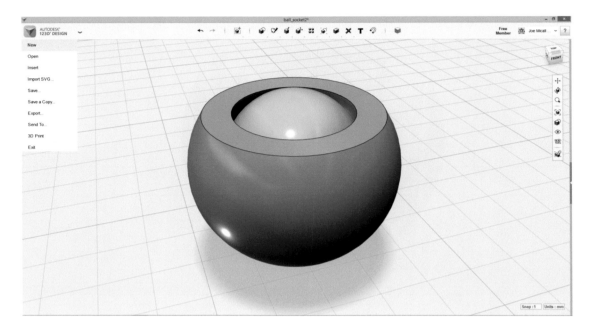

Figure 11-6. *The smaller sphere is lowered into the hollow sphere to create the ball and socket*

10. Add cylinders to both sphere objects. Add a narrow cylinder to the inner sphere to create a handle. Make the height 25mm and the radius 2mm (Figure 11-7).

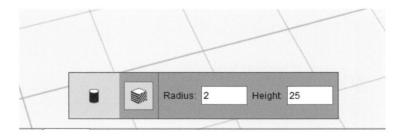

Figure 11-7. *Create a narrow cylinder with a radius of 2 and a height of 25*

11. Intersect the narrow cylinder with the inner sphere and merge them into one object using the Combine function. The narrow cylinder will need to penetrate into the lower sphere. The easiest way to align the two objects for the interpenetration to occur is to turn on orthographic mode (right-click the view cube to access orthographic mode) and then click the front view. This will help the narrow cylinder remain in the proper position as it is placed into the sphere (Figure 11-8).

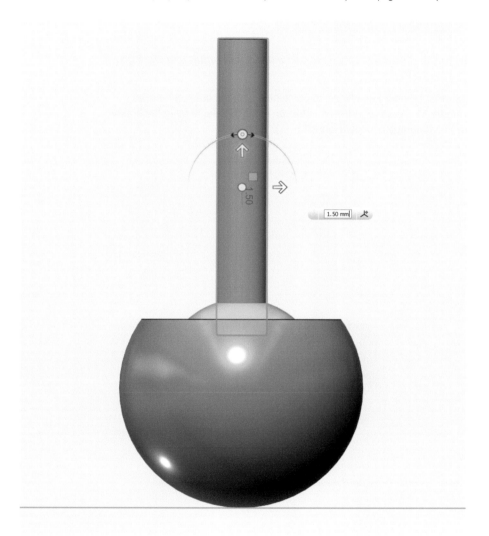

Figure 11-8. *Move the narrow cylinder into place. The narrow cylinder needs to interpenetrate the smaller inner sphere*

12. Add a wider but shorter cylinder to the outer sphere to create a base. Give that cylinder a height of 3mm and a width of 6mm (Figure 11-9).

Figure 11-9. *Create a base for the socket using a cylinder with a 6mm radius and 3mm height*

13. Move the shorter cylinder into place and combine it with the outer sphere, as shown in Figure 11-10. To align the two objects, it may helpful to be in the bottom view while in orthographic mode (Figure 11-11).

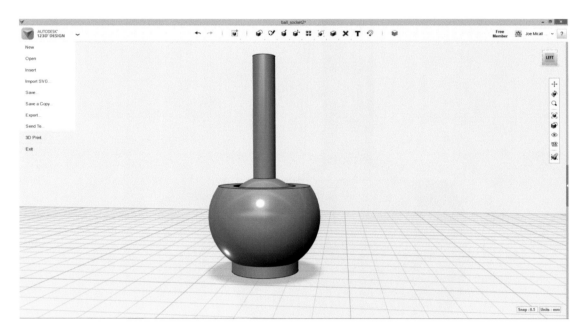

Figure 11-10. *Fit the base cylinder beneath the socket by moving it into position*

Figure 11-11. *It may help to view the socket from the bottom down, while in orthographic mode, to ensure that the base is properly aligned with the socket*

14. Finally, add a thin cylinder that will be used as a support to keep the inner sphere elevated while it's being printed. This cylinder should be .75mm thick and 3mm tall. Move the connector piece into position and connect the bottom of the inner sphere to the top surface of the bottom sphere. It may help to be in outline mode as the thin cylinder is lowered to connect the two spheres (Figure 11-12). Once the ball and socket joint is printed, the connecter is meant to be snapped off (do this by rocking the inner sphere object back and forth), allowing for the inner sphere to move within the outer sphere. The final ball and socket will not require any additional supports, and the ball will move freely once the main support is broken. Figure 11-13 shows a final 3D-printed version of the ball and socket.

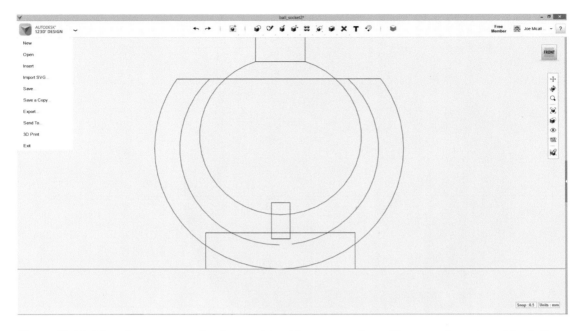

Figure 11-12. *Move the connector piece into position. The connect piece will connect the socket with a ball*

Figure 11-13. *Here is the final 3D-printed version of the ball and socket joint*

Solid Modeling in FreeCAD

Before we end this chapter, let's examine another 3D-modeling package, which you will use in the following gear design exercise. The package being explored, FreeCAD, emulates a number of commercial design applications such as Revit and CATIA in its functionality. For this reason, technical designers and engineers may find FreeCAD to be an appealing tool to design precise parts and assemblies.

FreeCAD: Getting Started

To download FreeCAD, please visit www.freecadweb.org. FreeCAD is available for Windows, Mac OS, and Linux.

How to Use FreeCAD

FreeCAD is divided up into working spaces known as *workbenches*. Workbenches group tools that are used for specific tasks. A workbench is essentially a customized instance of the interface that groups only the tools necessary for the job at hand. For example, there are specific workbenches for architectural design, part development, and nautical shipbuilding (Figure 11-14).

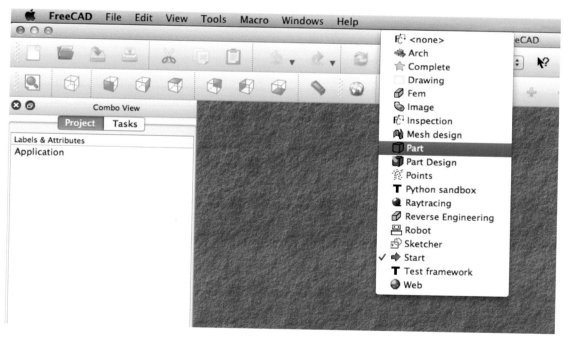

Figure 11-14. *FreeCAD is divided into workbenches that have specific tools for specific design applications*

Launching FreeCAD for the first time, users will be introduced with a wiki page introduction screen that provides version update information and sample projects. Provided here is a Getting Started link leading to the help section that contains in-depth tutorials on learning FreeCAD (Figure 11-15).

Figure 11-15. *FreeCAD's wiki page has a wealth of features and tutorials to help new users get up and running*

You will also notice that the FreeCAD interface is a bit more complex than the previous applications that have been explored in earlier chapters. The interface is broken down into three main sections: the 3D view, the tree view, and the properties editor (Figure 11-16).

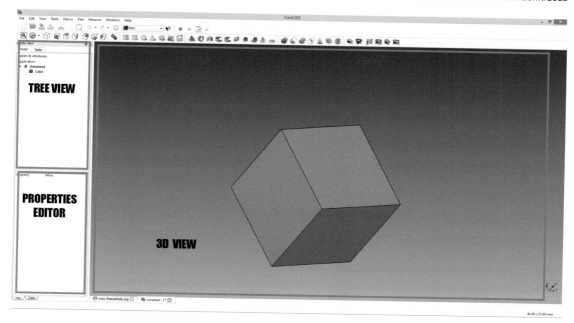

Figure 11-16. *FreeCAD's interface is broken down into three distinct sections: the 3D view, the tree view, and the properties editor*

Navigation in FreeCAD

Using the middle mouse button in FreeCAD allows designers to pan. The scroll wheel allows designers to zoom in and out. To rotate (orbit) the view, first press down on the middle mouse button and then press down on the left mouse button.

GEAR LAB

FreeCAD has an easy way to make gears quickly. In this project, you will create two interacting gears, where one gear drives the other. Before beginning, it is necessary to understand some of the mechanical properties of gears.

When designing gears that drive other gears, the ratio of gear teeth from one gear to the next plays an important role. Gears work on a ratio based on the number of teeth found in the gears. This ratio also determines how many times a gear will rotate.

First, in systems where one gear controls another, the controlling gear is known as the *driver gear*. The control gear is the *driven gear*.

If the driver gear has 10 teeth and the driven gear has 30 teeth, the gear ration is 3 to 1 (or when properly written, 3:1) . With a 3:1 ratio, the driver gear must rotate three times for the driven gear to rotate once.

First you will make the driven gear; then you will make the driver gear.

1. Begin this exercise by working in the Part Design workbench (Figure 11-17). The Part Design workbench will give you access to the Involute Gear function.

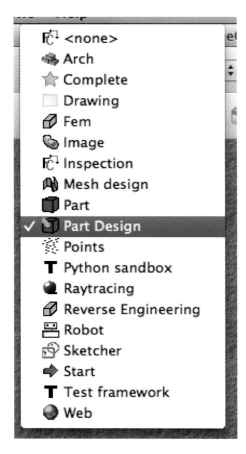

Figure 11-17. Begin the gear projects by accessing the Part Design workbench

2. In the Part Design menu, select Involute Gear. In the Properties Editor window, under the Task tab will be a gear generator with a number of inputs. Make the number of teeth 30 (Figure 11-18). All the other values can be left at their defaults.

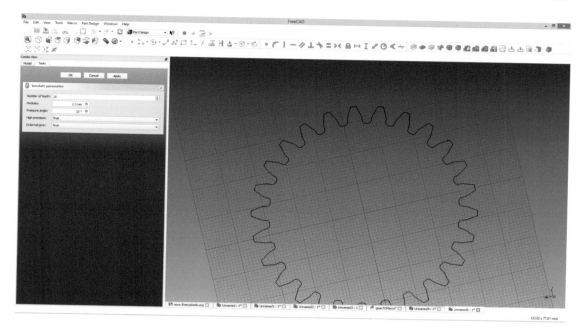

Figure 11-18. *For the initial gear, set the number of teeth to 30. All other values can be kept at their defaults*

3. Once you are satisfied with Gear, hit OK.

4. Select the gear outline (double-click a segment, and the whole gear will turn green).

5. Then hit the Pad icon in the upper horizontal toolbar (Figure 11-19). This will turn the sketch into a solid object. If satisfied, hit OK in the Task tab.

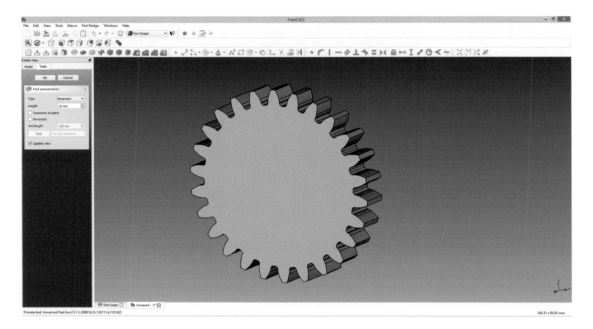

Figure 11-19. *Use the Pad function to turn the gear line drawing into a three-dimensional solid object*

6. The Pad function turns the gear into a solid object that is nonparametric, meaning the gear can't adjusted after it's built. To adjust the solid gear object, change its position in 3D view using the Refine function. To access the Refine function, go to the OpenSCAD workbench and select Refine Shape Feature, which is found in the OpenSCAD menu.

7. Now you can move the gear in the 3D view. To move and change the position of the gear, select the gear object in the 3D view and change the X position value on the Data tab to **31mm** (Figure 11-20).

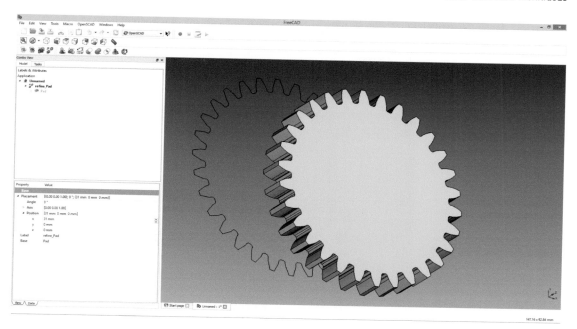

Figure 11-20. *To adjust the solid object, user must apply the Refine function, which is found in the OpenSCAD workbench*

8. In the next steps you will make a 10-toothed gear; follow the same procedure as in steps 2–6. You will have to return to the Part Design workbench to begin the process anew.

9. Move the gears into position so the teeth of one gear fit nicely into the teeth of the other gear (Figure 10-21).

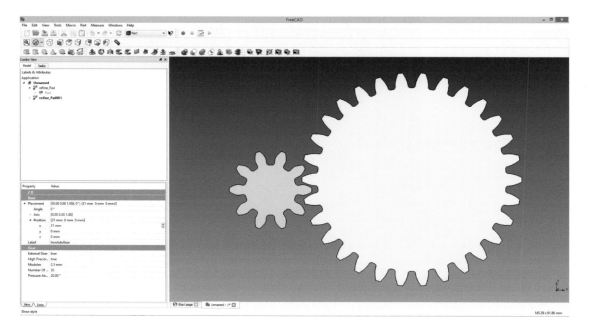

Figure 11-21. *For the final assembly, move the smaller gear into position. The teeth of the smaller gear should fit within the teeth of the larger gear*

10. At this stage, explore building a base for the gears and possibly a handle to turn the gears. These steps are for you to explore, but with FreeCAD's ample tutorial section, this shouldn't be a problem. For final 3D printing, it may be possible to print the gears as one assembly, but (for FDM 3D printing in particular) it would probably be easier to print the parts as separate pieces that could then be assembled afterwards.

Summary

The ability to make articulated designs and assemblies will allow designers to explore a full-range of 3D-printed, mechanical contractions. The projects in this chapter should be seen as launch points for other designs, such as articulated puppets and mechanical toys.

■■■

CHAPTER 12

Advanced Techniques Using Blender

The promise of 3D printing is that shape complexity is free, meaning that 3D printing an ornate or intricate object will not require more time or cost than a simple cube of the same mass. With 3D printing, highly complex objects are possible, but there are two issues that make living up to this promise of "shape complexity freedom" a challenge: designers must have the imagination and skill to make complex designs a reality, and the software being used must have the capabilities to make those designs possible. Most likely, artists and engineers will bravely step forward to meet the demand of dreaming up new complex designs; therefore, the biggest issue is the software having the right features to meet the designer's needs.

This book was written to present aspiring 3D-print designers with a wide range of (free) tools to make their ideas conceivable, but to make some designs possible, many of those tools need to be used in combination. For example, to make the vase heads in Chapter 9, the parts designed in 123D Design and Sculptris were combined in Meshmixer. But jumping from software to software can be time-consuming, and it would be nice to have one universal modeling tool that could cover all the basics. Well, such a universal tool exists; it is called Blender.

If you ever seen a complex 3D-printed sculpture but couldn't pinpoint how it was created, possibly it was created in Blender. Blender is a highly diverse 3D-modeling tool with a broad range of capabilities. Some of the functions allow for digital sculpting, while other functions resemble solid-modeling techniques found in 123D Design. Whatever your need is, most likely Blender will have the tools for the job.

This chapter will introduce you to Blender with a couple of exercises to get you familiar with Blender's capabilities. Note that Blender takes time getting used to, and this chapter covers Blender at the most basic level. One exercise will introduce designers to a modeling technique called *box modeling*. Another exercise focuses on the creation of wireframe polyhedrons. The final exercise will show how textures can be used to generate geometry.

Exploring New Ideas with Blender

In previous chapters, you started to use a combination of tools to get the desired results. Blender presents an opportunity to explore some new concepts that are popular in the world of 3D-printable designs. These ideas include math-based art, box modeling, and turning 3D images into 3D designs.

What Can Blender Do?

The great thing about Blender is that it can do a little bit of everything. It has the capabilities of both solid-modeling and digital-sculpting software tools. But the true magic behind Blender is that it's open source, and anyone with programming skills can make Blender do whatever they want. But it must be said that Blender can be challenging to learn in the beginning, and users coming from other software packages find Blender's multipanel interface to be a bit alien and a little frustrating.

Blender: Getting Started

Blender is a free download available for both Windows and Mac OS; see `www.blender.org/`.

How to Use Blender

Blender represents a new stage of complexity in the number of icons and menus that appear in the interface (Figure 12-1). As you advance beyond the more toned-down interfaces found in other applications such as Tinkercad, 123D Design, and Sculptris (these applications were intended to have simplified interfaces to make new users feel at ease), busier interfaces will be the norm. As you explore more advanced tools such as Blender, you will see that highly complex interfaces are quite normal.

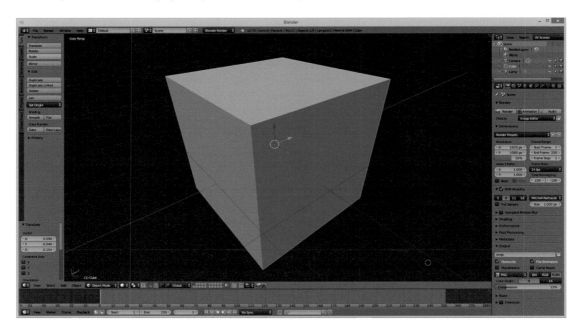

Figure 12-1. *Upon launching Blender for the first time, you will be greeted with a complex interface consisting of multiple menus and numerous icons*

Blender's Interface

Known primarily as an animation tool, Blender has a number of panels and functions that can be ignored when you're using it strictly as a 3D-modeling tool. Therefore, Figure 12-2 is a breakdown of Blender's interface that focuses on the areas that are most relevant for 3D-print design purposes.

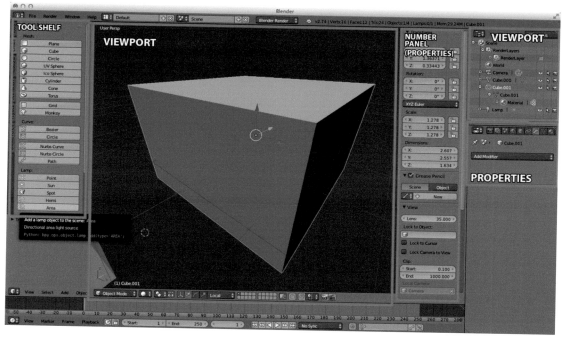

Figure 12-2. *Blender's interface is broken down into five main sections*

On the far right is the Tool Shelf. You can toggle the Tool Shelf's visibility on and off using the T keyboard shortcut. The Tool Shelf consists of a number of tabs. Clicking each tab reveals a different menu. The two tabs that will be most relevant for 3D-modeling purposes are the Create tab and the Tools tab.

The Create tab unveils a list of icons/buttons that will create geometry, mostly primitive objects that should already be familiar, such as the cube, cone, and torus. To generate geometry in the viewport, click the appropriate icon.

The Tools tab has a number of functions that will move, scale, and rotate the geometry that is created.

The main workspace where the modeling takes place is the *viewport*. .By default, this is the largest panel in the interface.

Next to the viewport is the .Numbers panel (which is also called the Properties window). The Numbers panel shows the various numeric layouts relating to the geometry in the scene, such as the distance an object has moved.

Navigation in Blender

Like other software tools featured in earlier chapters, Blender uses the mouse buttons in combination with the Shift and Ctrl keys. The easy thing to remember about Blender's navigation is that the middle mouse button is used in all navigation operations. Used alone, the middle mouse button orbits around the main objects in the scene. Pressing Shift in combination with the middle mouse button pans up and down and left and right, and pressing Ctrl in combination with the middle mouse zooms in and out.

CREATE A CHAIR

The purpose of this initial exercise is to get you familiar with one of the more common modeling techniques in Blender known as *box modeling*.

1. Launch Blender. The cube in the middle of the viewport will serve as the basis for the chair model.

2. Scale down the cube in the Z direction. To scale down, use the S keyboard shortcut, followed by the Z keyboard shortcut (hit S and then Z in quick succession). Scale down to about approximately .11 (you can view the scaling amount in the lower-hand corner of the interface) and then hit the left mouse button to accept the new size.

3. To make the legs and the back of the chair, you will first add some edge loops using Blender's Loop Cut and Slide tool, but in order to use the Loop Cut and Slide tool we must first be in Blender's Edit Mode. First hit tab to enter Edit Mode then Press the keyboard shortcut Ctrl+R to access the Loop Cut and Slide tool. You will notice a magenta line appear through the center of the box (i.e. the flattened cube that was created in Step 2). Hit the left mouse button and then move the mouse to change the position of the line (Figure 12-3). Once you are satisfied with the location of the edge loop hit the left mouse button again to complete the Loop Cut and Slide operation.

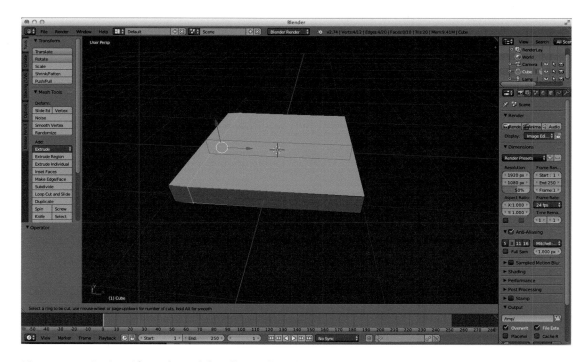

Figure 12-3. *Begin with a cube and then flatten the cube in the Z direction using the Scale tool. Begin adding edge loops using the Ctrl+R keyboard shortcut*

In Blender, the Loop Cut and Slide tool creates an edge loop. Edge loops are necessary for the box-modeling process. An edge loop is an edge that completely wraps around a model. When using the box modeling technique edge loops can be combined to form additional polygons on a model. The additional polygons that are created allow the designer to add more detail the model.

4. To create the polygons that will become the back and legs of the chair, you will need to create four edge loops around the flattened cube (Figure 12-4). After each edge loop is created (using Loop Cut and Slide tool as described in Step 3), it is always a good idea to hit the A key to deselect the edge loop. If the edge loop remains selected, it may be moved inadvertently, which will distort the model.

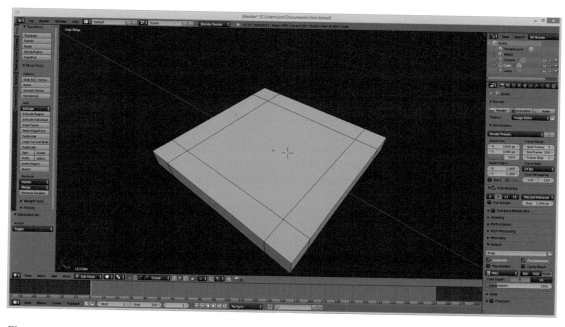

Figure 12-4. *Add four edge loops to the flattened cube*

5. Next you will extrude the back and legs of the chair. To do this, you need to select the faces of the rectangle you want to extrude. Since edge loops were added using the Loop Cut and Slide tool, you now have the proper number of faces to extrude in order to create the necessary chair geometry. To select faces, press Ctrl+Tab and select Faces the in the small pop-up menu (Figure 12-5).

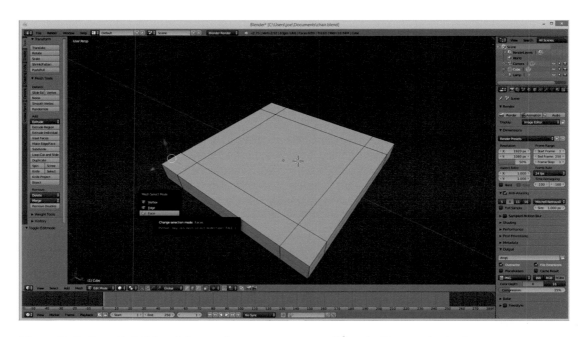

Figure 12-5. *Press Ctrl+Tab to bring up the component menu. Select the Faces option in the component menu*

6. Select the three faces that will represent the back of the chair. Right-click a face to select it. Keep the Shift key held down as the faces are selected in order to select the faces as a group. The selected faces will be highlighted in orange (Figure 12-6).

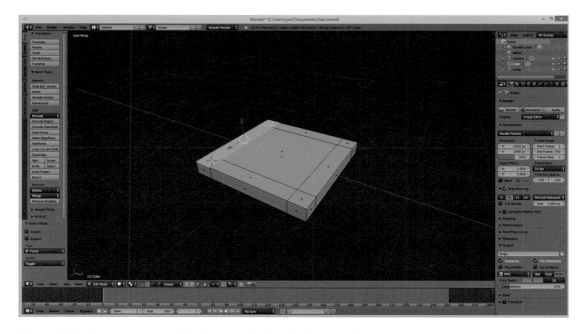

Figure 12-6. *Create the back of the chair by selecting the three rear faces*

7. After the faces are selected, press E to extrude them to form the back of the chair. Drag upward and then left click to finalize the extrusion. Once the back is extruded, press the A key to deselect the faces that were selected in Step 5 (Figure 12-7).

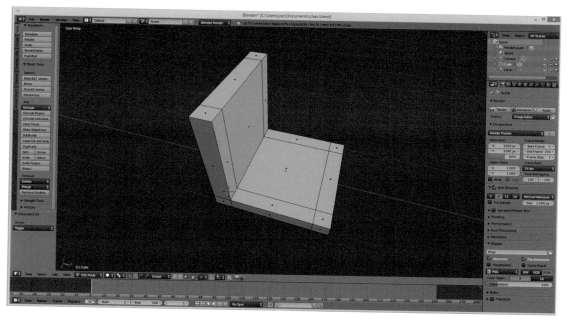

Figure 12-7. Use the E keyboard shortcut to extrude the back of the chair

8. Using the middle mouse button, drag to rotate the view to the underside of the chair. Here you will Shift+select the faces in the four corners on the bottom of the chair (Figure 12-8).

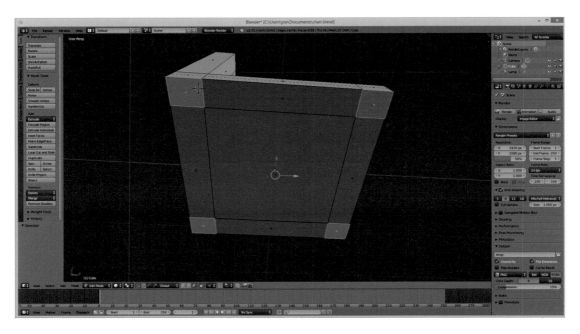

Figure 12-8. *Select the faces that will represent the legs*

9. Hit E again and extrude downward. Once the legs are extruded sufficiently, hit A to deselect the geometry. Now you should have a simple chair (Figure 12-9).

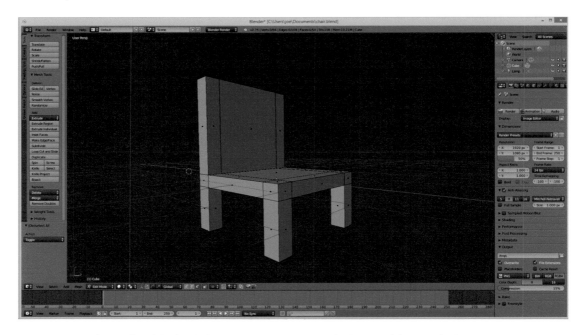

Figure 12-9. *The results of the final chair model created using the box modeling method*

10. Once the chair is complete export the .stl file by selecting Export in Blender's File.

11. To generate supports for chair, import the .stl file into Meshmixer.

12. If, in Meshmixer, the chair appears is pink in color (Figure 12-10), this may indicate a problem with the chair geometry. To correct any potential errors it may be necessary to use the Flip Normals function in Meshmixer. To correct potential errors select Flip Normals, which is found in the Edit menu of the Select tool.

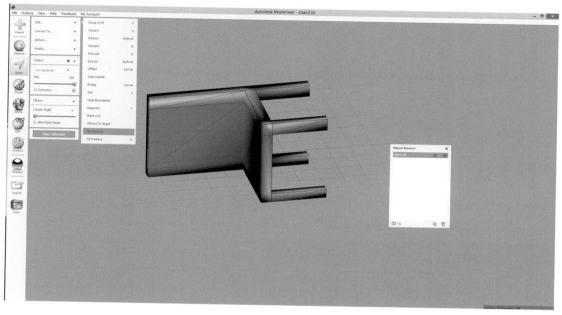

Figure 12-10. If, when imported into Meshmixer the chair is pink, there may be a problem with the geometry. To fix the issue use the Flip Normals operation which is found in the Edit menu of the Select tool

13. If necessary, scale up the chair and then rotate it 270 degrees using the Transform function in the Edit menu.

14. Also use the Layout/Packing option in the Analysis menu to ensure that the feet of the chair are flush with the printer bed grid.

15. Add supports using the Overhangs option in the Meshmixer's Analysis menu. Once supports are added (Figure 12-11), export an .stl file from Meshmixer for Cura or MatterControl for 3D printing, or 3D print the file directly from Meshmixer. Figure 12-12 shows a version of the chair being printed on a Deezmaker Bukito 3D printer.

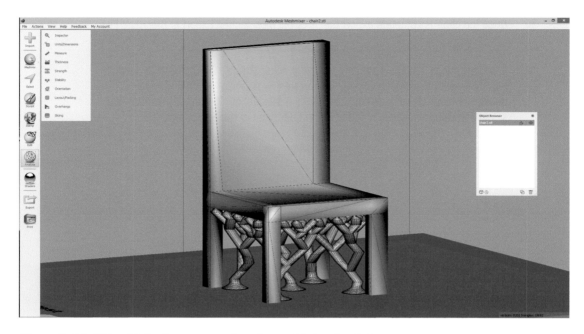

Figure 12-11. *Using Meshmixer, supports have been added to the chair*

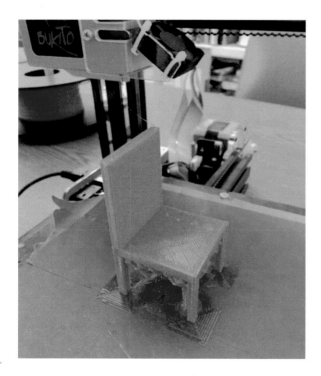

Figure 12-12. *Here is a 3D printed version of the chair*

Use Blender to Create 3D-Printed Polyhedrons

A polyhedron is a three-dimensional object whose sides are composed of regular polygonal shapes such as triangles, octagons, and hexagons. The Platonic solids (Figure 12-13) are well-known examples of polyhedrons, revered throughout history for their aesthetic beauty and considered by ancient philosophers to be the most perfect structural forms achievable.

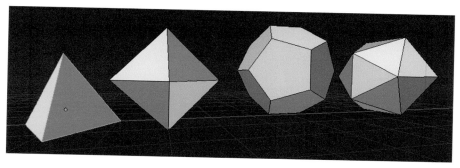

Figure 12-13. *Examples of Platonic solids (polyhedrons)*

Many 3D artists revere polyhedrons as well since they can be interesting to behold as 3D-printed objects. One approach to generating polyhedral shapes for 3D printing is (instead of printing the whole solid form) to 3D print just outer edges as a three-dimensional frame. The final results of the 3D-printed polyhedron frame can be compelling to behold, as the mathematical precise that makes up the polyhedron frame creates a compelling, interconnecting lattice structure (Figure 12-14).

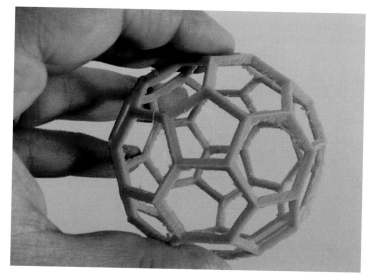

Figure 12-14. *The 3D-printed version of a polyhedron frame*

Anyone wanting to 3D print polyhedral objects can easily do so with Blender. Blender provides a nice assortment of polyhedral objects that can be output as interesting 3D-printed designs. Complementing the generation of polyhedral shapes is Blender's Wireframe function. Blender's

Wireframe function will convert the edges of a solid, multisided object into a three-dimensional frame (Figure 12-15). Anyone can easily create their own polyhedral frameworks and explore Blender's Wireframe function by following these steps:

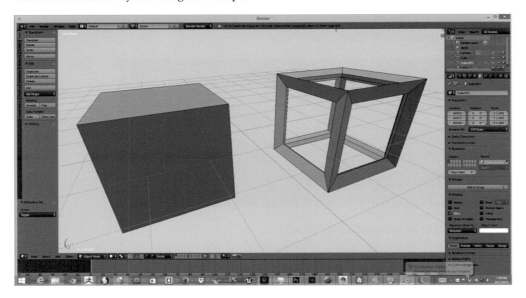

Figure 12-15. *On the left is the original solid cube, on the right is a wireframe version*

1. Blender has many unique shapes to take advantage of (such as the polyhedrons) that are not initially available by default. To access these additional shapes, select User Preferences, which is found in Blender's File menu (Figure 12-16). This will bring up the User Preferences window.

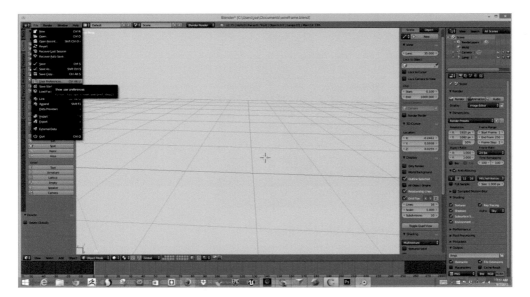

Figure 12-16. *Select User Preferences in the File menu to access the User Preferences window*

2. In the User Preference window that appears, find the Add-ons tab and look for the Add Mesh: Extra Object section (Figure 12-17). Along with giving access to a range of polyhedral solids, the Add Mesh: Extra Object section contains a number of additional geometric objects that can be used within Blender. Clicking the check box (Figure 12-18) will make these extra geometries, along with the polyhedral shapes, accessible in Blender's Add menu.

Figure 12-17. *The Add-ons menu in User Preferences will allow users to turn on the Add Mesh: Extra Objects feature in order to make the polyhedron shapes available in Blender*

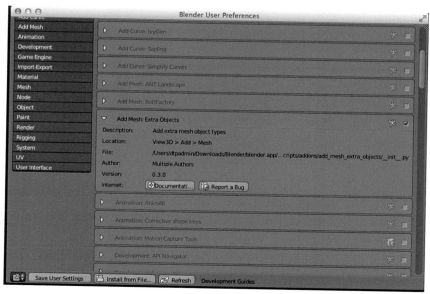

Figure 12-18. *Click the check box in the Add Mesh: Extra Objects panel to add access to the polyhedron shapes in Blender's Add menu*

3. You can now find the polyhedron shapes that will be used for this exercise in the Add menu (Figure 12-19), which appears at the bottom of the 3D viewport. To access the polyhedral shapes, select Mesh, then Math Function, and then Regular Solid. A pyramid object (a tetrahedron) will appear in the Blender scene.

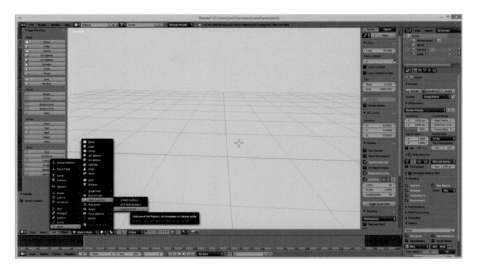

Figure 12-19. *You can access the polyhedron shapes in the Add menu*

4. In the Regular Solid panel that appears to the left of viewport is a drop-down menu that gives users access to different polyhedrons. Under Source you can choose a number of initial polyhedral shapes to explore such as Icosahedrons, Dodecahedrons, Octahedrons, and a few others. Select a shape in the drop-down menu, and it will appear in the viewport (Figure 12-20). In the Presets section, there are many more options to choose from.

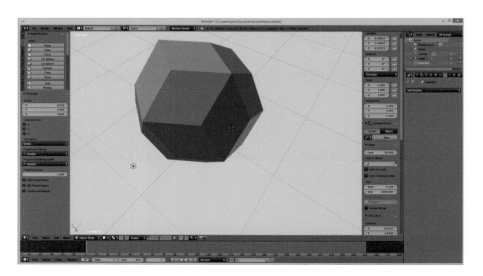

Figure 12-20. *Different polyhedron shapes are available in the Regular Solid panel that appears*

380

5. Once you select a favorite polyhedral shape, begin the process of turning it into a 3D wireframe for 3D printing. First, right-click the polyhedral shape to select it. Then, on the right-side of the Blender interface in the Properties window, look for the wrench icon (Figure 12-21). Click the wrench icon and the Add Modifier menu will appear. In the Add Modifier menu, apply the Wireframe modifier to the currently selected polyhedral shape. The solid shape consists of 3D frames that follow the edges of the shape.

Figure 12-21. *Click the wrench icon in the Properties window to access the Add Modifier menu*

6. Once the Wireframe modifier is applied, you can play with the Thickness settings in the Wireframe settings. A setting of .1 will work best for 3D-printing purposes (Figure 12-22).

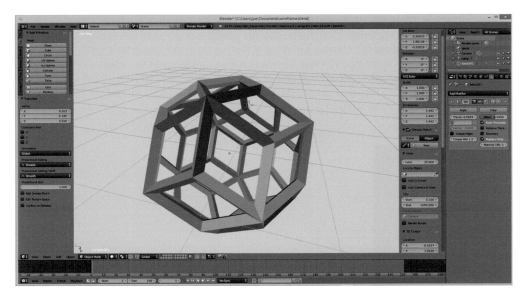

Figure 12-22. *The thickness of the wireframes can be adjusted in the Wireframe modifier menu*

7. Once you are satisfied with your wireframe shape, export the `.stl` file by going to the File menu and selecting Export.

8. To generate supports for the polyhedral frame, import the `.stl` file into Meshmixer. If necessary, scale up the object using the Transform function in the Edit menu.

9. Add supports using the Overhangs option in the Analysis menu (Figure 12-23). Once supports are added, export an `.stl` file for Cura or MatterControl for 3D printing or 3D print the file directly from Meshmixer.

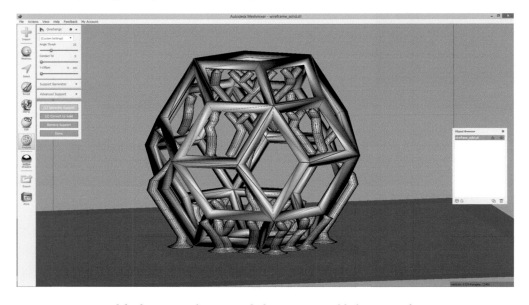

Figure 12-23. *A polyhedron in Meshmixer with the necessary added supports for 3D printing*

CREATING 3D BLUEPRINTS

The purpose of this final Blender project is to create a 3D blueprint, which can be helpful for architecture and home layouts. In this exercise, you will turn a shader into a height map in Blender. In Blender, a shader is used for color 3D geometry. In this technique, the shader is a black-and-white graphic that has been imported into Blender.

To begin the project, find a suitable black-and-white blueprint online (or draw your own). Make sure that the image being used is nice and crisp. A pure black-and-white image will work best. Any grayscale pixels and noise in the image will produce jaggy, unwanted geometry. Also, blueprints with thick black lines work better than blueprints with thin lines (Figure 12-24).

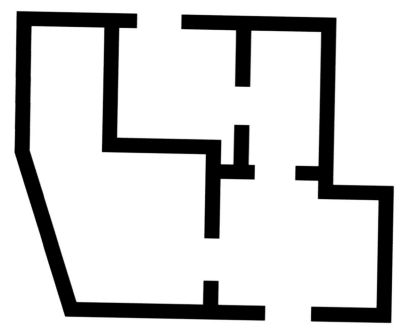

Figure 12-24. *Black-and-white blueprints with thick, black lines work best. Also, make sure there is no noise in the image*

1. Launch Blender. Delete the cube in the viewport. Add a grid to the scene. The Grid object is found in the Create tab of the main Tool Shelf (Figure 12-25).

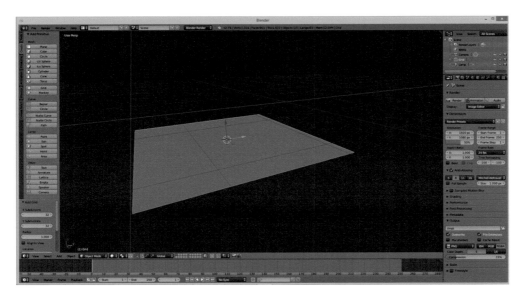

Figure 12-25. *Add a grid to the scene*

2. Hit Tab to enter Edit mode. In the Tools tab in the Tool Shelf, click Subdivide. Enter **10** for the number of cuts. Click the Subdivide button three more times (Figure 12-26).

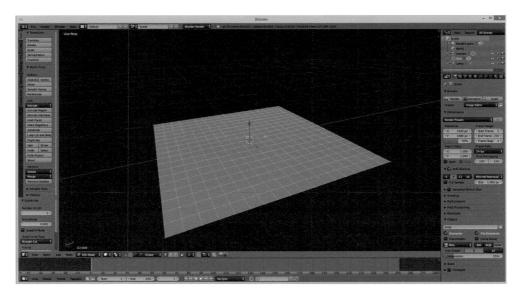

Figure 12-26. *Add subdivisions to the grid to increase its resolution*

3. Press Tab to go back into Object mode. In the Properties window, click the icon that looks like a wrench. This will let you add a Displace modifier to the grid. Select the Displace modifier, and in the Displace modifier's properties window, click the New Texture button. Then click the icon next to the X to show the texture view (Figure 12-27).

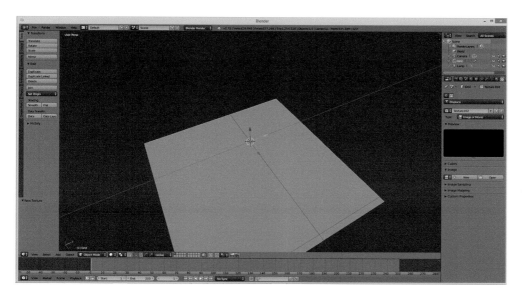

Figure 12-27. *In the Modifier menu, select the Displace modifier*

4. In the Preview window that appears, click Open and import the blueprint image. Right now the extrusion is facing the wrong direction. Let's fix that (Figure 12-28).

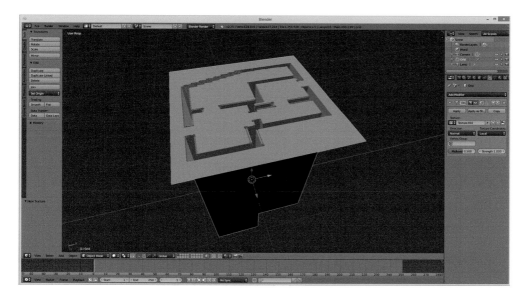

Figure 12-28. *Add an image to the texture being applied with the Displace modifier*

5. To have the extrusion face up, change the strength of the Displace modifier to -.4 (Figure 12-29). The Displace modifier will determine the height of the walls for the 3D blueprint.

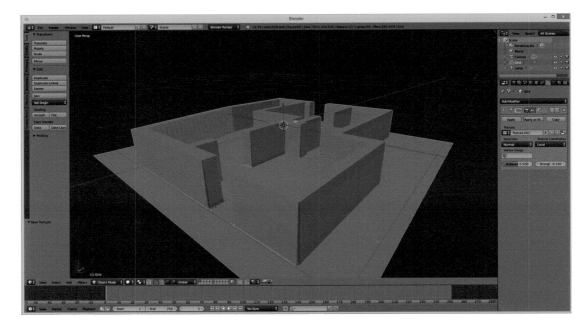

Figure 12-29. *Reverse the direction of the displacement by entering -.4 in the Strength setting of the Displace modifier. The Displace modifier will determine the wall height of the blueprint*

6. To clean up the geometry, click the Texture icon in the Properties window. Open Image Sampling and increase Filter Size to 4 (Figure 12-30).

Figure 12-30. *Increase the Filter Size in the Texture window to help clean up the 3D blueprint geometry*

7. Since the 3D blueprint is hollow, a base should be added to help avoid the unnecessary use of supports.

8. A base can be created with a cube. To begin the process of creating a base click on the Cube button in the Create menu (Figure 12-31).

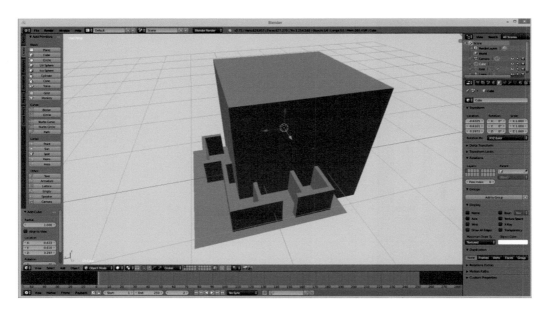

Figure 12-31. *Add a base to blueprint by with a cube*

9. To finalize the base, scale the cube down in the Z direction (hit S to scale, then hit Z to constrain the scaling to the Z direction) and then move it beneath the 3D blueprint (use the G keyboard shortcut to move the base) as seen in Figure 12-32.

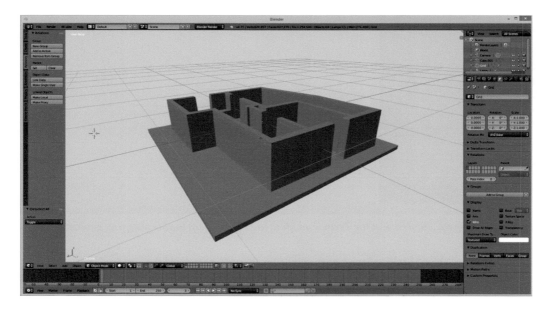

Figure 12-32. *Transform the cube into a base for the 3D blueprint by scaling it down in the Z direction. Move the base beneath the blueprint to finalize the design*

10. Once you are satisfied with the model, export it as an .stl file using the Export function, found in the File menu. To ensure that both the base and the blueprint are exported, hit the A key twice.

11. To finalize the 3D blueprint, import it into Meshmixer.

12. In Meshmixer, scale up the 3D blueprint (give it a height of 20mm in the Size Z setting) and then rotate it 270 degrees in the X direction (use the Rotate X setting) with the Transform function in the Edit menu.

13. To help optimize the size of the mesh, apply the Make Solid function (use the default settings) in the Edit menu.

14. Also make sure that the blueprint is lying flat and flush on the printer bed (Figure 12-33) by using the Transform tool in the Edit menu. Drag the blueprint upwards in the Z direction with green arrow.

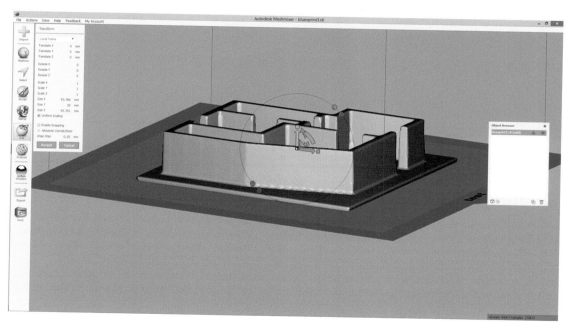

Figure 12-33. *Use the Transform function to make sure the 3D blueprint lies flat on the printer bed*

15. Since there are no overhangs, the 3D blueprint can be exported as an .stl and then imported into Cura or MatterControl to generate g-code for 3D printing. Figure 12-34 shows a slight variation of this project 3D printed as a three-dimensional maze.

Figure 12-34. *Here is slight variation of the 3D blueprint project – a 3D printed maze*

Summary

I hope the techniques presented here will encourage you to explore Blender in greater detail. Blender's capabilities are truly vast, providing an assortment tools to create nearly any 3D printable project imagined. The techniques presented here only touch upon what is possible since Blender provides a whole assortment of modeling methods ranging from organic sculpting tools to the hard edge functions found in solid modeling software packages (such as extrusions, curves and Booleans). While difficult to master at first, having some knowledge of how to use Blender will come in handy for a wide range of 3D printable projects.

■ ■ ■

CHAPTER 13

Working with 3D-Printing Service Bureaus

With the growing number of 3D-printing service bureaus available, anyone interested in getting their 3D designs printed now have many options available. From online services to local 3D-print shops, there are many opportunities to get 3D prints in a growing range of materials. The rise of 3D-printing service bureaus brings 3D printing to the masses, and as mentioned in Chapter 1, not owning a 3D printer shouldn't stop anyone from experiencing the joys of 3D printing.

But 3D printing through an outside company presents a few challenges, and to develop a good relationships with 3D-printing service providers, best practices should be followed to ensure successful outcomes. Not following best practices can result in costly mistakes in the 3D-printing process.

This chapter will outline the general procedures designers should follow when submitting files, emphasizing the importance of following 3D etiquette when working with 3D-printing services. The chapter will also dispel some common misconceptions regarding the preparation of 3D models for outside 3D-printing services.

What Is a 3D-Printing Service Bureau?

A 3D-printing service bureau is a company that provides 3D printing for a fee. With the number of service bureaus in operation growing, even large, established companies such as UPS and Lowe's are beginning to offer 3D-printing services.

There are generally two types of services bureaus: independent, brick-and-mortar shops and web-based 3D-printing companies. Both have their pros and cons, which are discussed in this chapter. (Note that many of the online service bureaus were already discussed in Chapter 2.)

Independent Service Bureaus

Initially, in the early days of 3D printing, 3D print service bureaus were rare and were more commonly known as prototype shops. These early prototype shops typically served engineers, architects, and manufacturers. Now, with the rising popularity of 3D printing, prototype shops have become full-fledged 3D-printing service bureaus, making their services available to a much wider audience.

Typically, independent-run service bureaus will have one to two high-end machines, and many of these machines have capabilities beyond the scope of consumer-level 3D printers, such as multimaterial output. These high-end machines include the Stratasys Fortus series of FDM printers, the Stratasys Connex multimaterial printers, and the Projet line of 3D printers from 3D Systems. Some of the more established service bureaus will have access to many of these high-end 3D printers, giving consumers the opportunity to print in full-color sandstone, metal, ceramics, and other materials that wouldn't be available on desktop 3D printers.

With the recent growth of 3D printing, finding a local independent 3D-printing service bureau shouldn't be too difficult. The smaller service bureaus will be more common, but they may also be more limited in the type of 3D printers they offer. To explore 3D printing service bureaus locally, 3D Hubs (`www.3dhubs.com`) is a great place to start (Figure 13-1). The 3D Hubs service provides a wealth of information regarding local service bureaus, such as types of materials offered and estimated delivery times.

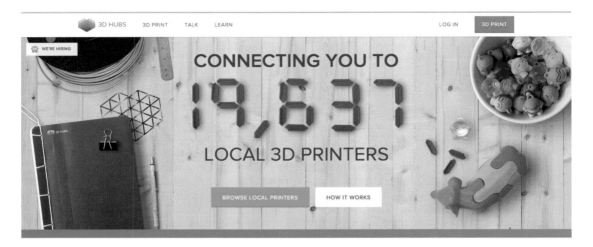

Figure 13-1. *3D Hubs offers a great deal of information on local service bureaus*

The advantages of going to an independent service bureau include, if the service bureau is local, face-to-face consulting and the opportunity to approve the file onsite before it is printed.

■ **Note**   Visiting the service bureaus to approve the file being printed is highly recommended. This will help assure that the file being submitted meets the proper specifications outlined by both the service bureau and the designer.

Online Service Bureaus

Online service bureaus include Sculpteo, Shapeways, MyMiniFactory, and Pinshape. Such service bureaus have access to a wider range of printers, including 3D printers that print in metal. The advantage of using these sites is convenience. Simply upload your file and pick the materials you desire, and the online service bureaus do the rest. This convenience tends to make online service bureaus more expensive than their brick-and-mortar counterparts. Also, delivery times can take longer since online shops print jobs together in large batches. They do this to take advantage of available space on the print bed, and jobs tend to print only when the print bed is filled. But the biggest challenge with using an online 3D-printing company is the lack of a face-to-face contact that can help ensure that a design will print correctly.

■ **Note**   To learn more about online service bureaus, please refer to Chapter 2.

Checklist When Submitting Files

Here is a checklist when submitting files:

- Review the service bureau's web site to ensure the correct procedures are being followed.

- Export the file as an `.stl` file. Even with the growing number of 3D-printing file formats, many service bureaus still prefer `.stl` files.

- Make sure all geometry is watertight (for more information on watertight geometry, please refer to Chapter 4).

- Run the file through Netfabb to ensure there are no errors and nonmanifold geometry that would otherwise cause the file to fail (for more information on NetFabb, refer to Chapter 4).

- Make sure there are no areas that are excessively thin; a rule of thumb is that all surfaces should be at least .5mm thick.

- Don't add supports. If you are printing using a polyjet process, then supports are unnecessary. If you are using an FDM or SLA, the service bureau will most likely handle the supports for you.

- Give the service a spec sheet listing the dimensions of the file to be printed.

General Best Practices

The following are some best practices.

Get to Know Your Service Bureau

When working with a local service bureau, pay them a visit and get to know the people running the machines. Most service bureaus are open to having visitors. Developing a close relationship with your service bureau provider can help ensure the proper procedures are being followed. If there are errors in the file you are submitting, it's good to establish a point of contact to ensure any problems can be quickly corrected.

File Formats

While many new file formats are being established, `.stl` files are still preferred by the majority of service bureaus as the best file format to work with for single-colored 3D prints (typically FDM, SLA, and SLS prints).

Full-color 3D prints, which are possible with ZCorp (sandstone material) and Projet 4500 (plastic material) printers, require a VRML file format. If your model has colored details, it can be exported as a VRML file through Meshmixer. Most of the online service bureaus, as well as several independent service bureaus, have the proper machines to print designs in full color. You can find more information on creating 3D objects with color details in Chapter 12.

Optimizing File Size

Sometimes files can reach a large size, especially designs using organic workflows (for more information on organic workflows, please refer to Chapter 8). In the past, service bureaus worked primarily with architects and engineers who would provide CAD files that were typically less than 10MB. Now that more professions are investigating the use of 3D printing, larger file types are much more common, and it's not unusual for files to reach sizes of 1GB.

Most service bureaus should not have problem dealing with large files although some may be apprehensive at first since they are not used to dealing with file sizes of such magnitude. Therefore, when sending over a large file, it is best to discuss how the files will be handled. Most service bureaus offer services similar to Dropbox where a file can be sent directly to a company through their web site, but many of those services will have a cap to the size of files that can be sent (usually around 50MB), and it will be necessary to deliver files via a third party such as www.wetransfer.com.

When working on designs that end up being 50MB and over, examine the file to ensure that there is no unintended geometry within the file that is adding to the file size. There are many ways to optimize files; one of the best practices involves using Meshmixer to reduce the size of the file while keeping the details intact. These workflows were discussed in Chapter 9 and should be reviewed if you find your files are becoming exceeding large. Also, review the Make Solid function in Meshmixer (the workflow is repeated in the "Making Meshes Watertight" section) to help optimize 3D geometry.

Making Meshes Watertight

I will end with a discussion of making meshes watertight; the importance of making meshes watertight was discussed in Chapter 4. Meshmixer also provides a quick solution using its Make Solid function, which will perform a "shrink-wrap" operation over any geometry imported into Meshmixer and make that geometry watertight.

CREATING WATERTIGHT FILES USING MESHMIXER'S MAKE SOLID FUNCTION

1. Import the geometry into Meshmixer. You will notice in Figure 13-2 that there is a large hole on the bottom of the imported cube. Because of the large hole, the geometry is not watertight and needs to be fixed before being sent to the service bureau. To make the geometry watertight, use the Make Solid function, which is found in the Edit menu in the main Meshmixer toolbar.

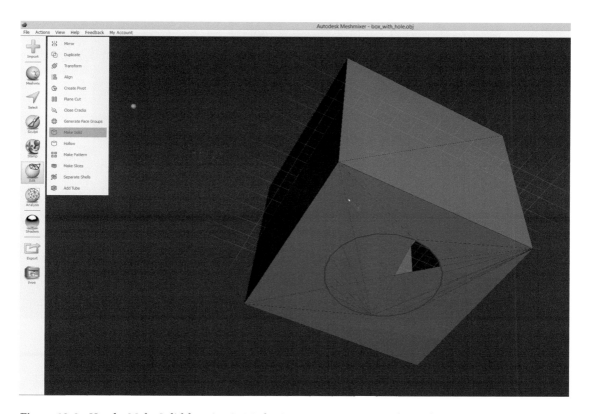

Figure 13-2. *Use the Make Solid function in Meshmixer to create a watertight mesh*

2. When activated, the Make Solid command will present a number of options. To make the model watertight, raise the Solid Accuracy and Mesh Density values to around 200 and hit Update. This will increase the resolution of the model and fix the hole in the bottom of the cube, making the mesh watertight (Figure 13-3). You can always reduce the size of the mesh by inputting smaller values into Solid Accuracy and Mesh Density and updating the Make Solid function a second time.

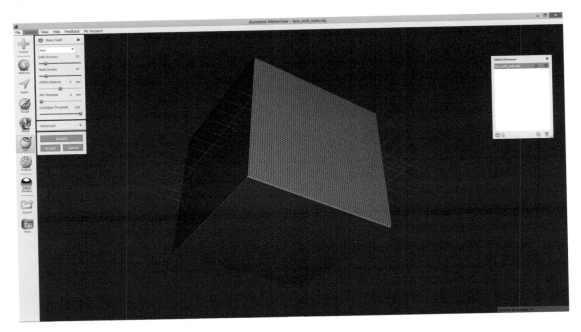

Figure 13-3. *Here are the results of the Make Solid function in Meshmixer*

Summary

The goal of this chapter was to help 3D-print designers and service bureaus establish best practices to ensure the success of your 3D-printing project. Service bureaus offer a great opportunity for anyone to get their designs 3D printed, but for the relationship between the designer and 3D-printing service bureau to be successful, proper communication protocols should be established. Following the best practices in this chapter will ensure that files print correctly, meeting the expectations of the designer who created the model and making the service bureau's job as stress free as possible.

■ ■ ■

Timeline of 3D Printing Design Milestones

To bring a clearer understanding of the many design achievements that have occurred in the world of 3D printing, this appendix presents a timeline of design milestones. This should not be regarded as a conclusive list; many more applications for 3D printing are being born daily, and featuring every 3D-printed, first-time accomplishment would be beyond the scope of this book. Nor is this timeline a history of the 3D printing process. Rather, the chronology lists objects grown from the 3D printing process for the first time (such as the world's first 3D-printed shoe or the first 3D-printed guitar, just to name a few examples). For more history on the evolution of the 3D printing process, Joan Horvath's *Mastering 3D Printing* is highly recommended.

Within this brief history is a great deal of variety that should be inspiring for other designers looking to explore what is possible with 3D printing. Born from Chuck Hull's initial patent, this is the history of the democratic spirit of 3D printing, where industrial-age manufacturing is transitioning to a digital age of additive production. Now that 3D printing has grown from being a means of prototyping ideas to a tool for direct manufacturing, there is a vast world of human-made objects being introduced to the 3D printing process. Laying out this evolution of things being created with 3D printing should provide additional incentive for the many additive artists, designers, and engineers pushing forward with their own ideas for 3D-printed breakthroughs and inventions.

	Premillenial (3D printing is invented. Prototyping with 3D printing begins.)
1984	Stereolithography is patented by Chuck Hull of 3D Systems.
1985	Selective laser sintering is developed by Dr. Carl Deckard and Dr. Joe Beaman at the University of Texas in Austin, resulting in the startup company DTM.
1988	Scott Crump uses a primitive form of 3D printing (a glue gun loaded with polyethylene and candle wax) to make a toy frog for his daughter.
1990	Fused depostion modeling is commercialized by Stratasys.
1992	First 3D printer is built by 3D Systems.
1993	Powder-bed 3D printing is developed at MIT. The technology is called *Z printing* and results in the company Z-corp.
1996	3D Systems introduces Actua 2100. This is the first time the term *3D printer* is used to refer to rapid prototyping machines.
1998	Objet develops the photo-polymer process.
1999	Wake Forest Institute for Regenerative Medicine creates a 3D synthetic scaffold coated with human cells, opening the doors to the first 3D-printed bioengineering of human organs.

2000–2009 (Prototyping with 3D printing continues. 3D printing is used for direct manufacturing for the first time.)

2002	Scientists engineer and print first functional miniature 3D-printed kidney.
2005	The Rep Rap blog begins.
2006	The first selective laser sintering machines are introduced.
2006	Objet develops a machine that prints in multiple materials.
2007	Peter Wejiwarshausen, Robert Schouwneburg, and Marlee Vege Laar found Shapeways.
2008	First usable 3D-printed prosthetic leg.
2008	Laika begins experimenting with 3D printing with its film Coraline.
2009	With inspiration provided by Robert Swartz, Peter Schmitt creates a 3D-printed clock, a complete and assembled clock entirely created by a 3D printer all at once.

2010 (3D printing is used for direct manufacturing.)

January 2010	First 3D printer (a Makerbot) appears at the Consumer Electronics Show (CES).
February 2010	Freedom of Creation (FOC) creates custom 3D-printed chairs for the Chisco superyacht.
February 2010	Apple Europe sells 3D-printed iPhone cases.
March 8, 2010	The first prototype of a full-scale 3D printed building.
March 14, 2010	Scientists 3D print first human vein.
April 14, 2010	Shapeways introduces 3D-printed glass.
May 1, 2010	McGill University creates a process to 3D print with ice.
May 25, 2010	EOS prints stainless steel medical prototypes.
June 8, 2010	Life-sized re-creation of King Tut 3D printed.
July 15, 2010	3D-printed fashion: Iris Van Herpen presents her first 3D print that she created in collaboration with the London-based architect Daniel Widrig and that was printed by .MGX by Materialise.
August 2, 2010	3D-printed trophies: Materialise.com manufactures trophies for the Hungary Formula 1 Grand Prix, designed by Italian Architect Antonio Pia Saracino.
November 2010	World's first 3D-printed goods store opens in Brussels.
November 2010	Urbee, the world's first prototype car is presented.
November 2010	3D prints are added to the Smithsonian collection.
December 2010	First 3D-printed flute created by Amit Zorn of MIT Media lab is printed on an Objet Connex 500.
December 2010	3D-printed ceramic objects are created by Mark Ganter at Solheim Labs.

2011

2011	i.materialize begins offering 14k gold and sterling silver as a printable material.
2011	A small group of students and scientists at Cornell University begin researching and testing a 3D printer that prints food.
2011	General Electric engineers decide to start using three-dimensional printers for constructing complex jet engine components, such as for example fuel injectors.
February 26, 2011	Karl Willis develops Fabricate Yourself, a wonderful software application that uses Microsoft's Kinect to turn your poses into a 3D printer work of art.
March 11, 2011	3D printing bone now possible.
March 17, 2011	The world's smallest stop-motion video makes use of 3D printing.
March 28, 2011	Materialise 3D prints an incredibly detailed scaled version of an industrial facility.
April 27, 2011	The web-based 3D modeling package TinkerCAD is born.
June 2011	University of Exeter researchers develop a 3D printer that uses chocolate.
June 2011	World's first 3D-printed bikini.
June 4, 2011	Autodesk introduces its free-for-use 3D modeling package 123D.
June 10, 2011	MakerBot offers assembled 3D printers.
June 24, 2011	The Obama administration pumps $500 million into 3DP.
August 2011	Master hat maker Elvis Pompilo begins 3D printing designer hats.
August 2011	Google 3D prints a small town for its "Uncover Your World" ad campaign.

2012

December 2012	World's first 3D scanning "photo booth" (produces 3D prints from 3D scans).
February 2012	World's first 3D-printed jaw constructed for facial reconstruction.
June 2012	Dr. Kenneth Lacovara of Drexel University re-creates life-size robotic dinosaurs using 3D printing.
August 2012	Japanese company Fasotec 3D prints fetuses based on ultrasounds.
August 2012	3D-printed exoskeleton allows young girl to use her arms for the first time.
August 2012	New software tool developed at Harvard allows for the creation of fully articulated 3D models.
August 2012	Gershon Elber 3D prints the optical illusions of MC Escher.
August 2012	World's first 3D-printed Formula 1 racer takes a test-drive.
September 2012	Form Labs launches the Form 1, the world's first low-cost SLA printer.
October 2012	Olaf Deigel creates the world's first 3D-printed guitar.
November 2012	Kacie Hultgren creates a 3D-printed purse.
November 2012	InMoov creates a 3D-printed animatronic robot.
November 2012	Israel opens its first open source 3D printing lab.

2013

December 2013	Chinese company manufactures a 5-meter central wing spar using Laser Additive Manufacturing for the Cormac C919 passenger plane.
February 2013	Scientists in Scotland use a 3D printer to arrange human embryonic stem cells.
February 2013	President Obama mentions 3D in his State of the Union address, stating 3D printing has "the potential to revolutionize the way we make almost everything."
February 2013	Nike creates the world's first football cleat using 3D printing.
March 2013	Dutch architects develop plans for the first 3D-printed canal house.
March 2013	World's first 3D-printed dress created for Dita von Teese.
May 2013	World's first working 3D-printed gun.
April 2012	New 3D scanner developed by a research team led by Gerald Buller can gather high-resolution 3D data from objects up to a kilometer away.
May 2013	The Smithsonian begins 3D scanning its 137-million-object collection for future preservation.
May 2013	Doctors from the University of Michigan save a baby's life with a 3D-printed splint.
June 2013	Microsoft adds 3D printing support to Windows 8.1.
June 2013	U.S. researchers develop 3D-printed lithium batteries.
July 2013	Ivan Sentch of Auckland, Newland, builds his an Aston Martin DB4 replica using a Solidoodle 2 3D printer.
August 2013	World's first 3D-printed skateboard, created by Sam Abbet.
October 2013	The first 3D printers arrive in Haiti. Local Haitians are taught 3D modeling skills and how to operate the printers.
December 2013	Scientists at the Michigan Technological University develop their own open source 3D metal printer.

2014–2015

January 2014	World's first 3D-printed house (the Canal House) begins construction.
February 2014	World's first 3D-printed bike frame.
August 2014	Olaf Diegel creates the world's first 3D-printed saxophone.
August 2014	GE considers 3D printing turbine blades for the next-generation 777X's GE9X engines.
August 15, 2014	AV-8B Harrier aircraft landing gear is repaired with 3D printing after emergency landing.
August 2014	Lockheed Martin begins implementing 3D printing for its A2100 satellite to reduce costs and improve the life cycle of its products.
August 2014	Amazon begins offering custom 3D-printed products.
September 2014	Scientists at the Victorian Organic Solar Cell Consortium (VICOSC) develop 3D-printed solar panels.
October 2014	HP reveals plan for break-through 3D printer that is ten times faster than any current 3D printer on the market.
December 17, 2014	The first usable tool, a wrench, is 3D printed in outer space using the first zero-gravity 3D printer. Developed by Made in Space.
December 22, 2014	Barilla announces its 3D-printed pasta contest winners.
January 2015	WinSun 3D-prints an apartment building in China.
March 2015	Carbon3D Unveils CLIP 3D Printing, which is 25 to 100 times faster than pre-exsisting 3D printing technologies.

Index

■ T, U, V, W, X, Y, Z

Printed in the United States
By Bookmasters